CASIAN ANTON (born July 30, 1988) private analyst in International Relations with concerns in the study of interdisciplinary methodology, world state and structures of explanation. QTS in Humanities (2016 in England, 2011 in Romania, Petru Maior's University of Târgu Mureş), MA in *Security and International Relations* ('Lucian Blaga' University of Sibiu, Romania, 2013), BA in *International Relations and European Studies* (Petru Maior's University of Târgu Mureş, Romania, 2011), Erasmus Student to *University of Social Science and Humanities* (Warsaw, Poland, 2012-2013).

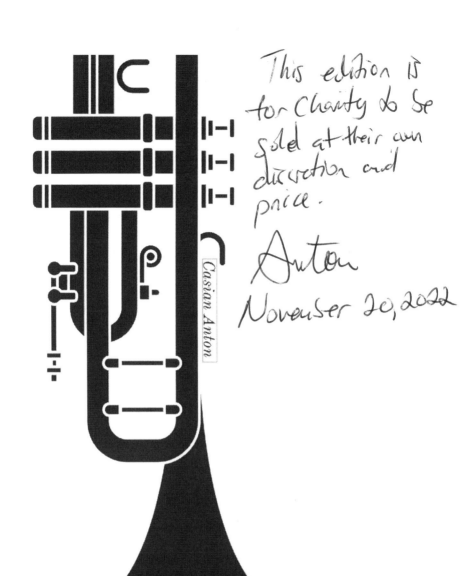

This edition is for Charity to be sold at their own discretion and price.

Anton
November 20, 2022

Casian Anton

BLACK
AND
WHITE
MUSIC

Author: Casian Anton
Cover: created inside the app Adobe Express (free licence)

Printed by Amazon

© 2022 CASIAN ANTON via Revi Project 88

"Black and White Music: A Journey Behind the Musical Notes"

ISBN: 9798844465284

Revi Project 88 (London, UK): *is dedicated to create knowledge and advance the understanding of various topics in the field of Humanities (International Relations as a specific area of study). All the activities within this project is to guide, exchange, sustain and share unique and original ideas that can help people to understand the world.*

Online orders: www.amazon.com
Contact: www.reviproject88.com
Social Media: Revi Project 88 (Twitter, Facebook, Instagram, Tumblr)

FIRST EDITION

The content of this report may influence your view about the artists investigated. Please be aware that this report is not a source of a final truth and might interfere (positive and negative) with what you know about the artists investigated. The information from this report should be seen with a higher level of suspicion than what you might be used to.

This report used data available only online (internet pages) which can be changed at any time and without any announcement from the data producer. From this point of view, and because several years have passed since the data was collected, the data in this report may differ slightly from the data available online.

The writer of this report confirms that there is no conflict of interest of any kind with the artists, music labels, news agencies or any other entity that are written and part of this report.

Revi Project 88

Table of Contents

Introduction: *music* and *White privilege*

The Recording Academy was formally established in 1957 with the purpose to recognise and award achievements in the music industry in the United States of America (henceforth USA). In the last 64 years the Grammy Awards (created by the Recording Academy) have gained impressive prestige. The number of awards have been changed over the years with categories added and removed depending on various events that have had a positive or negative impact on the music industry and the artists. The Grammy Award is considered the most significant award in the music industry of the USA and most of the artists nominated dream to be recognised for their music (which expresses creativity, talent, originality and value).

However, in the last five years many articles have been written about the white privilege and have been distributed on social networks. The main idea of these articles is the existence of a privilege that the white artists (more in the USA and the United Kingdom) benefit, a privilege that lacks or is at a lower level for black people and other minorities. Why black artists do not win the *Album of the Year* so often as white artists?

The articles published in major newspapers argue with examples in which the contribution of the black artists in the music industry is not recognised and celebrated as often as it happens with the contribution of the white artists. For example, since the Grammy Awards (1957-2021) ten black artists have won the *Album of the Year* award; this number is promoted negatively (only ten) because, for black artists, the actual number of albums that should have received this recognition is higher. Moreover, black artists have a superb presence in the charts[1], for example Billboard

---

[1] It is based on the numbers of songs/albums sold every week and it is hard to show if the higher number of sales is equal with high quality of the song/album; many albums topped the chart with high sales, but with lower grades from critics.

in the USA, and yet the number of nominations for the Grammy Awards was lower than their presence in the charts.

Supporters of black artists have two arguments against the rules and awards offered by The Recording Academy:

1. the higher recognition of music received by the white artists is not about the quality and originality of their music, but because of the colour of their skin; in other words, the white artists received the higher recognition because the institutions behind the awards is ruled by white people;
2. black artists create music and white artists take advantage and profit from their creation.

In this report I explored a very small part of the music industry from the USA, more precisely, I investigated the contribution, greater or lesser, of black and white artists in the production and writing of their albums. The artists investigated in this report are Taylor Swift, Kanye West, Beyoncé, Kendrick Lamar, Macklemore & Ryan, Adele and Beck. I selected these artists because the music produced and released by them were used by various artists and journalists as examples of racial discrimination that takes place in the music industry. For example, Kendrick Lamar (black man) was promoted by western journalists the winner of the Best Rap Album days before the 2014 ceremony, but was defeated by Macklemore & Ryan (white artists) and in 2016 by Taylor Swift (white artist); Beyoncé (black artist) lost in 2015 to Beck (white artist) and in 2017 she lost to Adele (white artist); Kanye West was not nominated with for *Album of the Year* although he had one of the most recommended and positive reviewed albums of his life, *My Beautiful Dark Twisted Fantasy*, and in the music industry. In other words, today's music industry is caught in a difficult situation that is severely undermining The Recording Academy's credibility and the Grammy Awards.

The purpose of this report is to show (within the limits of the information used):

1. the creativity, originality and novelty of the investigated artists;
2. the artist(s) with a greater contribution in the production and writing of a song(s) and album(s) that have been released;

3. whether the awards and recognition offered by the USA music industry are based on originality, creativity and novelty in music, or are offered based on the colour of the skin;
4. what are the differences between the music recognized by receiving an award and the music that did not receive an award, but was nominated for the music award (either by the vote of the general public or by the vote of the members of the jury);
5. whether the loss of the award is a direct and personal non-recognition of the black artist(s) who performed the song(s) and under whose name the song(s) and album(s) were released;
6. whether the loss of the award is a direct and personal non-recognition of the black producer(s) and lyricist(s) who created a part(s) (or full) of a song(s) and the album(s);
7. reasons that might justify why white artists receive more recognition than black artists in the music industry (only the artists in this report and Grammy Awards: Album of the Year, Best Rap Album; MTV Awards: Beyoncé (*Single Ladies (Put a Ring On It), If I were a Boy*) versus Taylor Swift (*You Belong With Me, The Man*) regarding the originality of these songs.

This report was born out of the urgent need to confront and challenge the core arguments of the black artists who feel and promote the idea of injustice regarding their music, hoping to provide clearer, more transparent information and better-founded reasons for the institution's decision to award the white artists from this report.

Black artists and white artists are in need of answers and this report is a meditative resource about the recognition of their contribution in the music industry. In this report interested people about music and awards will find the space to read about it and confront their knowledge with the investigation's findings.

The report can be used to calm the realities of racism and can provide a point of reference of the quality, originality and novelty of the music used in this report, but also for future artists waiting to be discovered. The findings of the report might be a challenge for people with a fixed opinion about who is the best artist despite the evidence used. In the end, the findings of this report are a challenge for the music industry as well, as it contributes to the wider discussion about creativity, originality and novelty of the artists and who/which artist/song/album should get the higher award.

By no means this report is made with the intentional purpose to present the artists investigated in a negative light. I followed and interpreted raw numbers. In this report you will find numbers, not reviews of the quality of the music by a professional in instruments and lyrics.

This report aligns with three articles published in *Russia Today* on racial discrimination in the United States in film and music. Parts of each article are listed below:

1. Michael McCaffrey, *#GrammysSoWhite: Is White privilege really repressing Black entertainers?*[2]

- "It is obvious upon reviewing the data that, over the last 30 years, Black artists are, in fact, substantially over-represented at the Grammys in relation to their percentage of the US population."
- "Of the top four Grammy winners in history, three are Black artists – Stevie Wonder, Quincy Jones, and Beyonce. Alyson Krause is the only white artist on that list."
- "Simply put, Black artists are thriving in show business."
- "These scurrilous accusations of award show prejudice make a mockery of the struggle against the scourge of racial inequality and injustice. There's no accounting for taste, but to chalk up awards losses by Black artists to racial animus is a cheap way to avoid artistic responsibility and ignore demographic reality."

2. Chris Sweeney, *The Grammys aren't racist, claiming so is just a cynical attempt to play the race card*[3]:

---

[2] Michael McCaffrey, *#GrammysSoWhite: Is White privilege really repressing Black entertainers?*, Russia Today, February 26, 2017, available at: https://www.rt.com/op-ed/378651-grammys-oscars-favor-whites/, last accessed: July 25, 2021. **Michael McCaffrey** *is a writer and cultural critic who lives in Los Angeles. His work can be read at RT, Counterpunch and at his website mpmacting.com/blog. He is also the host of the popular cinema podcast Looking California and Feeling Minnesota. Follow him on Twitter @MPMActingCo .*

[3] Chris Sweeney, *The Grammys aren't racist, claiming so is just a cynical attempt to play the race card*, Russia Today, November 27, 2020, available at: https://www.rt.com/op-ed/508053-drake-weeknd-grammys-racism/, last accessed: July 25, 2021. *Chris Sweeney is an author and columnist who has written for newspapers such as The Times, The Sun and the Daily Record, along with several international-selling magazines. His most recent book, Mad Dog Gravesen, was a bestseller on Amazon UK. Follow him on Twitter @Writes_Sweeney*

- "The shortlist for the most prestigious award, Record of the Year, is really varied. Beyonce is there, along with soul duo Black Pumas, who are black singer Eric Burton and latino musician Adrian Quesada. Others include; Dua Lipa (British with Kosovan heritage), Da Baby (black American), Doja Cat (Jewish American mother/South African Zulu father), Billie Eilish (white American), Megan Thee Stallion (black American from Texas) and Post Malone (white American with Italian roots)."
- "America's population is crudely divided into; White (60 percent), Black (13 percent), Asian (6 percent), Hispanic (18 percent) and American Indian (1.3 percent). So if we go by the logic of connecting impact to race, then so-called white music and white artists would dominate. Sometimes your skin colour has nothing to do with critical acclaim."

3. Michael McCaffrey, *Riz Ahmed says Hollywood under-represents and toxically portrays Muslims. But he isn't telling the whole truth*[4]:

- "Its disingenuousness is clear when it declares that Muslims make up 24% of the world's population, but represent only 1.6% of speaking characters in films. This is a deceptive statistic, as the Muslim populations of the US, UK, Australia and New Zealand combined actually constitute roughly 1.5%. In other words, Muslims are slightly over-represented in film in comparison to their population percentage in the countries measured."
- "For example, it decries the fact that the US films on which it focused featured only 1.1% of characters who were Muslim, despite the fact the US has a Muslim population of… 1.1%. It also finds but fails to highlight that Australia actually features more than twice as many Muslims in its films, at 5.6%, than there are Muslims in its population, at 2.6%."
- "For example, in a section titled 'Modern-day Muslim Characters are Rare', it uses statistics that reveal that 48.9% of Muslim characters are shown in "present-day settings". Is slightly less than 50% now considered "rare"?"
- "The pat answer would be white people. They make up 76.3% of the US and 86% of the UK population, yet, in 2018, represented only 69.1% of characters in films. So, which group or groups should have their representation in film decreased to make room for the Muslims Ahmed fails to prove are under-represented?"

---

[4] Michael McCaffrey, *Riz Ahmed says Hollywood under-represents and toxically portrays Muslims. But he isn't telling the whole truth*, Russia Today, June 13, 2021, available at: https://www.rt.com/op-ed/526452-riz-ahmed-hollywood-muslims/, last accessed: July 25, 2021.

This report has three chapters.

In the first chapter, **the music sheet: methodology**, I described the main research methods and the limits of the research.

In the second chapter, **black and white music**, I offered a comparative study between the following artists: Taylor Swift versus Kanye West, Beyoncé versus Kendrick Lamar, Beyoncé versus Taylor Swift, Kendrick Lamar versus Taylor Swift, Beyoncé versus Adele, Beyoncé versus Beck and Macklemore & Ryan versus Kendrick Lamar; in the *Awards* section I investigated the originality of the songs released by Beyoncé (*Single Ladies (Put a Ring On It), If I were a Boy*) versus Taylor Swift (*You Belong With Me, The Man*).

In chapter three, **What if**, I wrote scenarios based on the information found. These scenarios are speculative and negative. After writing this chapter, I decided to delete it, but, in the end, I changed my mind because I remembered that in each scenario there is a bit of truth; maybe the speculative scenarios in this chapter are true or partially true and could help to create a better understanding of the unfolding events behind the curtain between the following artists: Kanye West, Beyoncé, Jay Z and Taylor Swift.

Finally, **the end of the journey: black and white music**, I reformulated the main purpose of this report, I wrote the conclusions I reached for the two arguments of the supporters of black artists, and the seven points of research.

I. *the music sheet*: methodology

In this chapter I described the research methodology used in this report.

Sample:

- "Reuse of portion (or sample) of a sound recording in another recording, such as rhythm, melody, speech, sounds, or entire bars of music; may be layered, equalized, sped up or slowed down, repitched, looped, manipulated;"[5]

Lyricist:

- "Is a songwriter who writes lyrics – words for songs.[6]"

Lyricist (Composer Lyricist):

- "Writes the song's music which may include but not limited to the melody, harmony, arrangement and accompaniment.[7]"

Original Song:

- "the first and genuine form of something, from which others are derived; able to think or carry out new ideas and concepts; the way the person who sang it, wanted the song to be;[8]"

---

[5] *Sampling (music)*, Wikipedia, available at: https://en.m.wikipedia.org/wiki/Sampling_(music), last accessed: February 25, 2021.
[6] *Lyricist*, Wikipedia, available at: https://en.m.wikipedia.org/wiki/Lyricist, last accessed: February 25, 2021).
[7] *Ibidem.*
[8] This information is a mix of ideas from Quora website and first page of results from Google with the keywords: what is original song.

- song written and performed for the first time in the world by an artist and does not contain any samples.

Creativity:

- the ability to create something new, making connections and observations; original ideas;
- I read the lyrics of the songs that used samples to find out the connection between the original song and the song that sampled the original song.

Novelty:

- the quality of being new, original, unfamiliar thing or experience;
- I read the lyrics of the songs that used samples to find out the connection between the original song and the song that sampled the original song.

All the artists in this report had a source of inspiration, but I focused on samples as sources of inspiration and as a method of comparison between the investigated artists.

In this report I used only the number of lyricists and general producers, not Mixer(s), Mastering Engineer(s) and so forth.

The information collected from the credit page will be used for the rest of this report without recitation.

The list of songs in this report are not used to argue that the artists infringed the copyrights of other artists or to claim any wrongdoing from any point of view of music copyrights. This list is used *only* to *show* and *understand* the background narrative of composing music.

The main research methods are: counting, total calculation and general average of the songs and albums used in this report.

Counting and calculating the songs written by each artist:

- sole lyricist;

- two lyricists;
- three lyricists;
- at least four lyricists;
- the number of producers and lyricists;
- the length of songs: sole and two lyricists (one is the main artists used in this report);
- the number of songs with or with no samples (percentage included).

The Average Method:

- the rating on Metacritic;
- the average number of lyricists and producers for songs and albums and total career.

The List of Samples:

- I collected as much as possible the sources of the samples used by artists. Unfortunately, I was unable to offer information for each song.

The Fame of the Sample:

- I investigated the fame (charts, awards, popular opinion, reviews, influence and legacy) of the samples to show if there is a connection between the old and the new song, the differences and similarities between the samples used and the final songs of the artists from this report. This information is available only in a comparison table, no further explanation is given.

The Album Release:

- I used the information to find patterns that could show how artists are releasing their albums: similarities, differences, predictable and fixed release patterns, changing release patterns, surprise pattern.

What if:

- during the investigation my mind (based on what I read) created a few scenarios related to the artists involved that I will describe in this chapter; the scenarios are reproduced in order to help, if possible, to observe the events behind the creation of the music released by the following artists: Kanye West, Beyoncé, Jay Z (only in this chapter) and Taylor Swift.

The Race of the Samples:

- it is used only for the comparative study between Taylor Swift and Kanye West: I investigated only their albums released in 2010 because I wanted to expose how many black and white people inspired the artists in creating their music.

The Race of the Artists:

- *Black artists*: Kanye West, Beyoncé, Kendrick Lamar, Jay Z (only in the *What If* chapter;
- *White artists*: Taylor Swift, Adele, Beck, Macklemore & Ryan.

The Limits of the Research:

- this report was not created or revised by professionals in the music industry;
- all the information in this report should not be used as a source of final truth: only a few research ideas and the calculations of numbers under certain conditions are used to show information (perhaps unknown until now) about the creation of music by artists, the connections between methods of creating music, similarities, differences;
- Metacritic website does not include all the reviews written about the albums, there are reviews with higher and lower grades which are not included, and, therefore, the real and the final grade could be higher or lower than what it is available on Metacritic and in this report;
- *the lyrics and production*: I did not find the real contribution (in percentage sense: 20% or 90%, 100%) of each artist in writing and producing songs and albums and therefore the informations in this report can be misleading about the real contribution of the

artist in writing and the production of the released songs and albums;

- *the length of songs and albums*: the information about the length (in minutes and seconds) on Wikipedia and Tidal are different, on Wikipedia some songs have 1 - 3 seconds more or less than what is available on Tidal which means the length of the albums is higher or lower on both services; from this point of view the length of the songs in this report can be misleading;
- from the album released by Taylor Swift, *1989*, we know three ways to write a song:

  1. songs based on your own life or events in the lives of the people you live around;
  2. to listen to instrumental music sent by a producer and write the lyrics;
  3. ideas that appeared during a music session;

  it is very possible that these three techniques to be valid for the other artists included in this report;

- the information and conclusions in this report are limited and should be used only in terms of the information used here;
- there may be a wrong interpretation of the information used and I could not see or think about it as a wrong way to use it;
- this report explored mostly mathematical / suggestion correlations and does not provide clear causal evidence to support the findings.

II. *black* and *white* music

II.1 *Taylor Swift* versus *Kanye West*

Taylor Swift (white woman) and Kanye West (black man) are the main actors in the *Famous* feud and for its understanding few hundreds of articles have been written in the Western mass-media.[9] For this reason, Taylor Swift and Kanye West are the best source of comparison in terms of original songs and albums as Kanye West has often expressed his disagreement with the music released by Taylor Swift.

In this chapter I investigated which artist provided the original music, which artist needed support to write and produce songs and what this support consists of. At the same time, I explored who was the most original artist after the MTV Music Video Awards event and the albums released in 2010.

II.1.1 Sample

II.1.1.1 Use of Sample

TABLE 1. USE OF SAMPLE	
TAYLOR SWIFT	**KANYE WEST**
Taylor Swift (Deluxe, 2006): 0 out of 14[10]	The College Dropout (2004): 11 out of 22[11]

---

[9] See Casian Anton, *On the Famous* Feud, July 2022, Amazon (printed edition), iTunes, Kobo and Google Play Books (eBook edition).
[10] Taylor Swift, 'Taylor Swift Credits', *Tidal*, 2006, https://listen.tidal.com/album/116125894/credits, last accessed: September 1, 2019.
[11] Kanye West, 'The College Dropout Credits Tracks 1 -21', *Tidal*, 2004, https://listen.tidal.com/album/92099357, last accessed September 1, 2019. Track 22 from *The College*

Fearless (Platinum, 2008): 1 out of 19[12]	Late Registration (2005): 14 out of 22[13]
Speak Now (Deluxe, 2010): 0 out of 17[14]	Graduation (2007): 11 out of 14[15]
RED (Deluxe, 2012): 0 out of 19[16]	My Beautiful Dark Twisted Fantasy (2010): 10 out of 14[17]
1989 (Deluxe, 2013): 0 out of 16[18]	Yeezus (2013): 8 out of 10[19]
reputation (2017): 1 out of 15[20]	The Life of Pablo (2016): 15 out of 20[21]
Lover (2019): 3 out of 18[22]	Ye (2018): 5 out of 7[23]
folklore (Deluxe, 2020): 0 out of 17[24]	Jesus is King (2019): 8 out of 11[25]
Evermore (Deluxe, 2020): 0 out of 17[26]	
Fearless (Taylor's Version, 2021): 0 out of 7	

Dropout, Wikipedia, https://en.wikipedia.org/wiki/The_College_Dropout, last accessed September 1, 2019. The data collected from this credit page will be used for the rest of this report without recitation.

[12] Taylor Swift, 'Fearless (Platinum Edition) Credits', *Tidal*, 2008, https://listen.tidal.com/album/3169103/credits, last accessed: September 1, 2019. 'Forever & Always' has two versions which were included in this chart since both have a different length.

[13] Kanye West, 'Late Registration Credits', *Tidal*, 2005, https://listen.tidal.com/album/34739750, last accessed September 1, 2019. The data collected from this credit page will be used for the rest of this report without recitation.

[14] Taylor Swift, 'Speak Now Credits', *Tidal*, 2010, https://listen.tidal.com/album/4726104/credits, last accessed: September 1, 2019.

[15] Kanye West, 'Graduation Credits Tracks 1 – 13', *Tidal*, https://listen.tidal.com/album/103805723, last accessed September 1, 2019. The data collected from this credit page will be used for the rest of this report without recitation.

[16] Taylor Swift, 'RED (Deluxe Edition) Credits', *Tidal*, 2012, https://listen.tidal.com/album/92138674/credits, last accessed: September 1, 2019.

[17] Kanye West, 'My Beautiful Dark Twisted Fantasy Credits Tracks 1 – 13', *Tidal*, 2010, https://listen.tidal.com/album/4875681, last accessed: September 1, 2019. Track 14 from Wikipedia, *My Beautiful Dark Twisted Fantasy*, https://en.wikipedia.org/wiki/My_Beautiful_Dark_Twisted_Fantasy, last accessed: September 1, 2019. The data collected from this credit page will be used for the rest of this report without recitation.

[18] Taylor Swift, '1989 (Deluxe Edition) Credits', *Tidal*, 2014, https://listen.tidal.com/album/121444594/credits, last accessed: September 1, 2019.

[19] Kanye West, 'Yeezus Credits', *Tidal*, 2013, https://listen.tidal.com/album/20753857, last accessed: September 1, 2019. The data collected from this credit page will be used for the rest of this report without recitation.

[20] Taylor Swift, 'reputation Credits', *Tidal*, 2017, https://listen.tidal.com/album/121255042/credits, last accessed: September 1, 2019.

[21] Kanye West, 'The Life of Pablo Credits', *Tidal*, 2016, https://listen.tidal.com/album/57273408/credits, last accessed: September 1, 2019. The data collected from this credit page will be used for the rest of this report without recitation.

[22] Taylor Swift, 'Lover Credits', *Tidal*, 2019, https://listen.tidal.com/album/116125894/credits, last accessed: September 1, 2019.

[23] Kanye West, 'Ye Credits', *Tidal*, 2018, https://listen.tidal.com/album/98156343, last accessed: September 1, 2019. The data collected from this credit page will be used for the rest of this report without recitation.

[24] Taylor Swift, 'folklore (Deluxe Edition)', *Tidal*, 2020, https://listen.tidal.com/album/152246341/credits, last accessed: February 3, 2021.

[25] Kanye West, 'Jesus is King', *Tidal*, 2019, https://listen.tidal.com/album/121012112, last accessed: November 21, 2019. The data collected from this credit page will be used for the rest of this report without recitation.

[26] Taylor Swift, 'Evermore (Deluxe Edition)', *Tidal*, 2020, https://listen.tidal.com/album/168101331/credits, last accessed: February 3, 2021.

Total: 5 out of 159 songs (3%)	Total: 85 out of 132 songs (64%)

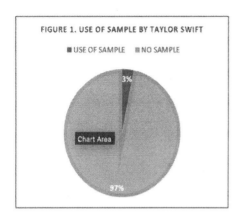

FIGURE 1. USE OF SAMPLE BY TAYLOR SWIFT

■ USE OF SAMPLE   ■ NO SAMPLE

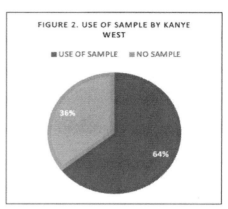

FIGURE 2. USE OF SAMPLE BY KANYE WEST

■ USE OF SAMPLE   ■ NO SAMPLE

II.1.1.2 No Use of Samples

TABLE 2. ORIGINAL SONGS WITH NO SAMPLE	
TAYLOR SWIFT	**KANYE WEST**
Taylor Swift (Deluxe, 2006): 14 out of 14	The College Dropout (2004): 11 out of 22
Fearless (Platinum, 2008): 18 out of 19	Late Registration (2005): 7 out of 22
Speak Now (Deluxe, 2010): 17 out of 17	Graduation (2007): 4 out of 1
RED (Deluxe, 2012): 19 out of 19	88s & Heartbreak (2008): 9 out of 12
1989 (Deluxe, 2014): 16 out of 16	My Beautiful Dark Twisted Fantasy (2010): 4 out of 14
reputation (2017): 14 out of 15	Yeezus (2013): 2 out of 10
Lover (2019): 15 out of 18	The Life of Pablo (2016): 5 out of 20
folklore (Deluxe, 2020): 17 out of 17	Ye (2018): 2 out of 7
Evermore (Deluxe): 17 out of 17	Jesus is King (2019): 3 out of 11
Fearless (Taylor's Version, 2021): 7 out of 7	
Total: 154 out of 159 songs (97%)	*Total: 47 out of 132 songs (36%)*

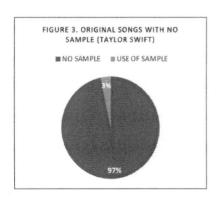

FIGURE 3. ORIGINAL SONGS WITH NO SAMPLE (TAYLOR SWIFT)

■ NO SAMPLE   ■ USE OF SAMPLE

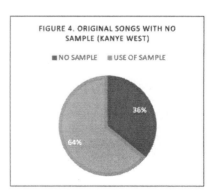

FIGURE 4. ORIGINAL SONGS WITH NO SAMPLE (KANYE WEST)

■ NO SAMPLE   ■ USE OF SAMPLE

CONCLUSIONS:

- Taylor Swift has a higher number of original songs than Kanye West with 97% of her music having no samples, while Kanye West has 36% of music with no samples;
- from the point of view of *Use of Samples*, Taylor Swift's music is 21.33(3) times more original than Kanye West's music;
- from the point of view of *No Use of Samples*, Taylor Swift's music is 2.694(4) times more original than Kanye West's music.

II.1.2 Lyricists

II.1.2.1 Sole Lyricist

TABLE 3. ORIGINAL SONG AS SOLE LYRICIST	
TAYLOR SWIFT	**KANYE WEST**
Taylor Swift (Deluxe, 2006): 3 out of 14	The College Dropout (2004): 6 out of 22[27]
Fearless (Platinum, 2008): 10 out of 19	Late Registration (2005): 1 out of 22
Speak Now (Deluxe, 2010): 16 out of 17	Graduation (2007): 0 out of 14
RED (Deluxe, 2012): 11 out of 19	88s & Heartbreak (2008): 1 out of 12[28]
1989 (Deluxe, 2014): 1 out of 16	My Beautiful Dark Twisted Fantasy (2010): 0 out of 14
reputation (2017): 0 out of 15	Yeezus (2013): 0 out of 10
Lover (2019): 3 out of 18	The Life of Pablo (2016): 0 out of 20
folklore (Deluxe, 2020): 1 out of 17	Ye (2018): 0 out of 7
Evermore (Deluxe, 2020): 1 out of 17	Jesus is King (2019): 0 out of 11
Fearless (Taylor's Version, 2021): 2 out of 7	
Total: 48 out of 159 (30%)	***Total: 8 out of 132 songs (6%)***

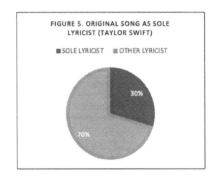

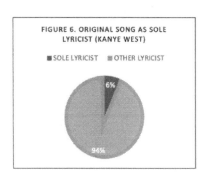

---

[27] 'Skit No. 1', 'Skit No. 2', 'Skit No. 3', 'Skit No. 4' are instrumental song with no lyricist.
[28] The song name is 'Pinocchio Story'.

CONCLUSIONS:

- Taylor Swift has a higher level of songs written by herself with 30% of her catalogue, while Kanye West has 6%; however, the songs written by Kanye West are not only full songs, but also a short text spoken in the *Intro, Outro* and *Skit;*
- as *Sole Lyricist,* Taylor Swift released 5 times more songs than Kanye West.

II.1.2.2 Two Lyricists

TABLE 4. ORIGINAL SONGS WITH TWO LYRICISTS	
TAYLOR SWIFT	**KANYE WEST**
Taylor Swift (Deluxe, 2006): 7 out of 14	The College Dropout (2004): 4 out of 22
Fearless (Platinum, 2008): 7 out of 19	Late Registration (2005): 4 out of 22
Speak Now (Deluxe, 2010): 1 out of 17	Graduation (2007): 5 out of 14
RED (Deluxe, 2012): 4 out of 19	88s & Heartbreak (2008): 1 out of 12
1989 (Deluxe, 2014): 7 out of 16	My Beautiful Dark Twisted Fantasy (2010): 0 out of 14
reputation (2017): 5 out of 15	Yeezus (2013): 0 out of 10
Lover (2019): 9 out of 18	The Life of Pablo (2016): 0 out of 20
folklore (Deluxe, 2020): 15 out of 17	Ye (2018): 0 out of 7
Evermore (Deluxe, 2020): 13 out of 17	Jesus is King (2019): 0 out of 11
Fearless (Taylor's Version, 2021): 4 out of 7	
Total: 72 out of 159 songs (45%)	***Total: 14 out of 132 songs (11%)***

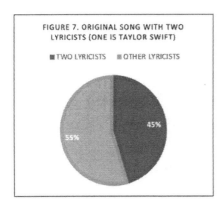

FIGURE 7. ORIGINAL SONG WITH TWO LYRICISTS (ONE IS TAYLOR SWIFT)

TWO LYRICISTS   OTHER LYRICISTS

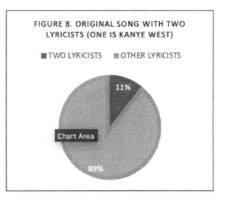

FIGURE 8. ORIGINAL SONG WITH TWO LYRICISTS (ONE IS KANYE WEST)

TWO LYRICISTS   OTHER LYRICISTS

CONCLUSION:

- Taylor Swift has a higher number of songs written in partnership with a second writer, which is 45% of her total songs, while Kanye West has a lower number of songs, 11%, which is 4.09(09) times lower than Taylor Swift.

II.1.2.3 Three Lyricists

TABLE 5. ORIGINAL SONGS WITH THREE LYRICISTS	
TAYLOR SWIFT	**KANYE WEST**
Taylor Swift (Deluxe, 2006): 4 out of 14	The College Dropout (2004): 3 out of 22
Fearless (Platinum, 2008): 1 out of 19	Late Registration (2005): 8 out of 22
Speak Now (Deluxe, 2010): 0 out of 17	Graduation (2007): 3 out of 14
RED (Deluxe, 2012): 4 out of 19	88s & Heartbreak (2008): 1 out of 12
1989 (Deluxe, 2014): 7 out of 16	My Beautiful Dark Twisted Fantasy (2010): 1 out of 14
reputation (2017): 5 out of 15	Yeezus (2013): 0 out of 10
Lover (2019): 5 out of 18	The Life of Pablo (2016): 0 out of 20
folklore (Deluxe, 2020): 1 out of 17	Ye (2018): 0 out of 7
Evermore (Deluxe, 2020): 2 out of 17	Jesus is King (2019): 1 out of 11
Fearless (Taylor's Version, 2021): 1 out of 7	
Total: 30 out of 159 songs (19%)	***Total: 17 out of 132 songs (13%)***

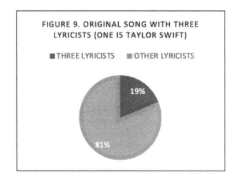

FIGURE 9. ORIGINAL SONG WITH THREE LYRICISTS (ONE IS TAYLOR SWIFT)

■ THREE LYRICISTS　■ OTHER LYRICISTS

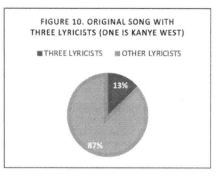

FIGURE 10. ORIGINAL SONG WITH THREE LYRICISTS (ONE IS KANYE WEST)

■ THREE LYRICISTS　■ OTHER LYRICISTS

II.1.2.4 At Least Four Lyricists

TABLE 6. ORIGINAL SONGS WITH AT LEAST FOUR LYRICISTS	
TAYLOR SWIFT	**KANYE WEST**
Taylor Swift (Deluxe, 2006): 0 out of 14	The College Dropout (2004): 8 out of 22[29]
Fearless (Platinum, 2008): 1 out of 19	Late Registration (2005): 4 out of 22
Speak Now (Deluxe, 2010): 0 out of 17	Graduation (2007): 8 out of 14
RED (Deluxe, 2012): 0 out of 19	88s & Heartbreak (2008): 8 out of 12
1989 (Deluxe, 2014): 1 out of 16	My Beautiful Dark Twisted Fantasy (2010): 13 out of 14
reputation (2017): 5 out of 15	Yeezus (2013): 10 out of 10
Lover (2019): 1 out of 18	The Life of Pablo (2016): 20 out of 20
folklore (Deluxe, 2020): 0 out of 16	Ye (2018): 7 out of 7
Evermore (Deluxe, 2020): 1 out of 17	Jesus is King (2019): 10 out of 11
Fearless (Taylor's Version, 2021): 0 out of 7	
Total: 9 out of 159 songs (6%)	***Total: 88 out of 132 songs (67%)***

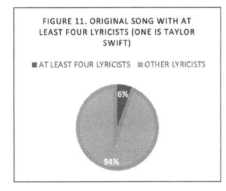

FIGURE 11. ORIGINAL SONG WITH AT LEAST FOUR LYRICISTS (ONE IS TAYLOR SWIFT)

■ AT LEAST FOUR LYRICISTS ■ OTHER LYRICISTS

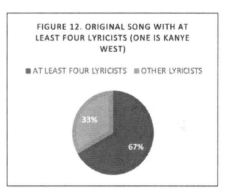

FIGURE 12. ORIGINAL SONG WITH AT LEAST FOUR LYRICISTS (ONE IS KANYE WEST)

■ AT LEAST FOUR LYRICISTS ■ OTHER LYRICISTS

CONCLUSIONS:

- Kanye West has a higher number of songs written in partnership with at least four lyricists (67%), than Taylor Swift with 6%, which is 11.16 times higher than Taylor Swift;
- overall, Taylor Swift seems to be highly more capable than Kanye West to write her own music (full songs), while Kanye West needed highly additional support (a reason behind this high support might be due to use of samples from other songs,

---

[29] 'I'll Fly Away' was written by Albert E. Brumley soley for Kanye West debut album.

which includes instrumental and lyrics, and adaptation of these instrumentals and lyrics into a new song with a different or close musical notes, which might be difficult to be achieved solely by Kanye West).

II.1.3 The Origins of Music

In this subchapter I investigated the sources of the music creativity of both artists: which artist has more original ideas and brings sounds and lyrics never heard before in any format.

II.1.3.1 The Origins of Music by Taylor Swift

TABLE 7. THE LIST OF SAMPLES USED BY TAYLOR SWIFT	
Taylor Swift (Deluxe, 2006)	N/A
Fearless (Platinum, 2008)	'Untouchable'[30] is a reworked version of Luna Halo's 'Untouchable'[31], written by Cary Barlowe, Nathan Barlowe, and Tommy Lee James.
Speak Now (Deluxe, 2010)	N/A
RED (Deluxe, 2010)	N/A
1989 (Deluxe, 2014)	N/A
reputation (2017)	'Look What You Made Me Do'[32] contains an interpolation of the 1991 song 'I'm Too Sexy'[33] by the band Right Said Fred.

---

[30] Audio: Taylor Swift, 'Untouchable', *Youtube*, December 12, 2018, available at: https://www.youtube.com/watch?v=WR6LNojTHG0, last accessed: February 25, 2020; Lyrics: Taylor Swift, 'Untouchable Lyrics', *Genius*, available at: https://genius.com/Taylor-swift-untouchable-lyrics, last accessed: February 25, 2020.

[31] Audio: Luna Halo, 'Untouchable', *Youtube*, January 26, 2009, available at: https://www.youtube.com/watch?v=6vmVhaFDe4A, last accessed: February 25, 2020; Lyrics: Luna Halor, 'Untouchable Lyrics', *Genius*, available at: https://genius.com/Luna-halo-untouchable-lyrics, last accessed: February 25, 2020.

[32] Audio: Taylor Swift, 'Look What You Made Me Do', *Youtube*, August 28, 2017, available at: https://www.youtube.com/watch?v=3tmd-ClpJxA, last accessed: February 25, 2020; Lyrics: Taylor Swift, 'Look What You Made Me Do', *Genius*, available at: https://genius.com/Taylor-swift-look-what-you-made-me-do-lyrics, last accessed: February 25, 2020.

[33] Audio: Right Said Fred, 'I'm Too Sexy (Original Mix – 2006 Version)', *Youtube*, June 14, 2009, available at: https://www.youtube.com/watch?v=P5mtclwloEQ, last accessed: February 25, 2020. Lyrics: Right Said Fred, 'I'm Too Sexy', *Genius*, available at: https://genius.com/Right-said-fred-im-too-sexy-lyrics, last accessed: February 25, 2020.

Lover (2019)	1. 'The Archer'[34] contains an interpolation of the nursery rhyme 'Humpty Dumpty'[35];
	2. 'London Boy'[36] contains a sample of 'Cold War'[37] by Cautious Clay and a snippet of James Corden interviewing Idris Elba;
	3. 'It's Nice to Have a Friend'[38] contains a sample of 'Summer in the South' by the Toronto-based Regent Park School of Music.
folklore (Deluxe, 2020)	N/A
Evermore (Deluxe, 2020)	N/A
Fearless (Taylor's Version, 2021)	N/A

CONCLUSIONS:

- Taylor Swift's sources of samples are at low level in creating her music, the first source of sample used was a full song named 'Untouchable' (modified by Taylor Swift in her own vision) while the rest of her songs contains bits of instrumental and lyrics from other songs;
- Taylor Swift is highly capable to create her own music world with songs based on her life (from family to relationships and enemies) never heard before;
- Taylor Swift demonstrated a high level of musical imagination and ideas in the music industry.

---

[34] Audio: Taylor Swift, 'The Archer', *Youtube*, July 23, 2019, available at: https://www.youtube.com/watch?v=8KpKc3C9V3w, last accessed: February 25, 2020; Lyrics: Taylor Swift, 'The Archer' *Genius*, available at: https://genius.com/Taylor-swift-the-archer-lyrics, last accessed: February 25, 2020.

[35] Lyrics: Humpty, Dumpty, *Genius*, available at: https://genius.com/Children-songs-humpty-dumpty-annotated, last accessed: February 25, 2020.

[36] Audio: Taylor Swift, 'London Boy', *Youtube*, available at: https://www.youtube.com/watch?v=VsKoOH6DVys, last accessed: February 25, 2020; Lyrics: Taylor Swift, 'London Boy', *Genius*, available at: https://genius.com/Taylor-swift-london-boy-lyrics, last accessed: February 25, 2020.

[37] Audio: Cautious Clay, 'Cold War', *Youtube*, April 30, 2018, available at: https://www.youtube.com/watch?v=S1kyno4u9cQ, last accessed: February 25, 2020; Lyrics: Cautious Clay, 'Cold War', *Genius*, available at: https://genius.com/Cautious-clay-cold-war-lyrics, last accessed: February 25, 2020.

[38] Audio: Taylor Swift, 'It's Nice To have A Friend', *Youtube*, August 23, 2019, available at: https://www.youtube.com/watch?v=eaP1VswBF28, last accessed: February 25, 2020; Lyrics: Taylor Swift, 'It's Nice To have A Friend', *Genius*, available at: https://genius.com/Taylor-swift-its-nice-to-have-a-friend-lyrics, last accessed: February 25, 2020.

II.1.3.2 The Origins of Music by Kanye West

In this table I also included the following albums (only to show the background work (similarities and differences) of the music by Kanye West and which will not be part of the investigation): *Watch the Throne* (2011), *Cruel Summer* (2012) and *Kids See Ghosts* (2017).

TABLE 8. THE LIST OF SAMPLES USED BY KANYE WEST	
The College Dropout (2004)	1. 'We Don't Care'[39] contains samples of 'I Just Wanna Stop'[40], written by Ross Vannelli and performed by The Jimmy Castor Bunch. 2. 'All Falls Down'[41] contains interpolations of 'Mystery of Iniquity'[42], written and performed by Lauryn Hill. 3. 'Spaceship'[43] contains samples of 'Distant Lover'[44], written by Marvin Gaye, Gwen Gordy Fuqua and Sandra Greene, and performed by Marvin Gaye.

[39] Audio: Kanye West, 'We Don't Care', *Youtube*, July 16, 2018, available at: https://www.youtube.com/watch?v=0Tdpq3FRGhY&list=OLAK5uy_l139P2p521JCZVZX8S_PuGFUKyD1b rXWY&index=2, last accessed: February 25, 2020; Lyrics: Kanye West, 'We Don't Care, *Genius*, available at: https://genius.com/Kanye-west-we-dont-care-lyrics, last accessed: February 25, 2020.

[40] Audio: The Jimmy Castor Bunch, 'I Just Wanna Stop', *Youtube*, January 23, 2017, available at: https://www.youtube.com/watch?v=xf9CKTk37-I, last accessed: February 25, 2020. Lyrics: The Jimmy Castor Bunch, 'I Just Wanna Stop', *Genius*, available at: https://genius.com/The-jimmy-castor-bunch-i-just-wanna-stop-lyrics, last accessed: February 25, 2020 .

[41] Audio: Kanye West, 'All Falls Down', *Youtube*, December 24, 2009, available at: https://www.youtube.com/watch?v=8kyWDhB_Qel&list=OLAK5uy_l139P2p521JCZVZX8S_PuGFUKyD1b rXWY&index=4, last accessed: February 25, 2020; Lyrics: Kanye West, 'All Falls Down', *Genius*, available at: https://genius.com/Kanye-west-all-falls-down-lyrics, last accessed: February 25, 2020.

[42] Audio: Lauryn Hill, 'Mystery of Iniquity', *Youtube*, February 2, 2012, available at: https://www.youtube.com/watch?v=BUZzW3wQg7Q, last accessed: February 25, 2020. Lyrics: Lauryn Hill, 'Mystery of Iniquity', *Genius*, available at: https://genius.com/Lauryn-hill-the-mystery-of-iniquity-lyrics, last accessed: February 25, 2020.

[43] Audio: Kanye West, 'Spaceship', *Youtube*, July 16, 2018, available at: https://www.youtube.com/watch?v=mn77gzjBl1U&list=OLAK5uy_l139P2p521JCZVZX8S_PuGFUKyD1br XWY&index=6, last accessed: February 25, 2020. Lyrics: Kanye West, 'Spaceship', *Genius*, available at: https://genius.com/Kanye-west-spaceship-lyrics, last accessed: February 25, 2020.

[44] Audio: Marvin Gaye, 'Distant Lover', *Youtube*, September 18, 2010, available at: https://www.youtube.com/watch?v=NShJXGrNotU, last accessed: February 25, 2020. Lyrics: Marvin Gaye, 'Distant Lover', *Genius*, available at: https://genius.com/Marvin-gaye-distant-lover-lyrics, last accessed: February 25, 2020.

	4. 'Jesus Walks'[45] contains samples of 'Walk with Me'[46], performed by The ARC Choir and '(Don't Worry) If There's a Hell Below, We're All Going to Go'[47], written and performed by Curtis Mayfield; interpolation of 'Hovi Baby (remix)'[48], written by Shawn Carter, Justin Smith and Kenneth Edmonds, and preformed by Jay Z. 5. 'Never Let Me Down'[49] contains samples of 'Maybe It's the Power of Love'[50], written by Michael Bolton and Bruce Kulick, and performed by Blackjack. 6. 'Slow Jamz'[51] contains samples of 'A House Is Not a Home'[52], written by Burt Bacharach and Hal David, and performed by Luther Vandross.

---

[45] Audio: Kanye West, 'Jesus Walks', *Youtube*, December 24, 2009, available at: https://www.youtube.com/watch?v=MYF7H_fpc-g&list=OLAK5uy_l139P2p521JCZVZX8S_PuGFUKyD1brXWY&index=7, last accessed: February 25, 2020; Lyrics: Kanye West, 'Jesus Walks', *Genius*, available at: https://genius.com/Kanye-west-jesus-walks-lyrics, last accessed: February 25, 2020.

[46] Audio: The ARC Choir, 'Walk With Me', *Youtube*, November 2, 2008, available at: https://www.youtube.com/watch?v=-Ib36OXrEL8, last accessed: February 25, 2020. Lyrics: The ARC Choir, 'Walk With Me', *Genius*, available at: https://genius.com/The-arc-choir-walk-with-me-lyrics, last accessed: February 25, 2020.

[47] Audio: Curtis Mayfield, '(Don't Worry) If There's a Hell Below, We're All Going To Go', *Youtube*, June 5, 2011, available at: https://www.youtube.com/watch?v=x1xmXOP3lhM, last accessed: February 25, 2020. Lyrics: Curtis Mayfield, '(Don't Worry) If There's a Hell Below, We're All Going To Go', *Genius*, available at: https://genius.com/Curtis-mayfield-dont-worry-if-theres-a-hell-below-were-all-going-to-go-lyrics, last accessed: February 25, 2020.

[48] Audio: Blackjack, 'Maybe It's The Power Of Love', *Youtube*, March 12, 2012, available at: https://www.youtube.com/watch?v=C71EfYUIrYo, last accessed: February 25, 2020. Lyrics: Blackjack, 'Maybe It's The Power Of Love', *Genius*, available at: https://genius.com/Blackjack-maybe-its-the-power-of-love-lyrics, last accessed: February 25, 2020.

[49] Audio: Kanye West, 'Never Let Me Down', *Youtube*, July 16, 2018, available at: https://www.youtube.com/watch?v=p4NvOKy7GOU&list=OLAK5uy_l139P2p521JCZVZX8S_PuGFUKyD1brXWY&index=8, last accessed: February 25, 2020; Lyrics: Kanye West, 'Never Let Me Down', *Genius*, available at: https://genius.com/Kanye-west-never-let-me-down-lyrics, last accessed: February 25, 2020.

[50] Audio: Blackjack, 'Maybe It's The Power Of Love', *Youtube*, March 12, 2012, available at: https://www.youtube.com/watch?v=C71EfYUIrYo, last accessed: February 25, 2020. Lyrics: Blackjack, 'Maybe It's The Power Of Love', *Genius*, available at: https://genius.com/Blackjack-maybe-its-the-power-of-love-lyrics, last accessed: February 25, 2020.

[51] Audio: Kanye West, 'Slow Jamz', *Youtube*, December 12, 2012, available at: https://www.youtube.com/watch?v=jl-w4gvkCkQ&list=OLAK5uy_l139P2p521JCZVZX8S_PuGFUKyD1brXWY&index=12, last accessed: February 25, 2020; Lyrics: Kanye West, 'Slow Jamz', *Genius*, available at: https://genius.com/Twista-kanye-west-and-jamie-foxx-slow-jamz-lyrics, last accessed: February 25, 2020.

[52] Audio: Luther Vandross, 'A House Is Not a Home', *Youtube*, May 23, 2015, available at: https://www.youtube.com/watch?v=CGib6okEeZ4, last accessed: February 25, 2020. Lyrics: Luther Vandross, 'A House Is Not a Home', *Genius*, available at: https://genius.com/Luther-vandross-a-house-is-not-a-home-lyrics, last accessed: February 25, 2020.

<table>
<tr><td></td><td>

7. 'Breathe In Breathe Out'[53] contains samples of 'Precious Precious'[54], written and Performed by Jackie Moore.

8. 'School Spirit'[55] contains samples of 'Spirit in the Dark'[56], written and performed by Aretha Franklin.

9. 'Two Words'[57] contains samples of 'Peace & Love (Amani Na Mapenzi) – Movement IV (Encounter)'[58], written by Lou Wilson, Ric Wilson and Carlos Wilson, and performed by Mandrill; samples of 'The Rainmaker'[59], written by Harry Nilsson and Bill Martin and performed by The 5th Dimension.

10. 'Through the Wire'[60] contains samples of 'Through the Fire'[61], written by David Foster, Tom Keane and Cynthia Weil, and performed by Chaka Khan.

</td></tr>
</table>

---

[53] Audio: Kanye West, 'Breathe In Breathe Out', *Youtube*, July 16, 2018, available at: https://www.youtube.com/watch?v=E3dWKq3s6u0, last accessed: February 25, 2020. Lyrics: Kanye West, 'Breathe In Breathe Out', *Genius*, available at: https://genius.com/Kanye-west-breathe-in-breathe-out-lyrics, last accessed: February 25, 2020.

[54] Audio: Jackie Moore, 'Precious Precious', *Youtube*, April 23, 2013, available at: https://www.youtube.com/watch?v=dIaIRRcKkfU=, last accessed: February 25, 2020. Lyrics: Jackie Moore, 'Precious Precious', *Genius*, available at: https://genius.com/Jackie-moore-precious-precious-lyrics, last accessed: February 25, 2020.

[55] Audio: Kanye West, 'School Spirit', *Youtube*, July 16, 2018, available at: https://www.youtube.com/watch?v=-MOIPnu50O4&list=OLAK5uy_l139P2p521JCZVZX8S_PuGFUKyD1brXWY&index=15, last accessed: February 25, 2020; Lyrics: Kanye West, 'School Spirit', *Genius*, available at: https://genius.com/Kanye-west-school-spirit-lyrics, last accessed: February 25, 2020.

[56] Audio: Aretha Franklin, 'Spirit In The Dark', *Youtube*, March 7, 2011, available at: https://www.youtube.com/watch?v=qvGmbsLxF0w, last accessed: February 25, 2020. Lyrics: Aretha Franklin, 'Spirit In The Dark', *Genius*, available at: https://genius.com/Aretha-franklin-spirit-in-the-dark-lyrics, last accessed: February 25, 2020.

[57] Audio: Kanye West, 'Two Words', *Youtube*, June 16, 2009, available at: https://www.youtube.com/watch?v=tkFOBx6j0l8&list=OLAK5uy_l139P2p521JCZVZX8S_PuGFUKyD1brXWY&index=18, last accessed: February 25, 2020; Lyrics: Kanye West, 'Two Words', *Genius*, available at: https://genius.com/Kanye-west-two-words-lyrics, last accessed: February 25, 2020.

[58] Audio: Mandrill, 'Peace and Love (Amani Na Mapenzi) – Movement IV (Encounter)', *Youtube*, July 29, 2012, available at: https://www.youtube.com/watch?v=gXCcPAk2NBY, last accessed: February 25, 2020. Lyrics: Audio: Mandrill, 'Peace and Love (Amani Na Mapenzi) – Movement IV (Encounter)', *Genius*, available at: https://genius.com/Mandrill-peace-and-love-amani-na-mapenzi-movement-iv-encounter-lyrics, last accessed: February 25, 2020.

[59] Audio: The 5th Dimension, ‚The Rainmaker', *Youtube*, September 24, 2015, available at: https://www.youtube.com/watch?v=aQ4GgAvYBpY, last accessed: February 25, 2020; Lyrics: The 5th Dimension, ‚The Rainmaker', Genius, available at: https://genius.com/The-5th-dimension-time-and-love-lyrics, last accessed: February 25, 2020.

[60] Audio: Kanye West, 'Through the Wire', *Youtube*, July 16, 2018, available at: https://www.youtube.com/watch?v=AE8y25CcE6s&list=OLAK5uy_l139P2p521JCZVZX8S_PuGFUKyD1brXWY&index=19, last accessed: February 25, 2020; Lyrics: Kanye West, 'Through the Wire', *Genius*, available at: https://genius.com/Kanye-west-through-the-wire-lyrics, last accessed: February 25, 2020.

[61] Audio: Chaka Khan, 'Through The Fire', *Youtube*, February 26, 2009, available at: https://www.youtube.com/watch?v=ymuWb8xtCsc, last accessed: February 25, 2020. Lyrics: Chaka Khan, 'Through The Fire', *Genius*, available at: https://genius.com/Chaka-khan-through-the-fire-lyrics, last accessed: February 25, 2020.

	11. 'Family Business'[62] contains samples of 'Fonky Thang'[63], written by Terry Callier and Charles Stepney, and performed by The Dells; interpolations of 'Ambitionz As A Ridah'[64], written by Tupac Shakur and Delmar Arnaud and performed by 2Pac. 12. 'Last Call'[65] contains samples of 'Mr. Rockefeller'[66], written by Jerry Blatt and Bette Midler, and performed by Bette Midler; sample of 'She's Gone To Another'[67], written by Kenneth Ruffin and performed by The Whatnauts.
	1. 'Wake Up Mr. West'[68] and 'Heard Em Say'[69] both contain excerpts of 'Someone That I Used to Love'[70] as performed by Natalie Cole.
Late Registration (2005)	

[62] Audio: Kanye West, 'Family Business', *Youtube*, July 16, 2018, available at: https://www.youtube.com/watch?v=JwAjANmjajc&list=OLAK5uy_l139P2p521JCZVZX8S_PuGFUKyD1brXWY&index=20, last accessed: February 25, 2020; Lyrics: Kanye West, 'Family Business', *Genius*, available at: https://genius.com/Kanye-west-family-business-lyrics, last accessed: February 25, 2020.
[63] Audio: The Dells, 'Fonky Thang', *Youtube*, October 23, 2016, available at: https://www.youtube.com/watch?v=Rz9SLTRi_IE, last accessed: February 25, 2020. Lyrics: The Dells, 'Fonky Thang', *Genius*, available at: https://genius.com/The-dells-fonky-thang-diamond-rang-lyrics, last accessed: February 25, 2020.
[64] Audio: 2Pac, 'Mabitionz As A Ridah', *Youtube*, November 19, 201, available at: https://www.youtube.com/watch?v=cQZqPi1aHNo, last accessed: February 25, 2020; Lyrics: 2Pac, 'Mabitionz As A Ridah', *Genius*, available at: https://genius.com/2pac-ambitionz-az-a-ridah-lyrics, last accessed: February 25, 2020.
[65] Audio: Kanye West, 'Last Call', *Youtube*, July 16, 2018, available at: https://www.youtube.com/watch?v=cpbeS15sHZ0&list=OLAK5uy_l139P2p521JCZVZX8S_PuGFUKyD1brXWY&index=21, last accessed: February 25, 2020; Lyrics: Kanye West, 'Last Call', *Genius*, available at: https://genius.com/Kanye-west-last-call-lyrics, last accessed: February 25, 2020.
[66] Audio: Bette Midler, 'Mr. Rockefeller', *Youtube*, April 6, 2011, available at: https://www.youtube.com/watch?v=hao8NDTeREs, last accessed: February 25, 2020. Lyrics: Bette Midler, 'Mr. Rockefeller', *Genius*, available at: https://genius.com/Bette-midler-mr-rockefeller-lyrics, last accessed: February 25, 2020.
[67] Audio: The Whatnauts, 'She's Gone To Another', *Youtube*, May 25, 2008, available at: https://www.youtube.com/watch?v=fJXIGOizJsE, last accessed: February 25, 2020.
[68] Audio: Kanye West, 'Wake Up Mr. West', October 29, 208, *Youtube*, available at: https://www.youtube.com/watch?v=Bwyu-SZ7g_E&list=OLAK5uy_mS2sPIJinRK2fIXN9Ce756lZFRX2KT21o, last accessed: February 25, 2020; Lyrics: Kanye West, 'Wake Up Mr. West', *Genius*, available at: https://genius.com/Kanye-west-wake-up-mr-west-lyrics, last accessed: February 25, 2020.
[69] Audio: Kanye West, 'Heard Em Say', *Youtube*, June 16, 2009, available at: https://www.youtube.com/watch?v=elVF7oG0pQs&list=OLAK5uy_mS2sPIJinRK2fIXN9Ce756lZFRX2KT21o&index=2, last accessed: February 25, 2020; Lyrics: Kanye West, 'Heard Em Say', *Genius*, available at: https://genius.com/Kanye-west-heard-em-say-lyrics, last accessed: February 25, 2020.
[70] Audio: Natalie Cole, 'Someone That I Used To Love', *Youtube*, January 30, 2014, available at: https://www.youtube.com/watch?v=H89_X3v0c9g, last accessed: February 25, 2020. Lyrics: Natalie Cole, 'Someone That I Used To Love', *Genius*, available at: https://genius.com/Natalie-cole-someone-that-i-used-to-love-lyrics, last accessed: February 25, 2020.

	2. 'Touch the Sky'[71] contains samples of 'Move On Up'[72] as performed by Curtis Mayfield. 3. 'Gold Digger'[73] contains samples of 'I Got a Woman'[74] as performed by Ray Charles. 4. 'Drive Slow'[75] contains samples of 'Wildflower'[76] as performed by Hank Crawford. 5. 'My Way Home'[77] contains samples of 'Home Is Where the Hatred Is'[78] as performed by Gil Scott-Heron. 6. 'Crack Music'[79] contains samples of 'Since You Came in My Life'[80] as performed by New York Community Choir.

---

[71] Audio: Kanye West, 'Touch The Sky', *Youtube*, June 16, 2009, available at: https://www.youtube.com/watch?v=YkwQbuAGLj4&list=OLAK5uy_mS2sPIJinRK2fIXN9Ce756lZFRX2KT21o&index=3, last accessed: February 25, 2020; Lyrics: Kanye West, 'Touch The Sky', *Genius*, available at: https://genius.com/Kanye-west-touch-the-sky-lyrics, last accessed: February 25, 2020.

[72] Audio: Curtis Mayfield, 'Move On Up', *Youtube*, December 22, 2009, available at: https://www.youtube.com/watch?v=6Z66wVo7uNw, last accessed: February 25, 2020. Lyrics: Curtis Mayfield, 'Move On Up', *Genius*, available at: https://genius.com/Curtis-mayfield-move-on-up-lyrics, last accessed: February 25, 2020.

[73] Audio: Kanye West, 'Gold Digger', *Youtube,* June 16, 2009, available at: https://www.youtube.com/watch?v=6vwNcNOTVzY&list=OLAK5uy_mS2sPIJinRK2fIXN9Ce756lZFRX2KT21o&index=4, last accessed: February 25, 2020; Lyrics: Kanye West, 'Gold Digger', *Genius*, available at: https://genius.com/Kanye-west-gold-digger-lyrics, last accessed: February 25, 2020.

[74] Audio: Ray Charles, 'I Got A Woman', *Youtube*, August 3, 2009, available at: https://www.youtube.com/watch?v=Cnl_LuCJ4Ek, last accessed: February 25, 2020. Lyrics: Ray Charles, 'I Got A Woman', *Genius*, available at: https://genius.com/Ray-charles-i-got-a-woman-lyrics, last accessed: February 25, 2020.

[75] Audio: Kanye West, 'Drive Slow', *Youtube*, October 29, 2018, available at: https://www.youtube.com/watch?v=Q1ViJEYNki4&list=OLAK5uy_mS2sPIJinRK2fIXN9Ce756lZFRX2KT21o&index=6, last accessed: February 25, 2020; Lyrics: Kanye West, 'Drive Slow', *Genius*, available at: https://genius.com/Kanye-west-drive-slow-lyrics, last accessed: February 25, 2020.

[76] Audio: Hank Crawford, 'Wildflower', *Youtube*, June 9, 2012, available at: https://www.youtube.com/watch?v=QC88dJ4KuFw, last accessed: February 25, 2020. Lyrics: Hank Crawford, 'Wildflower', *Genius*, available at: https://genius.com/Hank-crawford-wildflower-lyrics, last accessed: February 25, 2020.

[77] Audio: Kanye West, 'My Way Home', *Youtube*, October 29, 2018, available at: https://www.youtube.com/watch?v=TgAomHGqKUM&list=OLAK5uy_mS2sPIJinRK2fIXN9Ce756lZFRX2KT21o&index=7, last accessed: February 25, 2020; Lyrics: Kanye West, 'My Way Home', *Genius*, available at: https://genius.com/Kanye-west-my-way-home-lyrics, last accessed: February 25, 2020.

[78] Audio: Gil Scott-Heron, 'Home Is Where The Hatred Is', *Youtube*, August 19, 2014, available at: https://www.youtube.com/watch?v=nSpBs1ghyoo, last accessed: . Lyrics: Gil Scott-Heron, 'Home Is Where The Hatred Is', *Genius*, available at: https://genius.com/Gil-scott-heron-home-is-where-the-hatred-is-pieces-of-a-man-version-lyrics, last accessed: .

[79] Audio: Kanye West, 'Crack Music', *Youtube*, October 29, 2018, available at: https://www.youtube.com/watch?v=2tmPSK-w90o&list=OLAK5uy_mS2sPIJinRK2fIXN9Ce756lZFRX2KT21o&index=8, last accessed: February 25, 2020; Lyrics: Kanye West, 'Crack Music', *Genius*, available at: https://genius.com/Kanye-west-crack-music-lyrics, last accessed: February 25, 2020.

[80] Audio: New York Community Choir, 'Since You Came In My Life', *Youtube*, December 16, 2017, available at: https://www.youtube.com/watch?v=RRcuYBg9S8w, last accessed: February 25, 2020. Lyrics: New York Community Choir, 'Since You Came In My Life', *Genius*, available at: https://genius.com/New-york-community-choir-since-you-came-in-my-life-lyrics, last accessed: February 25, 2020.

	7. 'Roses'[81] contains samples of 'Rosie'[82] as performed by Bill Withers. 8. 'Addiction'[83] contains elements of 'My Funny Valentine'[84] as performed by Etta James. 9. 'Diamonds from Sierra Leone'[85] contains samples of 'Diamonds Are Forever'[86] as performed by Shirley Bassey. 10. 'We Major'[87] contains samples of 'Action'[88] as performed by Orange Krush. 11. 'Hey Mama'[89] contains samples of 'Today Won't Come Again'[90] as performed by Donal Leace.

[81] Audio: Kanye West, 'Roses', *Youtube*, October 29, 2018, available at: https://www.youtube.com/watch?v=Qxlnb1lEdEs&list=OLAK5uy_mS2sPIJinRK2fIXN9Ce756lZFRX2KT21 o&index=9, last accessed: February 25, 2020; Lyrics: Kanye West, 'Roses', *Genius*, available at: https://genius.com/Kanye-west-roses-lyrics, last accessed: February 25, 2020.

[82] Audio: Bill Withers, 'Rosie', *Youtube*, March 22, 2013, available at: https://www.youtube.com/watch?v=TLdRoeO2OQ4, last accessed: February 25, 2020. Lyrics: Bill Withers, 'Rosie', *Genius*, available at: https://genius.com/Bill-withers-rosie-lyrics, last accessed: February 25, 2020.

[83] Audio: Kanye West, 'Addiction', *Youtube*, October 29, 2018, available at: https://www.youtube.com/watch?v=YuCwP-NbY0s&list=OLAK5uy_mS2sPIJinRK2fIXN9Ce756lZFRX2KT21o&index=11, last accessed: February 25, 2020; Lyrics: Kanye West, 'Addiction', *Genius*, available at: https://genius.com/Kanye-west-addiction-lyrics, last accessed: February 25, 2020.

[84] Audio: Etta James, 'My Funny Valentine', *Youtube*, June 20, 2008, available at: https://www.youtube.com/watch?v=Bt7eqkPXO8A, last accessed: February 25, 2020. Lyrics: Etta James, 'My Funny Valentine', *Genius*, available at: https://genius.com/Etta-james-my-funny-valentine-lyrics, last accessed: February 25, 2020.

[85] Audio: Kanye West, 'Diamonds From Sierra Leone', June 16, 2009, *Youtube*, available at: https://www.youtube.com/watch?v=92FCRmggNqQ&list=OLAK5uy_mS2sPIJinRK2fIXN9Ce756lZFRX2KT 21o&index=20, last accessed: February 25, 2020; Lyrics: Kanye West, 'Diamonds From Sierra Leone', *Genius*, available at: https://genius.com/Kanye-west-diamonds-from-sierra-leone-lyrics, last accessed: February 25, 2020.

[86] Audio: Shirley Bassey, 'Diamonds Are Forever', *Youtube*, November 4, 2010, available at: https://www.youtube.com/watch?v=QFSAWiTJsjc, last accessed: February 25, 2020. Lyrics: Shirley Bassey, 'Diamonds Are Forever', *Genius*, available at: https://genius.com/Shirley-bassey-diamonds-are-forever-lyrics, last accessed: February 25, 2020.

[87] Audio: Kanye West, 'We Major', *Youtube*, October 29, 2018, available at: https://www.youtube.com/watch?v=_fr4SV4fGAw&list=OLAK5uy_mS2sPIJinRK2fIXN9Ce756lZFRX2KT2 1o&index=14, last accessed: February 25, 2020; Lyrics: Kanye West, 'We Major', *Genius*, available at: https://genius.com/Kanye-west-we-major-lyrics, last accessed: February 25, 2020.

[88] Audio: Orange Krush, 'Action', *Youtube*, May 26, 2011, available at: https://www.youtube.com/watch?v=fGyTxXfV4FQ, last accessed: February 25, 2020.

[89] Audio: Kanye West, 'Hey Mama', *Youtube*, October 29, 2018, available at: https://www.youtube.com/watch?v=B3NmMKfl3lc&list=OLAK5uy_mS2sPIJinRK2fIXN9Ce756lZFRX2KT2 1o&index=16, last accessed: February 25, 2020; Lyrics: Kanye West, 'Hey Mama', *Genius*, available at: https://genius.com/Kanye-west-hey-mama-lyrics, last accessed: February 25, 2020.

[90] Audio: Donal Leace, 'Today Won't Come Again', *Youtube*, March 22, 2013, available at: https://www.youtube.com/watch?v=4PJ1YyCGg4k, last accessed: February 25, 2020. Lyrics: Donal Leace, 'Today Won't Come Again', *Musixmatch*, available at: https://www.musixmatch.com/lyrics/Donal-Leace/Today-Won-t-Come-Again, last accessed: February 25, 2020.

	12. 'Celebration'[91] contains samples of 'Heavenly Dream'[92] as performed by The Kay-Gees. 13. 'Gone'[93] contains samples of 'It's Too Late'[94] as performed by Otis Redding. 14. 'Late'[95] contains samples of 'I'll Erase Away Your Pain'[96] by The Whatnauts.
Graduation (2007)	1. 'Good Morning'[97] contains samples from 'Someone Saved My Life Tonight'[98] performed by Elton John. 2. 'Champion'[99] contains elements of 'Kid Charlemagne'[100] performed by Steely Dan.

[91] Audio: Kanye West, 'Celebration', *Youtube*, October 29, 2018, available at: https://www.youtube.com/watch?v=FZjlP-N7Hl4&list=OLAK5uy_mS2sPIJinRK2flXN9Ce756lZFRX2KT21o&index=17, last accessed: February 25, 2020; Lyrics: Kanye West, 'Celebration', *Genius*, available at: https://genius.com/Kanye-west-celebration-lyrics, last accessed: February 25, 2020.

[92] Audio: The Kay-Gees, 'Heavenly Dream', *Youtube*, September 18, 2008, available at: https://www.youtube.com/watch?v=oecXXqAPyQ0, last accessed: February 25, 2020. Lyrics: The Kay-Gees, 'Heavenly Dream', *Genius*, available at: https://genius.com/The-kay-gees-heavenly-dream-lyrics, last accessed: February 25, 2020.

[93] Audio: Kanye West, 'Gone', *Youtube*, October 29, 2018, available at: https://www.youtube.com/watch?v=TwPCaWQIJME&list=OLAK5uy_mS2sPIJinRK2flXN9Ce756lZFRX2KT21o&index=19, last accessed: February 25, 2020; Lyrics: Kanye West, 'Gone', *Genius*, available at: https://genius.com/Kanye-west-gone-lyrics, last accessed: February 25, 2020.

[94] Audio: Otis Redding, 'It's Too Late', *Youtube*, November 16, 2009, available at: https://www.youtube.com/watch?v=5bbv8PYQD-0, last accessed: February 25, 2020. Lyrics: Otis Redding, 'It's Too Late', *Genius*, available at: https://genius.com/Otis-redding-its-too-late-lyrics, last accessed: February 25, 2020.

[95] Audio: Kanye West, 'Late', *Youtube*, October 29, 2018, available at: https://www.youtube.com/watch?v=YRwTaWWK3dI&list=OLAK5uy_mS2sPIJinRK2flXN9Ce756lZFRX2KT21o&index=21, last accessed: February 25, 2020; Lyrics: Kanye West, 'Late', *Genius*, available at: https://genius.com/Kanye-west-late-lyrics, last accessed: February 25, 2020.

[96] Audio: The Whatnauts, 'I'll Erase Away Your Pain', *Youtube*, September 8, 2007, available at: https://www.youtube.com/watch?v=euSVtelwD_Q, last accessed: February 25, 2020. Lyrics: The Whatnauts, 'I'll Erase Away Your Pain', *Genius*, available at: https://genius.com/Whatnauts-ill-erase-away-your-pain-lyrics, last accessed: February 25, 2020.

[97] Audio: Kanye West, 'Good Morning', *Youtube*, December 13, 2009, available at: https://www.youtube.com/watch?v=6CHs4x2uqcQ&list=OLAK5uy_kVXQTEtfSWtL_gP_czGRaKH1KyfraNW80, last accessed: February 25, 2020; Lyrics: Kanye West, 'Good Morning', *Genius*, available at: https://genius.com/Kanye-west-good-morning-lyrics, last accessed: February 25, 2020.

[98] Audio: Elton John, 'Someone Saved My Life Tonight', *Youtube*, February 17, 2009, available at: https://www.youtube.com/watch?v=Sw2Lptf7K0E, last accessed: February 25, 2020. Lyrics: Elton John, 'Someone Saved My Life Tonight', *Genius*, available at: https://genius.com/Elton-john-someone-saved-my-life-tonight-lyrics, last accessed: February 25, 2020.

[99] Audio: Kanye West, 'Champion', *Youtube*, February 7, 2019, available at: https://www.youtube.com/watch?v=L1SEEMkc-qw&list=OLAK5uy_kVXQTEtfSWtL_gP_czGRaKH1KyfraNW80&index=2, last accessed: February 25, 2020; Lyrics: Kanye West, 'Champion', *Genius*, available at: https://genius.com/Kanye-west-champion-lyrics, last accessed: February 25, 2020.

[100] Audio: Steely Dan, 'Kid Charlemagne', *Youtube*, January 19, 2016, available at: https://www.youtube.com/watch?v=jJ9Xk-VoGqo, last accessed: February 25, 2020. Lyrics: Steely Dan, 'Kid Charlemagne', *Genius*, available at: https://genius.com/Steely-dan-kid-charlemagne-lyrics, last accessed: February 25, 2020.

	3. 'Stronger'[101] contains a sample of 'Harder, Better, Faster, Stronger'[102] performed by Daft Punk and master use of 'Cola Bottle Baby'[103] performed by Edwin Birdsong. 4. 'I Wonder'[104] contains a sample from 'My Song'[105] performed by Labi Siffre. 5. 'Good Life'[106] contains a sample of 'P.Y.T. (Pretty Young Thing)'[107] performed by Michael Jackson. 6. 'Barry Bonds'[108] contains a sample of 'Long Red'[109] performed by Mountain.

---

[101] Audio: Kanye West, 'Stronger', *Youtube*, June 16, 2009, available at: https://www.youtube.com/watch?v=PsO6ZnUZI0g&list=OLAK5uy_kVXQTEtfSWtL_gP_czGRaKH1KyfraN W80&index=3, last accessed: February 25, 2020; Lyrics: Kanye West, 'Stronger', *Genius*, available at: https://genius.com/Kanye-west-stronger-lyrics, last accessed: February 25, 2020.

[102] Audio: Daft Punk, 'Harder, Better, Faster, Stronger', *Youtube*, February 26, 2009, available at: https://www.youtube.com/watch?v=gAjR4_CbPpQ, last accessed: February 25, 2020. Lyrics: Daft Punk, 'Harder, Better, Faster, Stronger', *Genius*, available at: https://genius.com/Daft-punk-harder-better-faster-stronger-lyrics, last accessed: February 25, 2020.

[103] Audio: Edwin Birdsong, 'Cola Bottle', *Youtube*, February 7, 2009, available at: https://www.youtube.com/watch?v=Z3AKrwna2C8, last accessed: February 25, 2020. Lyrics: Edwin Birdsong, 'Cola Bottle', *Genius*, available at: https://genius.com/Edwin-birdsong-cola-bottle-baby-lyrics, last accessed: February 25, 2020.

[104] Audio: Kanye West, 'I Wonder', *Youtube*, February 7, 2019, available at: https://www.youtube.com/watch?v=z15wKo0r-74&list=OLAK5uy_kVXQTEtfSWtL_gP_czGRaKH1KyfraNW80&index=4, last accessed: February 25, 2020; Lyrics: Kanye West, 'I Wonder', *Genius,* available at: https://genius.com/Kanye-west-i-wonder-lyrics, last accessed: February 25, 2020.

[105] Audio: Labi Siffre, 'My Song', *Youtube*, August 7, 2015, available at: https://www.youtube.com/watch?v=aBhBG5lqpzM, last accessed: February 25, 2020. Lyrics: Labi Siffre, 'My Song', *Genius*, available at: https://genius.com/Labi-siffre-my-song-lyrics, last accessed: February 25, 2020.

[106] Audio: Kanye West, 'Good Life', *Youtube*, June 16, 2009, available at: https://www.youtube.com/watch?v=FEKEjpTzB0Q&list=OLAK5uy_kVXQTEtfSWtL_gP_czGRaKH1KyfraN W80&index=5, last accessed: February 25, 2020; Lyrics: Kanye West, 'Good Life', *Genius*, available at: https://genius.com/Kanye-west-good-life-lyrics, last accessed: February 25, 2020.

[107] Audio: Michael Jackson, 'P.Y.T. (Pretty Young Thing)', *Youtube*, February 20, 2017, available at: https://www.youtube.com/watch?v=1ZZQuj6htF4, last accessed: February 25, 2020. Lyrics: Michael Jackson, 'P.Y.T. (Pretty Young Thing)', *Genius*, available at: https://genius.com/Michael-jackson-pyt-pretty-young-thing-lyrics, last accessed: February 25, 2020.

[108] Audio: Kanye West, 'Barry Bonds', *Youtube*, February 7, 2019, available at: https://www.youtube.com/watch?v=6QARCF_dvWo&list=OLAK5uy_kVXQTEtfSWtL_gP_czGRaKH1Kyfra NW80&index=7, last accessed: February 25, 2020; Lyrics: Kanye West, 'Barry Bonds', *Genius*, available at: https://genius.com/Kanye-west-barry-bonds-lyrics, last accessed: February 25, 2020.

[109] Audio: Mountain, 'Long Red', *Youtube*, May 21, 2015, available at: https://www.youtube.com/watch?v=a-0selX930s, last accessed: February 25, 2020. Lyrics: Mountain, 'Long Red', *Genius*, available at: https://genius.com/Mountain-long-red-lyrics, last accessed: February 25, 2020.

	7. 'Drunk and Hot Girls'[110] contains elements of 'Sing Swan Song'[111] performed by Can.
	8. 'Everything I Am'[112] contains elements of 'If We Can't Be Lovers'[113] performed by Prince Phillip Mitchell, and 'Bring the Noise'[114] performed by Public Enemy.
	9. 'The Glory'[115] contains elements of 'Save the Country'[116] performed by Laura Nyro and contains a sample of 'Long Red'[117] performed by Mountain.

[110] Audio: Kanye West, 'Drunk and Hot Girls', *Youtube*, February 7, 2019, available at: https://www.youtube.com/watch?v=4UvPbIbLFAc&list=OLAK5uy_kVXQTEtfSWtL_gP_czGRaKH1KyfraNW80&index=8, last accessed: February 25, 2020; Lyrics: Kanye West, 'Drunk and Hot Girls', *Genius*, available at: https://genius.com/Kanye-west-drunk-and-hot-girls-lyrics, last accessed: February 25, 2020.

[111] Audio: Can, 'Sing Swan Song', *Youtube*, March 23, 2008, available at: https://www.youtube.com/watch?v=3VmM8qRRLwU, last accessed: February 25, 2020. Lyrics: Can, 'Sing Swan Song', *Genius*, available at: https://genius.com/Can-sing-swan-song-lyrics, last accessed: February 25, 2020.

[112] Audio: Kanye West, 'Everything I am', *Youtube*, February 7, 2019, available at: https://www.youtube.com/watch?v=1ey-fHASEuQ&list=OLAK5uy_kVXQTEtfSWtL_gP_czGRaKH1KyfraNW80&index=10, last accessed: February 25, 2020; Lyrics: Kanye West, 'Everything I am', *Genius*, available at: https://genius.com/Kanye-west-everything-i-am-lyrics, last accessed: February 25, 2020.

[113] Audio: Prince Phillip Mitchell, 'If We Can't Be Lovers', *Youtube*, June 11, 2012, available at: https://www.youtube.com/watch?v=0StV8XtoO34, last accessed: February 25, 2020. Lyrics: Prince Phillip Mitchell, 'If We Can't Be Lovers', *Cifras*, available at: https://www.cifras.com.br/cifra/prince-phillip-mitchell/if-we-cant-be-lovers, last accessed: February 25, 2020.

[114] Audio: Public Enemy, ‚Bring The Noise', *Youtube*, July 19, 2010 available at: https://www.youtube.com/watch?v=l_Jeyif7bB4, last accessed: February 25, 2020; Lyrics: Public Enemy, ‚Bring The Noise', *Genius*, available at: https://genius.com/Public-enemy-bring-the-noise-lyrics, last accessed: February 25, 2020.

[115] Audio: Kanye West, 'The Glory', *Youtube*, February 7, 2019, available at: https://www.youtube.com/watch?v=gfj5FYaCxIA&list=OLAK5uy_kVXQTEtfSWtL_gP_czGRaKH1KyfraNW80&index=11, last accessed: February 25, 2020; Lyrics: Kanye West, 'The Glory', *Genius*, available at: https://genius.com/Kanye-west-the-glory-lyrics, last accessed: February 25, 2020.

[116] Audio: Laura Nyro, 'Save The Country', *Youtube*, May 4, 2008, available at: https://www.youtube.com/watch?v=E21KH_YOk7Y, last accessed: February 25, 2020. Lyrics: Laura Nyro, 'Save The Country', *Genius*, available at: https://genius.com/Laura-nyro-save-the-country-single-version-lyrics, last accessed: February 25, 2020.

[117] Audio: Mountain, 'Long Red', *Youtube*, May 21, 2015, available at: https://www.youtube.com/watch?v=a-0selX930s, last accessed: . Lyrics: Mountain, 'Long Red', *Genius*, available at: https://genius.com/Mountain-long-red-lyrics, last accessed: .

	10. 'Big Brother'[118] contains elements of 'It's Gonna Be Lonley'[119] performed by Prince and an interpolation of 'Hola Hovito'[120] from Jay Z, The Blueprint album. 11. 'Good Night'[121] contains elements of 'Nuff Man a Dead'[122] performed by Super Cat and 'Wake The Town'[123] performed by U-Roy. 12. 'Bittersweet Poetry'[124] interpolates 'Bittersweet'[125] performed by Chairmen of the Board.
88s & Heartbreak (2008)	1. 'RoboCop'[126] embodies portions of 'Kissing in the Rain'[127], written by Patrick Doyle.

[118] Audio: Kanye West, 'Big Brother', *Youtube*, February 7, 2019, available at: https://www.youtube.com/watch?v=gfqmlkXjVJk, last accessed: February 25, 2020; Lyrics: Kanye West, 'Big Brother', *Genius*, available at: https://genius.com/Kanye-west-big-brother-lyrics, last accessed: February 25, 2020.

[119] Audio: Prince, 'It's Gonna Be Lonley', *Youtube*, November 7, 2014, available at: https://www.youtube.com/watch?v=csGzQep_DQc, last accessed: February 25, 2020. Lyrics: Prince, 'It's Gonna Be Lonley', *Genius*, available at: https://genius.com/Prince-its-gonna-be-lonely-lyrics, last accessed: February 25, 2020.

[120] Audio: Jay Z, 'Hola Hovito', *Youtube*, August 17, 2019, available at: https://www.youtube.com/watch?v=WNImnZ92CsM, last accessed: February 25, 2020. Lyrics: Jay Z, 'Hola Hovito', *Genius*, available at: https://genius.com/Jay-z-hola-hovito-lyrics, last accessed: February 25, 2020.

[121] Audio: Kanye West, 'Good Night', *Youtube*, July 20, 2018, available at: https://www.youtube.com/watch?v=cGkyVEpuR3o, last accessed: February 25, 2020; Lyrics: Kanye West, 'Good Night', *Genius*, available at: https://genius.com/Kanye-west-good-night-lyrics, last accessed: February 25, 2020.

[122] Audio: Super Cat, 'Nuff Man A Dead', *Youtube*, January 18, 2009, available at: https://www.youtube.com/watch?v=j7QWJXXqiOc, last accessed: February 25, 2020. Lyrics: Super Cat, 'Nuff Man A Dead', *Genius*, available at: https://genius.com/Super-cat-nuff-man-a-dead-lyrics, last accessed: February 25, 2020.

[123] Audio: U-Roy, 'Wake The Town', *Youtube*, January 23, 2020, available at: https://www.youtube.com/watch?v=w7BdFEccQ-0, last accessed: February 25, 2020. Lyrics: U-Roy, 'Wake The Town', *Genius*, available at: https://genius.com/U-roy-wake-the-town-lyrics, last accessed: February 25, 2020.

[124] Audio: Kanye West, 'Bittersweet Poetry', *Youtube*, September 21, 2007, available at: https://www.youtube.com/watch?v=35c8IW0vsSE, last accessed: February 25, 2020; Lyrics: Kanye West, 'Bittersweet Poetry', *Genius*, available at: https://genius.com/Kanye-west-bittersweet-poetry-lyrics, last accessed: February 25, 2020.

[125] Audio: Chairmen Of The Board, 'Bittersweet', *Youtube*, November 2, 2008, available at: https://www.youtube.com/watch?v=cta48KVs4bA, last accessed: February 25, 2020. Lyrics: Chairmen Of The Board, 'Bittersweet', *Genius*, available at: https://genius.com/Chairmen-of-the-board-bittersweet-lyrics, last accessed: February 25, 2020.

[126] Audio: Kanye West, 'RoboCop', *Youtube*, January 29, 2019, available at: https://www.youtube.com/watch?v=3aQQDh6N_zg&list=OLAK5uy_lxlAkj0irzRmBAbhZz3JJZRph6Crb3bCY&index=7, last accessed: February 25, 2020; Lyrics: Kanye West, 'RoboCop', *Genius*, available at: https://genius.com/Kanye-west-robocop-lyrics, last accessed: February 25, 2020.

[127] Audio: Patrick Doyle, 'Kissing The Rain', *Youtube*, July 5, 2010, available at: https://www.youtube.com/watch?v=y4fcqHVkxqE, last accessed: February 25, 2020.

	2. 'Bad News'[128] contains a sample of the recording 'See Line Woman'[129] as performed by Nina Simone and written by George Bass 3. 'Coldest Winter'[130] embodies an interpolation of 'Memories Fade'[131], written by Roland Orzabal.
My Beautiful Dark Twisted Fantasy (2010)	1. 'Dark Fantasy'[132] contains samples of 'In High Places'[133], written by Mike Oldfield and Jon Anderson, and performed by Anderson. 2. 'Gorgeous'[134] contains portions and elements of the composition 'You Showed Me'[135], written by Gene Clark and Roger McGuinn, and performed by The Turtles.

[128] Audio: Kanye West, 'Bad News', *Youtube*, January 31, 2019, available at: https://www.youtube.com/watch?v=ZBeXHnxu5PA&list=OLAK5uy_lxIAkj0irzRmBAbhZz3JJZRph6Crb3bCY&index=9, last accessed: February 25, 2020; Lyrics: Kanye West, 'Bad News', *Genius*, available at: https://genius.com/Kanye-west-bad-news-lyrics, last accessed: February 25, 2020.

[129] Audio: Nina Simone, 'See Line Woman', *Youtube*, February 6, 2015, available at: https://www.youtube.com/watch?v=hVEbzdN_7n0, last accessed: February 25, 2020. Lyrics: Nina Simone, 'See Line Woman', *Genius*, available at: https://genius.com/Nina-simone-see-line-woman-lyrics, last accessed: February 25, 2020.

[130] Audio: Kanye West, 'Coldest Winter', *Youtube*, February 11, 2010, available at: https://www.youtube.com/watch?v=n6rjQ9VVLDI&list=OLAK5uy_lxIAkj0irzRmBAbhZz3JJZRph6Crb3bCY&index=11, last accessed: February 25, 2020; Lyrics: Kanye West, 'Coldest Winter', *Genius*, available at: https://genius.com/Kanye-west-coldest-winter-lyrics, last accessed: February 25, 2020.

[131] Audio: Orzabal, 'Memories Fade', *Youtube*, July 31, 2018, (the song was performed by Tears for Fears), available at: https://www.youtube.com/watch?v=iuQSBr-YQYY, last accessed: February 25, 2020. Lyrics: Orzabal, 'Memories Fade', *Genius*, available at: https://genius.com/Tears-for-fears-memories-fade-lyrics, last accessed: February 25, 2020.

[132] Audio: Kanye West, 'Dark Fantasy', *Youtube*, July 12, 2011, available at: https://www.youtube.com/watch?v=PeFGaXCYktg&list=OLAK5uy_mRFuqe0IlrexXkU7JOxo4rOb0WLEcwuz8, last accessed: February 25, 2020; Lyrics: Kanye West, 'Dark Fantasy', *Genius*, available at: https://genius.com/Kanye-west-dark-fantasy-lyrics, last accessed: February 25, 2020.

[133] Audio: Mike Oldfield, 'In High Places', *Youtube*, available at: https://www.youtube.com/watch?v=AofUt0TQyf0, last accessed: February 25, 2020. Lyrics: Mike Oldfield, 'In High Places', *Genius*, available at: https://genius.com/Mike-oldfield-in-high-places-lyrics, last accessed: February 25, 2020.

[134] Audio: Kanye West, 'Gorgeous', *Youtube*, July 23, 2018, available at: https://www.youtube.com/watch?v=miJAfs7jhak&list=OLAK5uy_mRFuqe0IlrexXkU7JOxo4rOb0WLEcwuz8&index=2, last accessed: February 25, 2020; Lyrics: Kanye West, 'Gorgeous', *Genius*, available at: https://genius.com/Kanye-west-gorgeous-lyrics, last accessed: February 25, 2020.

[135] Audio: The Turtles, 'You Showed Me', *Youtube*, August 18, 2010, available at: https://www.youtube.com/watch?v=UI3K_e-ZgiE, last accessed: February 25, 2020. Lyrics: The Turtles, 'You Showed Me', *Genius*, available at: https://genius.com/The-turtles-you-showed-me-lyrics, last accessed: February 25, 2020.

	3. 'Power'[136] contains elements from 'It's Your Thing'[137], performed by Cold Grits; elements of '4. Afromerica'[138], written by Francois Bernheim, Jean-Pierre Lang, and Boris Bergman, and performed by Continent Number 6; and material sampled from '21st Century Schizoid Man'[139], composed by Robert Fripp, Michael Giles, Greg Lake, Ian McDonald, and Peter Sinfield, and performed by King Crimson. 4. 'So Appalled'[140] contains samples of 'You Are – I Am'[141], written by Manfred Mann, and performed by Manfred Mann's Earth Band. 5. 'Devil in a New Dress'[142] contains samples of 'Will You Love Me Tomorrow'[143], written by Carole King and Gerry Goffin, and performed by Smokey Robinson.

---

[136] Audio: Kanye West, 'Power', *Youtube*, August 5, 2010, available at: https://www.youtube.com/watch?v=L53gjP-TtGE&list=OLAK5uy_mRFuqe0IIrexXkU7JOxo4rOb0WLEcwuz8&index=3, last accessed: February 25, 2020; Lyrics: Kanye West, 'Power', *Genius*, available at: https://genius.com/Kanye-west-power-lyrics, last accessed: February 25, 2020.

[137] Audio: Cold Grits, 'It's Your Thing', *Youtube*, July 2, 2011, available at: https://www.youtube.com/watch?v=cozD75RcSRM, last accessed: February 25, 2020. Lyrics: Cold Grits, 'It's Your Thing', *Genius*, available at: https://genius.com/Cold-grits-its-your-thing-lyrics, last accessed: February 25, 2020.

[138] Audio: Continent Number 6, 'Afromerica', *Youtube*, November 25, 2008, available at: https://www.youtube.com/watch?v=e-dtwySzcQc, last accessed: February 25, 2020.

[139] Audio: King Crimson', 21st Century Schizoid Man', *Youtube*, December 7, 2019, available at: https://www.youtube.com/watch?v=t7n7KvWiCME, last accessed: February 25, 2020. Lyrics: King Crimson', 21st Century Schizoid Man', *Genius*, available at: https://genius.com/King-crimson-21st-century-schizoid-man-lyrics, last accessed: February 25, 2020.

[140] Audio: Kanye West, 'So Appalled', *Youtube*, July 23, 2018, available at: https://www.youtube.com/watch?v=0o9HzQ3zAcE&list=OLAK5uy_mRFuqe0IIrexXkU7JOxo4rOb0WLEcwuz8&index=7, last accessed: February 25, 2020; Lyrics: Kanye West, 'So Appalled', *Genius*, available at: https://genius.com/Kanye-west-so-appalled-lyrics, last accessed: February 25, 2020.

[141] Audio: Manfred Mann's Earth Band, 'You Are – I am', *Youtube*, April 8, 2010, available at: https://www.youtube.com/watch?v=cYJ0iLHeyNM, last accessed: February 25, 2020. Lyrics: Manfred Mann's Earth Band, 'You Are – I am', *Genius*, available at: https://genius.com/Manfred-manns-earth-band-you-are-i-am-lyrics, last accessed: February 25, 2020.

[142] Audio: Kanye West, 'Devil In A New Dress', *Youtube*, July 23, 2018, available at: https://www.youtube.com/watch?v=sk3rpYkiHe8&list=OLAK5uy_mRFuqe0IIrexXkU7JOxo4rOb0WLEcwuz8&index=8, last accessed: February 25, 2020; Lyrics: Kanye West, 'Devil In A New Dress', *Genius*, available at: https://genius.com/Kanye-west-devil-in-a-new-dress-lyrics, last accessed: February 25, 2020.

[143] Audio: Smokey Robinson, 'Will You Love me Tomorrow', *Youtube*, July 31, 2018, available at: https://www.youtube.com/watch?v=p8VDWxLj5Wk, last accessed: February 25, 2020. Lyrics: Smokey Robinson, 'Will You Love me Tomorrow', *Genius*, available at: https://genius.com/Smokey-robinson-will-you-love-me-tomorrow-lyrics, last accessed: February 25, 2020.

	6. 'Runaway'[144] contains a sample of 'Expo 83'[145], written by J. Branch, and performed by Backyard Heavies; and excerpts from Rick James Live at Long Beach, CA, 1981.[146] 7. 'Hell of a Life'[147] contains samples of 'She's My Baby'[148], written by Sylvester Stewart, and performed by The Mojo Men; samples of 'Stud-Spider'[149] by Tony Joe White; and portions of 'Iron Man'[150], written by Terence Butler, Anthony Iommi, John Osbourne, and William Ward, and performed by Black Sabbath. 8. 'Blame Game'[151] contains elements of 'Avril 14th'[152], written by Richard James, and performed by Aphex Twin.

[144] Audio: Kanye West, 'Runaway', *Youtube*, October 21, 20110, available at: https://www.youtube.com/watch?v=Bm5iA4Zupek&list=OLAK5uy_mRFuqe0IlrexXkU7JOxo4rOb0WLEc wuz8&index=9, last accessed: February 25, 2020; Lyrics: Kanye West, 'Runaway', *Genius*, available at: https://genius.com/Kanye-west-runaway-lyrics, last accessed: February 25, 2020.

[145] Audio: Backyard Heavies, 'Expo 83', *Youtube*, November 15, 2010, available at: https://www.youtube.com/watch?v=EjQ70gCx0H4, last accessed: February 25, 2020.

[146] Audio: Ricky James Live at Long Beach, CA, 1981, *Youtube*, May 27, 2011, available at: https://www.youtube.com/watch?v=Vp_Rxsat3FA&list=PLXMaLu7UP_qjn184yjcy9GmEG-J8IKmUx, last accessed: February 25, 2020.

[147] Audio: Kanye West, 'Hell Of A Life', *Youtube*, July 23, 2018, available at: https://www.youtube.com/watch?v=tJKNcl6jC6A&list=OLAK5uy_mRFuqe0IlrexXkU7JOxo4rOb0WLEcw uz8&index=10, last accessed: February 25, 2020; Lyrics: Kanye West, 'Hell Of A Life', *Genius*, available at: https://genius.com/Kanye-west-hell-of-a-life-lyrics, last accessed: February 25, 2020.

[148] Audio: The Mojo Men, 'She's My Baby', *Youtube*, October 8, 2011, available at: https://www.youtube.com/watch?v=KgLeOkSm56E, last accessed: February 25, 2020. Lyrics: The Mojo Men, 'She's My Baby', *Genius*, available at: https://genius.com/The-mojo-men-shes-my-baby-lyrics, last accessed: February 25, 2020.

[149] Audio: Tony Joe White, 'Stud-Spider', *Youtube*, February 10, 2010, available at: https://www.youtube.com/watch?v=6rkXth6pTr0, last accessed: February 25, 2020. Lyrics: Tony Joe White, 'Stud-Spider', *Genius*, available at: https://genius.com/Tony-joe-white-stud-spider-lyrics, last accessed: February 25, 2020.

[150] Audio: Black Sabbath, 'Iron Man', *Youtube*, August 14, 2012, available at: https://www.youtube.com/watch?v=8aQRq9hhekA, last accessed: February 25, 2020. Lyrics: Black Sabbath, 'Iron Man', *Genius*, available at: https://genius.com/Black-sabbath-iron-man-lyrics, last accessed: February 25, 2020.

[151] Audio: Kanye West, 'Blame Game', *Youtube*, July 23, 2018, available at: https://www.youtube.com/watch?v=6mp72xUirfs&list=OLAK5uy_mRFuqe0IlrexXkU7JOxo4rOb0WLEcw uz8&index=11, last accessed: February 25, 2020; Lyrics: Kanye West, 'Blame Game', *Genius*, available at: https://genius.com/Kanye-west-blame-game-lyrics, last accessed: February 25, 2020.

[152] Audio: Aphex Twin, 'Avril 14th', *Youtube*, May 7, 2015, available at: https://www.youtube.com/watch?v=F6dGAZTj8xA, last accessed: February 25, 2020. Lyrics: Aphex Twin, 'Avril 14th', *Genius*, available at: https://genius.com/Aphex-twin-avril-14th-lyrics, last accessed: February 25, 2020.

	9. 'Lost in the World'[153] contains portions of 'Soul Makossa'[154], written by Manu Dibango; a sample of 'Think (About It)'[155], written by James Brown, and performed by Lyn Collins; samples of 'Woods'[156], written by Justin Vernon, and performed by Bon Iver; and samples of 'Comment No. 1'[157], written and performed by Gil Scott-Heron. 10. 'Who Will Survive in America'[158] contains samples of 'Comment No. 1'[159] performed by Gil Scott-Heron.
	1. 'No Church in the Wild' contains samples from 'K-Scope', written and performed by Phil Manzanera; samples of 'Sunshine Help Me', written and performed by Spooky Tooth; and samples of 'Don't Tell a Lie About Me (and I Won't Tell the Truth About You)', written and performed by James Brown. 2. 'Niggas in Paris' contains samples of the Reverend W. A. Donaldson recording 'Baptizing Scene'; and dialogue between Will Ferrell and Jon Heder from the 2007 comedy film Blades of Glory. 3. 'Otis' contains samples of 'Try a Little Tenderness', written by [Jimmy Campbell and Reg Connelly, Harry M. Woods] and performed by Otis Redding; samples of 'Don't Tell a Lie About Me (and I Won't Tell the Truth About You)', written and performed by James Brown; and elements of 'Top Billin', written and performed by Audio Two.

---

[153] Audio: Kanye West, 'Lost In The World', *Youtube*, May 23, 2012, available at: https://www.youtube.com/watch?v=ofaRvNOV4SI&list=OLAK5uy_mRFuqe0IlrexXkU7JOxo4rOb0WLEc wuz8&index=12, last accessed: February 25, 2020; Lyrics: Kanye West, 'Lost In The World', *Genius*, available at: https://genius.com/Kanye-west-lost-in-the-world-lyrics, last accessed: February 25, 2020.
[154] Audio: Manu Dibango, 'Soul Makossa', *Youtube*, December 31, 2015, available at: https://www.youtube.com/watch?v=o0CeFX6E2yI, last accessed: February 25, 2020. Lyrics: Manu Dibango, 'Soul Makossa', *Genius*, available at: https://genius.com/Manu-dibango-soul-makossa-lyrics, last accessed: February 25, 2020.
[155] Audio: Lyn Collins, 'Think (About it)', *Youtube*, August 31, 2014, available at: https://www.youtube.com/watch?v=HKix_06L5AY, last accessed: February 25, 2020. Lyrics: Lyn Collins, 'Think (About it)', *Genius*, available at: https://genius.com/Lyn-collins-think-about-it-lyrics, last accessed: February 25, 2020.
[156] Audio: Bon Iver, 'Woods', *Youtube*, October 8, 2010, available at: https://www.youtube.com/watch?v=1_cePGP6lbU, last accessed: February 25, 2020. Lyrics: Bon Iver, 'Woods', *Genius*, available at: https://genius.com/Bon-iver-woods-lyrics, last accessed: February 25, 2020.
[157] Audio: Gil Scott-Heron, 'Comment No.1', *Youtube*, May 17, 2009, available at: https://www.youtube.com/watch?v=8B6DVdCzwy0, last accessed: . Lyrics: Gil Scott-Heron, 'Comment No.1', *Genius*, available at: https://genius.com/Gil-scott-heron-comment-1-annotated, last accessed: February 25, 2020.
[158] Audio: Kanye West, 'Who Will Survive In America', *Youtube*, July 23, 2018, available at: https://www.youtube.com/watch?v=UB6sXiZ1ldw&list=OLAK5uy_mRFuqe0IlrexXkU7JOxo4rOb0WLEcw uz8&index=13, last accessed: February 25, 2020; Lyrics: Kanye West, 'Who Will Survive In America', *Genius*, available at: https://genius.com/Kanye-west-who-will-survive-in-america-lyrics, last accessed: February 25, 2020.
[159] Audio: Gil Scott-Heron, 'Comment No.1', *Youtube*, May 17, 2009, available at: https://www.youtube.com/watch?v=8B6DVdCzwy0, last accessed: February 25, 2020. Lyrics: Gil Scott-Heron, 'Comment No.1', *Genius*, available at: https://genius.com/Gil-scott-heron-comment-1-annotated, last accessed: February 25, 2020.

Watch the Throne (2011)[160]	4. 'Gotta Have It' contains elements of 'Don't Tell a Lie About Me (and I Won't Tell the Truth About You)'; samples of 'People Get Up and Drive Your Funky Soul'; and elements of 'My Thang', written and performed by James Brown. 5. 'New Day' contains samples of 'Feeling Good', written and performed by Nina Simone. 6. 'That's My Bitch' contains samples of 'Get Up, Get Into It, Get Involved', written and performed by James Brown; and samples of 'Apache', written and performed by Incredible Bongo Band. 7. 'Who Gon Stop Me' contains samples of 'I Can't Stop', written and performed by Flux Pavilion. 8. 'Murder to Excellence' contains samples of 'LA LA LA', written and performed by The Indiggo Twins; and samples of 'Celie Shaves Mr./Scarification' from the 1985 drama film The Color Purple, written and performed by Quincy Jones. 9. 'Why I Love You' contains samples of 'I Love You So', written and performed by Cassius. 10. 'Primetime' contains samples of 'Action', written and performed by Orange Krush. 11. 'The Joy' contains samples of 'The Makings of You (Live)', written and performed by Curtis Mayfield; and elements of 'Different Strokes', written and performed by Syl Johnson. 12. Each interlude after the songs 'No Church in the Wild', 'New Day', and 'Welcome to the Jungle', as well as before 'Illest Motherfucker Alive' all contain samples of 'Tristessa', written and performed by Orchestra Njervudarov.
Cruel Summer (2012)[161]	1. 'Mercy' contains samples of the recording 'Dust a Sound Boy', written by Denzie Beagle and Winston Riley, and performed by Super Beagle; samples of the recording 'Cu-Oonuh', written by Reggie Williams and Winston Riley, and performed by Reggie Stepper; portions of the recording 'Lambo', performed by YB; and a sample of 'Tony's Theme', composed by Giorgio Moroder. 2. 'New God Flow' contains samples of the recording 'Synthetic Substitution', written by Herb Rooney, and performed by Melvin Bliss; samples of the recording 'Mighty Healthy', written by Herb Rooney, Ronald Bean, Highleigh Crizoe and Dennis Coles, and performed by Ghostface Killah; a sample of the Reverend G. I. Townsend recording 'Sermon Fragment', written and performed by Townsend; and samples from the recording 'Bôdas De Sangue', written and performed by Marcos Valle. 3. 'The Morning' contains portions of 'Get Me to the Church on Time', written and performed by Alan Jay Lerner and Frederick Loewe. 4. 'Cold' contains interpolations of 'Illegal Search', written by James T. Smith and Marlon L. Williams, and performed by LL Cool J; and 'Lookin' at Me' by Mase.

---

[160] The information for this album was retrieved from Watch the Throne, *Wikipedia*, available at: https://en.wikipedia.org/wiki/Watch_the_Throne, last accessed: February 25, 2020.
[161] The information for this album was retrieved from Cruel Summer, *Wikipedia*, available at: https://en.wikipedia.org/wiki/Cruel_Summer_(GOOD_Music_album), last accessed: February 25, 2020.

	5. 'The One' contains samples of the recording 'Public Enemy No. 1', written by Carlton Ridenhour and James Boxley, and performed by Public Enemy; and samples of the recording 'Double Barrel', written by Dave Barker, Winston Riley, and Ansell George Collins, and performed by Dave and Ansell Collins. 6. 'Don't Like' contains elements of 'Under Mi Sensi', written and performed by Barrington Levy and Paul Love.
Yeezus (2013)	1. 'On Sight'[162] contains an interpolation of 'Sermon (He'll Give Us What We Really Need)'[163], written by Keith Carter, Sr. 2. 'I Am a God'[164] contains samples of 'Forward Inna Dem Clothes'[165], written by Clifton Bailey III and H. Hart, performed by Capleton; and samples of 'Are Zindagi Hai Khel'[166], written by Anand Bakshi and Rahul Burman, performed by Burman, Manna Dey and Asha Bhosle. 3. 'New Slaves'[167] contains samples of 'Gyöngyhajú lány'[168], written by Gábor Presser and Anna Adamis, performed by Omega. 4. 'I'm In It'[169] contains samples of 'Lately'[170], written by Vidal Davis, Carvin Haggins, Andre Harris, Kenny Lattimore and Jill Scott, performed by Lattimore.

---

[162] Audio: Kanye West, 'On Sight', *Youtube*, July 21, 2018, available at: https://www.youtube.com/watch?v=uU9Fe-WXew4&list=OLAK5uy_m6VFZd8KNhbFoHGRhtzFakGNVSkMMGvbU&index=1, last accessed: February 25, 2020; Lyrics: Kanye West, 'On Sight', *Genius*, available at: https://genius.com/Kanye-west-on-sight-lyrics, last accessed: February 25, 2020.

[163] Audio: Keith Carter, Sr., 'Sermon (He'll Give Us What We Really Need)', *Youtube*, September 7, 2013, available at: https://www.youtube.com/watch?v=vyf7f7ouzjk, last accessed: February 25, 2020.

[164] Audio: Kanye West, 'I am A God', *Youtube*, July 21, 2018, available at: https://www.youtube.com/watch?v=KuQoQgL63Xo&list=OLAK5uy_m6VFZd8KNhbFoHGRhtzFakGNVSk MMGvbU&index=3, last accessed: February 25, 2020; Lyrics: Kanye West, 'I am A God', *Genius*, available at: https://genius.com/Kanye-west-i-am-a-god-lyrics, last accessed: February 25, 2020.

[165] Audio: Capleton, 'Forward Inna Dem Clothes', *Youtube*, April 27, 2017, available at: https://www.youtube.com/watch?v=HNVY4pTj6pk, last accessed: February 25, 2020.

[166] I did not find a version that is directly linked with the title of the song.

[167] Audio: Kanye West, 'New Slaves', *Youtube*, July 21, 2018, available at: https://www.youtube.com/watch?v=vQ0u09mFodw&list=OLAK5uy_m6VFZd8KNhbFoHGRhtzFakGNVSk MMGvbU&index=4, last accessed: February 25, 2020; Lyrics: Kanye West, 'New Slaves', *Genius*, available at: https://genius.com/Kanye-west-new-slaves-lyrics, last accessed: February 25, 2020.

[168] Audio: Omega, 'Gyöngyhajú lány', *Youtube*, April 12, 2007, available at: https://www.youtube.com/watch?v=CGt-rTDkMcM, last accessed: February 25, 2020. Lyrics: Omega, 'Gyöngyhajú lány', *Genius*, available at: https://genius.com/Omega-gyongyhaju-lany-lyrics, last accessed: February 25, 2020.

[169] Audio: Kanye West, 'I'am In It', *Youtube*, July 21, 2018, available at: https://www.youtube.com/watch?v=_jZuz3NEr18&list=OLAK5uy_m6VFZd8KNhbFoHGRhtzFakGNVSkM MGvbU&index=6, last accessed: February 25, 2020; Lyrics: Kanye West, 'I'am In It', *Genius*, available at: https://genius.com/Kanye-west-im-in-it-lyrics, last accessed: February 25, 2020.

[170] Audio: Lattimore, 'Lately', *Youtube*, November 8, 2014, available at: https://www.youtube.com/watch?v=mkJQzvrcBZM, last accessed: February 25, 2020. Lyrics: Lattimore, 'Lately', *Genius*, available at: https://genius.com/Kenny-lattimore-lately-lyrics, last accessed: February 25, 2020.

<table>
<tr><td></td><td>

5. 'Blood on the Leaves'[171] contains a sample of 'Strange Fruit'[172], written by Lewis Allan, performed by Nina Simone; samples of 'R U Ready'[173], written by Ross Birchard and Lunice Pierre, performed by TNGHT.

6. 'Guilt Trip'[174] contains interpolations of 'Chief Rocka'[175], written by Keith Elam, Kevin Hansford, Dupre Kelly, Christopher Martin, Alterick Wardrick and Marlon Williams, performed by Lords of the Underground; and a sample of 'Blocka (Ackeejuice Rockers Remix)'[176], written by Terrence Thornton and Tyree Pittman, performed by Pusha T featuring Travis Scott and Popcaan.

7. 'Send It Up'[177] contains a sample of 'Memories'[178], written by Anthony Moses Davis, Collin York and Lowell Dunbar, performed by Beenie Man.

</td></tr>
</table>

---

[171] Audio: Kanye West, 'Blood On The Leaves', *Youtube*, July 21, 2018, available at: https://www.youtube.com/watch?v=KEA0btSNkpw&list=OLAK5uy_m6VFZd8KNhbFoHGRhtzFakGNVSk MMGvbU&index=7, last accessed: February 25, 2020; Lyrics: Kanye West, 'Blood On The Leaves', *Genius*, available at: https://genius.com/Kanye-west-blood-on-the-leaves-lyrics, last accessed: February 25, 2020.

[172] Audio: Nina Simone, 'Strange Fruit', *Youtube*, July 7, 2009, available at: https://www.youtube.com/watch?v=BcCm_ySBslk, last accessed: February 25, 2020. Lyrics: Nina Simone, 'Strange Fruit', *Genius*, available at: https://genius.com/Nina-simone-strange-fruit-lyrics, last accessed: February 25, 2020.

[173] Audio: THGHT, 'R U Ready', *Youtube*, May 6, 2013, available at: https://www.youtube.com/watch?v=U_2gU4N9k3o, last accessed: February 25, 2020. Lyrics: THGHT, 'R U Ready', *Genius*, available at: https://genius.com/Tnght-r-u-ready-lyrics, last accessed: February 25, 2020.

[174] Audio: Kanye West, 'Guilt Trip', *Youtube*, July 21, 2018, available at: https://www.youtube.com/watch?v=5hthMeEqf40&list=OLAK5uy_m6VFZd8KNhbFoHGRhtzFakGNVSk MMGvbU&index=8, last accessed: February 25, 2020; Lyrics: Kanye West, 'Guilt Trip', *Genius*, available at: https://genius.com/Kanye-west-guilt-trip-lyrics, last accessed: February 25, 2020.

[175] Audio: Lords Of The Underground', 'Chief Rocka', *Youtube*, May 17, 2006, available at: https://www.youtube.com/watch?v=YFbLRZCExBk, last accessed: February 25, 2020. Lyrics: Lords Of The Underground', 'Chief Rocka', *Genius*, available at: https://genius.com/Lords-of-the-underground-chief-rocka-lyrics, last accessed: February 25, 2020.

[176] Audio: Pusha T, Travis Scott and Popcaan, 'Blocka (Ackeejuice Rockers Remix)', *Youtube*, May 30, 2013, available at: https://www.youtube.com/watch?v=OeNaX98bPE4, last accessed: February 25, 2020. Lyrics: Pusha T, Travis Scott and Popcaan, 'Blocka (Ackeejuice Rockers Remix)', *Genius*, available at: https://genius.com/Pusha-t-blocka-lyrics, last accessed: February 25, 2020.

[177] Audio: Kanye West, 'Send It Up', *Youtube*, July 21, 2018, available at: https://www.youtube.com/watch?v=vUFiVwa6U_c&list=OLAK5uy_m6VFZd8KNhbFoHGRhtzFakGNVSk MMGvbU&index=9, last accessed: February 25, 2020; Lyrics: Kanye West, 'Send It Up', *Genius*, available at: https://genius.com/Kanye-west-send-it-up-lyrics, last accessed: February 25, 2020.

[178] Audio: Beenie Man, 'Memories', *Youtube*, April 17, 2013, available at: https://www.youtube.com/watch?v=-jkmmZZfK-I, last accessed: February 25, 2020. Lyrics: Beenie Man, 'Memories', *Genius*, available at: https://genius.com/Beenie-man-memories-lyrics, last accessed: February 25, 2020.

	8. 'Bound 2'[179] contains interpolations of 'Aeroplane (Reprise)'[180], written by Norman Whiteside, performed by Wee; samples of 'Bound'[181], written by Bobby Massey and Robert Dukes, performed by Ponderosa Twins Plus One; a sample of 'Sweet Nothin's'[182], written by Ronnie Self, performed by Brenda Lee.
	1. 'Ultralight Beam'[183] contains uncredited elements of the video game Counter-Strike.[184] 2. 'Father Stretch My Hands, Pt. 1'[185] contains samples of 'Father I Stretch My Hands'[186], written and performed by Pastor T. L. Barrett featuring Youth for Christ. 3. 'Pt. 2'[187] contains samples of the song 'Panda'[188], written by Sidney Selby III and Adnan Khan, and performed by Desiigner;
The Life of Pablo (2016)	

[179] Audio: Kanye West, 'Bound 2', *Youtube*, November 19, 2013, available at: https://www.youtube.com/watch?v=BBAtAM7vtgc&list=OLAK5uy_m6VFZd8KNhbFoHGRhtzFakGNVSk MMGvbU&index=10, last accessed: February 25, 2020; Lyrics: Kanye West, 'Bound 2', *Genius*, available at: https://genius.com/Kanye-west-bound-2-lyrics, last accessed: February 25, 2020.

[180] Audio: Wee, 'Aeroplane (Reprise)', *Youtube*, August 1, 2011, available at: https://www.youtube.com/watch?v=ncB65dETKlM, last accessed: February 25, 2020. Lyrics: Wee, 'Aeroplane (Reprise)', *Genius*, available at: https://genius.com/Wee-aeroplane-reprise-lyrics, last accessed: February 25, 2020.

[181] Audio: Ponderosa Twins Plus One, 'Bound', *Youtube*, August 28, 2013, available at: https://www.youtube.com/watch?v=d6mGHwHMB5s, last accessed: February 25, 2020. Lyrics: Ponderosa Twins Plus One, 'Bound', *Genius*, available at: https://genius.com/Ponderosa-twins-plus-one-bound-lyrics, last accessed: February 25, 2020.

[182] Audio: Brenda Lee, 'Sweet Nothin's', *Youtube*, March 8, 2008, available at: https://www.youtube.com/watch?v=KWgyum5fjJc, last accessed: February 25, 2020. Lyrics: Brenda Lee, 'Sweet Nothin's', *Genius*, available at: https://genius.com/Brenda-lee-sweet-nothins-lyrics, last accessed: February 25, 2020.

[183] Audio: Kanye West, 'Ultralight Beam', *Youtube*, August 24, 2018, available at: https://www.youtube.com/watch?v=6oHdAA3AqnE, last accessed: March 1, 2020. Lyrics: Kanye West, 'Ultralight Beam', *Genius*, available at: https://genius.com/Kanye-west-ultralight-beam-lyrics, last accessed: March 1, 2020.

[184] Audio: Flash Bang Ultralight Beam, *Youtube*, January 16, 2017, available at: https://www.youtube.com/watch?v=ozCsGQIM29o, last accessed: March 1, 2020

[185] Audio: Kanye West, 'Father Stretch My Hands, Pt. 1', *Youtube*, July 24, 2018, available at: https://www.youtube.com/watch?v=wuO4_P_8p-Q&list=OLAK5uy_keyJA-JsoAdfCylvyyIQMRjenzX6MzmnE&index=2, last accessed: February 25, 2020; Lyrics: Kanye West, 'Father Stretch My Hands, Pt. 1', *Genius*, available at: https://genius.com/Kanye-west-father-stretch-my-hands-pt-1-lyrics, last accessed: February 25, 2020.

[186] Audio: Pastor T.L., Youth For Christ, 'Father I Stretch My Hands', *Youtube*, July 31, 2013, available at: https://www.youtube.com/watch?v=lBYcOGkWEJY, last accessed: February 25, 2020. Lyrics: Pastor T.L., Youth For Christ, 'Father I Stretch My Hands', *Genius*, available at: https://genius.com/Pastor-tl-barrett-father-stretch-my-hands-lyrics, last accessed: February 25, 2020.

[187] Audio: Kanye West, 'Pt. 2', *Youtube*, July 24, 2018, available at: https://www.youtube.com/watch?v=xp8z7pconzw&list=OLAK5uy_keyJA-JsoAdfCylvyyIQMRjenzX6MzmnE&index=3, last accessed: February 25, 2020; Lyrics: Kanye West, 'Pt. 2', *Genius*, available at: https://genius.com/Kanye-west-pt-2-lyrics, last accessed: February 25, 2020.

[188] Audio: Desiigner, 'Panda', *Youtube*, March 6, 2006, available at: https://www.youtube.com/watch?v=4NJlUribp3c, last accessed: February 25, 2020. Lyrics: Desiigner, 'Panda', *Genius*, available at: https://genius.com/Desiigner-panda-lyrics, last accessed: February 25, 2020.

samples of 'Father I Stretch My Hands'[189], written and performed by Pastor T. L. Barrett featuring Youth for Christ; and contains elements of the video game Street Fighter II: The World Warrior.
4. 'Famous'[190] contains samples of 'Do What You Gotta Do'[191], written by Jimmy Webb and performed by Nina Simone; samples of 'Bam Bam'[192], written by Winston Riley and performed by Sister Nancy; and contains samples of 'Mi Sono Svegliato E... Ho Chiuso Gli Occhi'[193], written by Luis Bacalov, Sergio Bardotti, Giampiero Scalamogna, and Enzo Vita, and performed by Il Rovescio della Medaglia.
5. 'Feedback'[194] contains samples of 'Talagh'[195], written by Ardalan Sarfaraz and Manouchehr Cheshmazar, and performed by Googoosh.
6. 'Low Lights'[196] contains samples of 'So Alive (Acapella)'[197], written by Sandy Rivera and performed by Kings of Tomorrow

[189] Audio: Pastor T.L., Youth For Christ, 'Father I Stretch My Hands', *Youtube*, July 31, 2013, available at: https://www.youtube.com/watch?v=lBYcOGkWEJY, last accessed: February 25, 2020. Lyrics: Pastor T.L., Youth For Christ, 'Father I Stretch My Hands', *Genius*, available at: https://genius.com/Pastor-tl-barrett-father-stretch-my-hands-lyrics, last accessed: February 25, 2020.

[190] Audio: Kanye West, 'Famous', *Youtube*, July 24, 2018, available at: https://www.youtube.com/watch?v=Lq2TmRzg19k&list=OLAK5uy_keyJA-JsoAdfCylvyyIQMRjenzX6MzmnE&index=4, last accessed: February 25, 2020; Lyrics: Kanye West, 'Famous', *Genius*, available at: https://genius.com/Kanye-west-famous-lyrics, last accessed: February 25, 2020.

[191] Audio: Nina Simone, 'Do What You Gotta Do', *Youtube*, June 29, 2014, available at: https://www.youtube.com/watch?v=E4xde537g1A, last accessed: February 25, 2020. Lyrics: Nina Simone, 'Do What You Gotta Do', *Genius*, available at: https://genius.com/Nina-simone-do-what-you-gotta-do-lyrics, last accessed: February 25, 2020.

[192] Audio: Sister Nancy, 'Bam Bam', *Youtube*, September 23, 2008, available at: https://www.youtube.com/watch?v=OcaPu9JPenU, last accessed: February 25, 2020. Lyrics: Sister Nancy, 'Bam Bam', *Genius*, available at: https://genius.com/Sister-nancy-bam-bam-lyrics, last accessed: February 25, 2020.

[193] Audio: Il Rovescio della Medaglia, 'Mi Sono Svegliato E ... Ho Chiuso Gli Occhi', *Youtube*, November 8, 2014, available at: https://www.youtube.com/watch?v=GrKyFS-22w8, last accessed: February 25, 2020. Lyrics: Il Rovescio della Medaglia, 'Mi Sono Svegliato E ... Ho Chiuso Gli Occhi', *Genius*, available at: https://genius.com/Il-rovescio-della-medaglia-mi-sono-svegliato-e-ho-chiuso-gli-occhi-lyrics, last accessed: February 25, 2020.

[194] Audio: Kanye West, 'Feedback', *Youtube*, July 24, 2018, available at: https://www.youtube.com/watch?v=Q-fluWQ6zW8&list=OLAK5uy_keyJA-JsoAdfCylvyyIQMRjenzX6MzmnE&index=5, last accessed: February 25, 2020; Lyrics: Kanye West, 'Feedback', *Genius*, available at: https://genius.com/Kanye-west-feedback-lyrics, last accessed: February 25, 2020.

[195] Audio: Googoosh, 'Talagh', *Youtube*, July 16, 2011, available at: https://www.youtube.com/watch?v=DF2sGMjEVHo, last accessed: February 25, 2020. Lyrics: Googoosh, 'Talagh', *Genius*, available at: https://genius.com/Googoosh-talagh-lyrics, last accessed: February 25, 2020.

[196] Audio: Kanye West, 'Low Lights', *Youtube*, July 24, 2018, available at: https://www.youtube.com/watch?v=wj0C2oet2r0&list=OLAK5uy_keyJA-JsoAdfCylvyyIQMRjenzX6MzmnE&index=6, last accessed: February 25, 2020; Lyrics: Kanye West, 'Low Lights', *Genius*, available at: https://genius.com/Kanye-west-low-lights-lyrics, last accessed: February 25, 2020.

[197] Audio: King Of Tomorrow, 'So Alive', *Youtube*, June 28, 2013, available at: https://www.youtube.com/watch?v=X0YxSuWvatE, last accessed: February 25, 2020. Lyrics: King Of

7. 'Freestyle 4'[198] contains samples of 'Human'[199], written by Alison Goldfrapp, William Gregory, Robert Locke, and Timothy Norfolk, and performed by Goldfrapp.

8. 'Waves'[200] contains samples and elements of 'Fantastic Freaks at the Dixie'[201], written by Fred Bratwaithe, Robin Diggs, Kevin Ferguson, Theodore Livingston, Darryl Mason, and James Whipper, and performed by Fantastic Freaks.

9. 'FML'[202] contains interpolations of 'Hit'[203], written by Lawrence Cassidy, Vincent Cassidy, and Paul Wiggin, and performed by Section 25.

10. 'Real Friends'[204] contains interpolations of 'Friends'[205], written by Jalil Hutchins and Lawrence Smith, and performed by Whodini.

Tomorrow, 'So Alive', *Genius*, available at: https://genius.com/Kings-of-tomorrow-so-alive-lyrics; last accessed: February 25, 2020.

[198] Audio: Kanye West, 'Freestyle 4', *Youtube*, July 24, 2018, available at: https://www.youtube.com/watch?v=yt3rfHIijZQ&list=OLAK5uy_keyJA-JsoAdfCylvyyIQMRjenzX6MzmnE&index=8, last accessed: February 25, 2020; Lyrics: Kanye West, 'Freestyle 4', *Genius*, available at: https://genius.com/Kanye-west-freestyle-4-lyrics, last accessed: February 25, 2020.

[199] Audio: Goldfrapp, 'Human', *Youtube*, September 5, 2016, available at: https://www.youtube.com/watch?v=ZAYt7Jf4uPc, last accessed: February 25, 2020. Lyrics: Goldfrapp, 'Human', *Genius*, available at: https://genius.com/Goldfrapp-human-lyrics, last accessed: February 25, 2020.

[200] Audio: Kanye West, 'Waves', *Youtube*, July 24, 2018, available at: https://www.youtube.com/watch?v=ML8Yq1Rd6I0&list=OLAK5uy_keyJA-JsoAdfCylvyyIQMRjenzX6MzmnE&index=10, last accessed: February 25, 2020; Lyrics: Kanye West, 'Waves', *Genius*, available at: https://genius.com/Kanye-west-waves-lyrics, last accessed: February 25, 2020.

[201] Audio: Fantastic Freaks, 'Fantastic Freaks At The Dixie', *Youtube*, May 25, 2012, available at: https://www.youtube.com/watch?v=94snQ9hXa7o, last accessed: February 25, 2020. Lyrics: Fantastic Freaks, 'Fantastic Freaks At The Dixie', *Genius*, available at: https://genius.com/Fantastic-freaks-fantastic-freaks-at-the-dixie-lyrics, last accessed: February 25, 2020.

[202] Audio: Kanye West, 'FML', *Youtube*, July 24, 2018, available at: https://www.youtube.com/watch?v=SHfB5HBFeTc&list=OLAK5uy_keyJA-JsoAdfCylvyyIQMRjenzX6MzmnE&index=11, last accessed: February 25, 2020; Lyrics: Kanye West, 'FML', *Genius*, available at: https://genius.com/Kanye-west-fml-lyrics, last accessed: February 25, 2020.

[203] Audio: Section 25, 'Hit', *Youtube*, June 12, 2012, available at: https://www.youtube.com/watch?v=J-IxWxbO7FI, last accessed: February 25, 2020. Lyrics: Section 25, 'Hit', *Genius*, available at: https://genius.com/Section-25-hit-lyrics, last accessed: February 25, 2020.

[204] Audio: Kanye West, 'Real Friends', *Youtube*, July 24, 2018, available at: https://www.youtube.com/watch?v=fWD9GF-Ogf4&list=OLAK5uy_keyJA-JsoAdfCylvyyIQMRjenzX6MzmnE&index=12, last accessed: February 25, 2020; Lyrics: Kanye West, 'Real Friends', *Genius*, available at: https://genius.com/Kanye-west-real-friends-lyrics, last accessed: February 25, 2020.

[205] Audio: Whodini, 'Friends', *Youtube*, February 12, 2010, available at: https://www.youtube.com/watch?v=LRn2VQWNkgA, last accessed: February 25, 2020. Lyrics: Whodini, 'Friends', *Genius*, available at: https://genius.com/Whodini-friends-lyrics, last accessed: February 25, 2020.

	11. 'Wolves'[206] contains samples of 'Walking Dub'[207], written and performed by Sugar Minott. 12. '30 Hours'[208] contains samples of 'Answers Me'[209], written and performed by Arthur Russell; interpolations of 'Hot in Herre'[210], written by Cornell Haynes, Pharrell Williams, and Charles Brown, and performed by Nelly; interpolations of 'EI'[211], written by Cornell Haynes and Jason Epperson, and performed by Nelly; and samples of 'Joy'[212], written and performed by Isaac Hayes. 13. 'No More Parties in LA'[213] contains samples of 'Give Me My Love'[214], written and performed by Johnny 'Guitar' Watson; samples of 'Suzie Thundertussy'[215], written and performed by

---

[206] Audio: Kanye West, 'Wolves', *Youtube*, July 29, 2016, available at: https://www.youtube.com/watch?v=LsA84bXrBZw&list=OLAK5uy_keyJA-JsoAdfCylvyyIQMRjenzX6MzmnE&index=13, last accessed: February 25, 2020; Lyrics: Kanye West, 'Wolves', *Genius*, available at: https://genius.com/Kanye-west-wolves-lyrics, last accessed: February 25, 2020.

[207] Audio: Sugar Minott, 'Walking Dub', *Youtube*, December 29, 2016, available at: https://www.youtube.com/watch?v=N3rOM-BjKEo, last accessed: February 25, 2020.

[208] Audio: Kanye West, '30 Hours', *Youtube*, July 24, 2018, available at: https://www.youtube.com/watch?v=OH3bNgA1rkE&list=OLAK5uy_keyJA-JsoAdfCylvyyIQMRjenzX6MzmnE&index=16, last accessed: February 25, 2020; Lyrics: Kanye West, '30 Hours', *Genius*, available at: https://genius.com/Kanye-west-30-hours-lyrics, last accessed: February 25, 2020.

[209] Audio: Arthur Russell, 'Answers Me', *Youtube*, November 20, 2014, available at: https://www.youtube.com/watch?v=VBJZ0t2avpI, last accessed: February 25, 2020. Lyrics: Arthur Russell, 'Answers Me', *Genius*, available at: https://genius.com/Arthur-russell-answers-me-lyrics, last accessed: February 25, 2020.

[210] Audio: Nelly, 'Hot In Herre', *Youtube*, December 24, 2009, available at: https://www.youtube.com/watch?v=GeZZr_p6vB8, last accessed: . Lyrics: Nelly, 'Hot In Herre', *Genius*, available at: https://genius.com/Nelly-hot-in-herre-lyrics, last accessed: February 25, 2020.

[211] Audio: Nelly, 'EI', *Youtube*, October 8, 2009, available at: https://www.youtube.com/watch?v=mNaMR8AyeWc, last accessed: February 25, 2020. Lyrics: Nelly, 'EI', *Genius*, available at: https://genius.com/Nelly-ei-lyrics, last accessed: February 25, 2020.

[212] Audio: Isaac Hayes, 'Joy', *Youtube*, January 25, 2011, available at: https://www.youtube.com/watch?v=OmZAvAuCDn4, last accessed: February 25, 2020. Lyrics: Isaac Hayes, 'Joy', *Genius*, available at: https://genius.com/Isaac-hayes-joy-lyrics, last accessed: February 25, 2020.

[213] Audio: Kanye West, 'No More Parties In LA', *Youtube*, July 24, 2018, available at: https://www.youtube.com/watch?v=NnMuFqsmYSE&list=OLAK5uy_keyJA-JsoAdfCylvyyIQMRjenzX6MzmnE&index=17, last accessed: February 25, 2020; Lyrics: Kanye West, 'No More Parties In LA', *Genius*, available at: https://genius.com/Kanye-west-no-more-parties-in-la-lyrics, last accessed: February 25, 2020.

[214] Audio: Johnny 'Guitar' Watson, 'Give Me My Love', *Youtube*, March 9, 2013, available at: https://www.youtube.com/watch?v=jawLEK8icbw, last accessed: February 25, 2020. Lyrics: Johnny 'Guitar' Watson, 'Give Me My Love', *Genius*, available at: https://genius.com/Johnny-guitar-watson-give-me-my-love-lyrics, last accessed: February 25, 2020.

[215] Audio: Walter 'Junie' Morrison, 'Suzie Thundertussy', *Youtube*, July 22, 2011, available at: https://www.youtube.com/watch?v=CtllZDSo2Mk, last accessed: February 25, 2020. Lyrics: Walter 'Junie' Morrison, 'Suzie Thundertussy', *Genius*, available at: https://genius.com/Junie-morrison-suzie-thundertussy-lyrics, last accessed: February 25, 2020.

Walter 'Junie' Morrison; samples of 'Mighty Healthy'[216], written by Herbert Rooney, Ronald Bean, Highleigh Crizoe, and Dennis Coles, and performed by Ghostface Killah; and samples of 'Stand Up and Shout About Love'[217], written by Larry Graham Jr., Tina Graham, and Sam Dees, and performed by Larry Graham. 14. 'Facts (Charlie Heat Version)'[218] contains samples of 'Dirt and Grime'[219], written by Nicholas Smith and performed by Father's Children; interpolations of 'Jumpman'[220], written by Aubrey Graham, Leland T. Wayne, and Nayvadius D. Wilburn, and performed by Drake and Future; and contains elements of the video game Street Fighter II: The World Warrior. 15. 'Fade'[221] contains samples of '(I Know) I'm Losing You'[222], written by Eddie Holland, Norman Whitfield, and Cornelius Grant, and performed by Rare Earth; samples of '(I Know) I'm Losing You'[223], written by Eddie Holland, Norman Whitfield, and Cornelius Grant, and performed by The Undisputed Truth; samples of 'Mystery of Love'[224], written by Larry Heard and

---

[216] Audio: Ghostface Killah, 'Mighty Healthy', *Youtube*, March 26, 2011, available at: https://www.youtube.com/watch?v=KBWXgVdAJiY, last accessed: February 25, 2020. Lyrics: Ghostface Killah, 'Mighty Healthy', *Genius,* available at: https://genius.com/Ghostface-killah-mighty-healthy-lyrics, last accessed: February 25, 2020.

[217] Audio: Larry Graham, 'Stand Up And Shout About Love', *Youtube*, February 27, 2012, available at: https://www.youtube.com/watch?v=KGtT5P28MnI, last accessed: February 25, 2020. Lyrics: Larry Graham, 'Stand Up And Shout About Love', *Genius,* available at: https://genius.com/Larry-graham-stand-up-and-shout-about-love-lyrics, last accessed: February 25, 2020.

[218] Audio: Kanye West, 'Facts (Charlie Heat Version)', *Youtube*, July 24, 2018, available at: https://www.youtube.com/watch?v=yiwDWKg9AMA&list=OLAK5uy_keyJA-JsoAdfCylvyyIQMRjenzX6MzmnE&index=18, last accessed: February 25, 2020; Lyrics: Kanye West, 'Facts (Charlie Heat Version)', *Genius,* available at: https://genius.com/Kanye-west-facts-charlie-heat-version-lyrics, last accessed: February 25, 2020.

[219] Audio: Father's Children, 'Dirt And Grime', *Youtube*, July 4, 2011, available at: https://www.youtube.com/watch?v=-X6B0_xd8Mg, last accessed: February 25, 2020. Lyrics: Father's Children, 'Dirt And Grime', *Genius,* available at: https://genius.com/Fathers-children-dirt-and-grime-lyrics, last accessed: February 25, 2020.

[220] Audio: Drake, Future, 'Jumpman', *Youtube*, June 12, 2016, available at: https://www.youtube.com/watch?v=elaR1IsAGwY, last accessed: February 25, 2020. Lyrics: Drake, Future, 'Jumpman', *Genius,* available at: https://genius.com/Drake-and-future-jumpman-lyrics, last accessed: February 25, 2020.

[221] Audio: Kanye West, 'Fade', *Youtube*, September 6, 2016, available at: https://www.youtube.com/watch?v=IxGvm6btP1A&list=OLAK5uy_keyJA-JsoAdfCylvyyIQMRjenzX6MzmnE&index=19, last accessed: February 25, 2020; Lyrics: Kanye West, 'Fade', *Genius,* available at: https://genius.com/Kanye-west-fade-lyrics, last accessed: February 25, 2020.

[222] Audio: Rare Earth, '(I Know) I'm Loosing You', *Youtube*, February 17, 2011, available at: https://www.youtube.com/watch?v=F28X8--2dFU, last accessed: February 25, 2020. Lyrics: Rare Earth, '(I Know) I'm Loosing You', *Genius,* available at: https://genius.com/Rare-earth-i-know-im-losing-you-lyrics, last accessed: February 25, 2020.

[223] Audio: The Undisputed Truth, '(I Know) I'm Loosing You', *Youtube*, December 4, 2012, available at: https://www.youtube.com/watch?v=2jtnCeV3rEk, last accessed: February 25, 2020. Lyrics: The Undisputed Truth, '(I Know) I'm Loosing You', *Genius,* available at: https://www.youtube.com/watch?v=ZNoFtLGZBwk, last accessed: February 25, 2020.

[224] Audio: Mr. Fingers, 'Mystery Of Love', *Youtube*, September 20, 2013, available at: https://www.youtube.com/watch?v=CvUp3P9sLO4, last accessed: February 25, 2020. Lyrics: Mr.

	Robert Owens, and performed by Mr. Fingers; samples of 'Deep Inside'[225], written by Louie Vega and performed by Hardrive; samples of 'I Get Lifted (The Underground Network Mix)'[226], written by Louie Vega, Ronald Carroll, Barbara Tucker, and Harold Matthews, and performed by Barbara Tucker; and contains an interpolation of 'Rock the Boat'[227], written by Stephen Garrett, Rapture Stewart, and Eric Seats, and performed by Aaliyah. 16. 'Saint Pablo'[228] contains samples of 'Where I'm From'[229], written by Shawn Carter, Marek Manning, Deric Angelettie, Ronald Lawrence, and Norman Whitfield, and performed by Jay-Z.
	1. The original version of 'I Thought About Killing You'[230] contains an uncredited sample from 'Fr3sh'[231], as performed by Kareem Lotfy. 2. 'Yikes'[232] contains a sample from 'Kothbiro'[233], as performed by Black Savage.

Fingers, 'Mystery Of Love', *Genius,* available at: https://genius.com/Mr-fingers-mystery-of-love-lyrics, last accessed: February 25, 2020.

[225] Audio: Hardrive, 'Deep Inside', *Youtube*, December 13, 2015, available at: https://www.youtube.com/watch?v=OJ0WL4TJVCg, last accessed: February 25, 2020. Lyrics: Hardrive, 'Deep Inside', *Genius,* available at: https://genius.com/Hardrive-deep-inside-lyrics, last accessed: February 25, 2020.

[226] Audio: Barbara Tucker, 'I Get Lifted (The Underground Network Mix), *Youtube*, December 19, 2008, available at: https://www.youtube.com/watch?v=4En_rYmiUMg, last accessed: February 25, 2020.

[227] Audio: Aaliyah, 'Rock The Boat', *Youtube*, August 26, 2008, available at: https://www.youtube.com/watch?v=A5AAcgtMjUI, last accessed: February 25, 2020. Lyrics: Aaliyah, 'Rock The Boat', *Genius,* available at: https://genius.com/Aaliyah-rock-the-boat-lyrics, last accessed: February 25, 2020.

[228] Audio: Kanye West, 'Saint Pablo', *Youtube*, July 24, 2018, available at: https://www.youtube.com/watch?v=w9rzz4pDFwA&list=OLAK5uy_keyJA-JsoAdfCylvyyIQMRjenzX6MzmnE&index=20, last accessed: February 25, 2020; Lyrics: Kanye West, 'Saint Pablo', *Genius,* available at: https://genius.com/Kanye-west-saint-pablo-lyrics, last accessed: February 25, 2020.

[229] Audio: Jay Z, 'Where I'm From', *Youtube*, November 12, 2018, available at: https://www.youtube.com/watch?v=UDAVDTN5zHw, last accessed: February 25, 2020. Lyrics: Jay Z, 'Where I'm From', *Genius,* available at: https://genius.com/Jay-z-where-im-from-lyrics, last accessed: February 25, 2020.

[230] Audio: Kanye West, 'I Thought About Killing You', *Youtube*, November 6, 2018, available at: https://www.youtube.com/watch?v=no1YszVVybo, last accessed: February 25, 2020; Lyrics: Kanye West, 'I Thought About Killing You', *Genius,* available at: https://genius.com/Kanye-west-i-thought-about-killing-you-lyrics, last accessed: February 25, 2020.

[231] Audio: Kareem Lotfy, 'Fr3sh', *Youtube*, March 21, 2017, available at: https://www.youtube.com/watch?v=Q0UMnxmMAZ8, last accessed: February 25, 2020. Lyrics: Kareem Lotfy, 'Fr3sh', *Genius,* available at: https://genius.com/Kareem-lotfy-fr3sh-lyrics, last accessed: February 25, 2020.

[232] Audio: Kanye West, 'Yikes', *Youtube*, November 6, 2018, available at: https://www.youtube.com/watch?v=kPPyUO6m3-4, last accessed: February 25, 2020; Lyrics: Kanye West, *Genius,* available at: https://genius.com/Kanye-west-yikes-lyrics, last accessed: February 25, 2020.

[233] Audio: Black Savage, 'Kothbiro', *Youtube*, March 25, 2016, available at: https://www.youtube.com/watch?v=btn9sV4D9tM, last accessed: February 25, 2020. Lyrics: Black Savage, 'Kothbiro', *Genius,* available at: https://genius.com/Black-savage-kothbiro-lyrics, last accessed: February 25, 2020.

Ye (2018)	3. 'Wouldn't Leave'[234] contains a sample from 'Baptizing Scene'[235], as performed by Reverend W.A. Donaldson. 4. 'No Mistakes'[236] contains a sample from 'Children (Get Together)'[237], as performed by Edwin Hawkins Singers; and 'Hey Young World'[238], as performed by Slick Rick. 5. 'Ghost Town'[239] contain a sample from 'Take Me for a Little While'[240], as performed by The Royal Jesters; and 'Someday'[241], as performed by Shirley Ann Lee. 6. 'Violent Crimes'[242] is a reworking of the track 'Brothers'[243], produced by Irv Gotti and 7 Aurelius.
	1. 'Fire' contains a sample of 'They're Coming to Take Me Away, Ha-Haaa!', written and performed by Jerry 'Napoleon XIV' Samuels. 2. '4th Dimension' contains samples of 'What Will Santa Claus Say (When He Finds Everybody Swingin')', written and performed by Louis Prima; and an uncredited sample of 'Someday', written and performed by Shirley Ann Lee.

---

[234] Audio: Kanye West, 'Wouldn't Leave', *Youtube*, November 6, 2018, available at: https://www.youtube.com/watch?v=nMkXJohQiuQ, last accessed: February 25, 2020; Lyrics: Kanye West, 'Wouldn't Leave', *Genius*, available at: https://genius.com/Kanye-west-wouldnt-leave-lyrics, last accessed: February 25, 2020.

[235] Audio: Reverend W.A. Donaldson, 'Baptizing Scene', *Youtube*, September 7, 2011, available at: https://www.youtube.com/watch?v=JpYPoMZhdyU, last accessed: February 25, 2020.

[236] Audio: Kanye West, 'No Mistakes', *Youtube*, November 6, 2018, available at: https://www.youtube.com/watch?v=4I8gDpuvZt4, last accessed: February 25, 2020; Lyrics: Kanye West, 'No Mistakes', *Genius*, available at: https://genius.com/Kanye-west-no-mistakes-lyrics, last accessed: February 25, 2020.

[237] Audio: Edwin Hawkins Singer, 'Children (Get Together)', *Youtube*, January 24, 2018, available at: https://www.youtube.com/watch?v=1f3KCCU4QUM, last accessed: February 25, 2020. Lyrics: Edwin Hawkins Singer, 'Children (Get Together)', *Genius*, available at: https://genius.com/The-edwin-hawkins-singers-children-get-together-lyrics, last accessed: February 25, 2020.

[238] Audio: Slick Rick, 'Hey Young World', *Youtube*, November 22, 2009, available at: https://www.youtube.com/watch?v=ea-ezolZq5k, last accessed: February 25, 2020. Lyrics: Slick Rick, 'Hey Young World', *Genius*, available at: https://genius.com/Slick-rick-hey-young-world-lyrics, last accessed: February 25, 2020.

[239] Audio: Kanye West, 'Ghost Town', *Youtube*, November 6, 2018, available at: https://www.youtube.com/watch?v=5S6az6odzPI, last accessed: February 25, 2020; Lyrics: Kanye West, 'Ghost Town', *Genius*, available at: https://genius.com/Kanye-west-ghost-town-lyrics, last accessed: February 25, 2020.

[240] Audio: The Royal Jesters, 'Little While', *Youtube*, June 24, 2015, available at: https://www.youtube.com/watch?v=AKG0j29VtIg, last accessed: February 25, 2020. Lyrics: The Royal Jesters, 'Little While', *Musixmatch*, available at: https://www.musixmatch.com/lyrics/The-Royal-Jesters/Take-Me-For-a-Little-While, last accessed: February 25, 2020.

[241] Audio: Shirley Ann Lee, 'Someday', *Youtube*, June 25, 2018, available at: https://www.youtube.com/watch?v=D7kSw_OFy2Y, last accessed: February 25, 2020. Lyrics: Shirley Ann Lee, 'Someday', *Genius*, available at: https://genius.com/Shirley-ann-lee-someday-lyrics, last accessed: February 25, 2020.

[242] Audio: Kanye West, 'Violent Crimes', *Youtube*, June 18, 2018, available at: https://www.youtube.com/watch?v=DSY7u8Jg9c0, last accessed: February 25, 2020; Lyrics: Kanye West, 'Violent Crimes', *Genius*, available at: https://genius.com/Kanye-west-violent-crimes-lyrics, last accessed: February 25, 2020.

[243] I did not find the original track to make a direct link with the song.

Kids See Ghosts (2017)[244]	3. 'Freeee (Ghost Town, Pt. 2)' contains samples of 'Stark', written and performed by Corin 'Mr. Chop' Littcler; an uncredited sample of a speech from Marcus Garvey; and portions of the previous 'Ghost Town'. 4. 'Cudi Montage' contains samples of 'Burn the Rain', written and performed by Kurt Cobain.
Jesus is King (2019)	1. 'Selah'[245] contains a cover of 'Revelation 19:1'[246] from 'Jesus Is Born', originally performed by the New Jerusalem Baptism Choir under the direction of Curtis Hayes and Jeffrey LaValley. 2. 'Follow God'[247] contains samples of 'Can You Lose By Following God'[248], written by Johnny Frieson, Curtis Eubanks, and Calvin Eubanks, and performed by Whole Truth. 3. 'Closed on Sunday'[249] contains samples of 'Martín Fierro'[250], written by Chango Farías Gómez and performed by Grupo Vocal Argentino. 4. 'On God'[251] contains samples of 'Lambo'[252], written and performed by YB; and 'Oh My God'[253], written by Jonathan Davis,

---

[244] The information for this album was retrieved from Kids See Ghosts, *Wikipedia*, available at: https://en.wikipedia.org/wiki/Kids_See_Ghosts_(album), last accessed: February 25, 2020.

[245] Audio: Kanye West, 'Selah', *Youtube*, October 25, 2019, available at: https://www.youtube.com/watch?v=6CNPg2IQoC0&list=OLAK5uy_nG0R7GxWTXwhsxxi_cwx8QwZe0QI1tED8&index=2, last accessed: February 25, 2020; Lyrics: Kanye West, 'Selah', *Genius*, available at: https://genius.com/Kanye-west-selah-lyrics, last accessed: February 25, 2020.

[246] Audio: New Jerusalem Baptism Choir, 'Revelation 19:1', *Youtube*, May 31, 2010, available at: https://www.youtube.com/watch?v=tF9uq9lj94s, last accessed: February 25, 2020.

[247] Audio: Kanye West, 'Follow God', *Youtube*, November 8, 2019, available at: https://www.youtube.com/watch?v=ivCY3Ec4iaU&list=OLAK5uy_nG0R7GxWTXwhsxxi_cwx8QwZe0QI1tED8&index=3, last accessed: February 25, 2020; Lyrics: Kanye West, 'Follow God', *Genius*, available at: https://genius.com/Kanye-west-follow-god-lyrics, last accessed: February 25, 2020.

[248] Audio: Whole Truth, 'Can You Lose By Following God', *Youtube*, March 17, 2017, available at: https://www.youtube.com/watch?v=AgsK5xpzT90, last accessed: February 25, 2020. Lyrics: Whole Truth, 'Can You Lose By Following God', *Genius*, available at: https://genius.com/Whole-truth-can-you-lose-by-following-god-lyrics, last accessed: February 25, 2020.

[249] Audio: Kanye West, 'Closed On Sunday', *Youtube*, October 25, 2019, available at: https://www.youtube.com/watch?v=Lp0q1wWe6XI&list=OLAK5uy_nG0R7GxWTXwhsxxi_cwx8QwZe0QI1tED8&index=4, last accessed: February 25, 2020; Lyrics: Kanye West, 'Closed On Sunday', *Genius*, available at: https://genius.com/Kanye-west-closed-on-sunday-lyrics, last accessed: February 25, 2020.

[250] Audio: Grupo Vocal Argentino, 'Martin Fierro', *Youtube*, December 18, 2015, available at: https://www.youtube.com/watch?v=2yV1IsTE97w, last accessed: February 25, 2020. Lyrics: Grupo Vocal Argentino, 'Martin Fierro', *Genius*, available at: https://genius.com/Grupo-vocal-argentino-martin-fierro-lyrics, last accessed: February 25, 2020.

[251] Audio: Kanye West, 'On God', *Youtube*, October 25, 2019, available at: https://www.youtube.com/watch?v=AOBQkHy8_p8&list=OLAK5uy_nG0R7GxWTXwhsxxi_cwx8QwZe0QI1tED8&index=5, last accessed: February 25, 2020; Lyrics: Kanye West, 'On God', *Genius*, available at: https://genius.com/Kanye-west-on-god-lyrics, last accessed: February 25, 2020.

[252] Audio: YB, Lambo', *Youtube*, May 7, 2012, available at: https://www.youtube.com/watch?v=LcOusBxmZF0, last accessed: February 25, 2020. Lyrics: YB, Lambo', *Genius*, available at: https://genius.com/Yung-bizzle-lambo-lyrics, last accessed: February 25, 2020.

[253] Audio: A Tribe Called Quest (featuring Busta Rhymes), 'Oh My God', *Youtube*, December 5, 2012, available at: https://www.youtube.com/watch?v=Olah18jcJko, last accessed: February 25, 2020. Lyrics:

	Ali Shaheed Muhammad, Trevor Smith, and Malik Taylor, and performed by A Tribe Called Quest featuring Busta Rhymes. 5. 'Water'[254] contains an interpolation of 'We're All Water'[255], written by Yoko Ono and performed by Ono and John Lennon; contains samples of 'Blow Job'[256], written and performed by Bruce Haack. 6. 'God Is'[257] contains samples of 'God Is'[258], written by Robert Fryson and performed by James Cleveland and The Southern California Community Choir. 7. 'Use This Gospel'[259] contains samples of 'Costume Party'[260], written by Alex Trimble, Kevin Baird, and Sam Halliday and performed by Two Door Cinema Club. 8. 'Jesus Is Lord'[261] contains samples of 'Un Homme Dans La Nuit'[262], written by Claude Léveillée.

A Tribe Called Quest (featuring Busta Rhymes), 'Oh My God', *Genius*, available at: https://genius.com/A-tribe-called-quest-oh-my-god-lyrics, last accessed: February 25, 2020.

[254] Audio: Kanye West, 'Water', *Youtube*, October 25, 2019, available at: https://www.youtube.com/watch?v=-YfG1Xbo4OA&list=OLAK5uy_nG0R7GxWTXwhsxxi_cwx8QwZe0QI1tED8&index=7, last accessed: February 25, 2020; Lyrics: Kanye West, 'Water', *Genius*, available at: https://genius.com/Kanye-west-water-lyrics, last accessed: February 25, 2020.

[255] Audio: Yoko Ono, John Lennon, 'We're All Water', *Youtube*, September 26, 2009, available at: https://www.youtube.com/watch?v=n_8dWTEWEKo, last accessed: February 25, 2020. Lyrics: Ono, John Lennon, 'We're All Water', *Genius*, available at: https://genius.com/Yoko-ono-were-all-water-lyrics, last accessed: February 25, 2020.

[256] Audio: Bruce Haack, 'Blow Job', *Youtube*, July 17, 2013, available at: https://www.youtube.com/watch?v=XaOwzqb1jDc, last accessed: February 25, 2020. Lyrics: Bruce Haack, 'Blow Job', *Genius*, available at: https://genius.com/Bruce-haack-blow-job-annotated, last accessed: February 25, 2020.

[257] Audio: Kanye West, 'God Is', *Youtube*, October 25, 2019, available at: https://www.youtube.com/watch?v=G8u3P7Xqlvo&list=OLAK5uy_nG0R7GxWTXwhsxxi_cwx8QwZe0QI1tED8&index=8, last accessed: February 25, 2020; Lyrics: Kanye West, 'God Is', *Genius*, available at: https://genius.com/Kanye-west-god-is-lyrics, last accessed: February 25, 2020.

[258] Audio: James Cleveland, The Southern California Community Choir, 'God Is', *Youtube*, April 13, 2014, available at: https://www.youtube.com/watch?v=dLyY8F96sfg, last accessed: February 25, 2020. Lyrics: James Cleveland, The Southern California Community Choir, 'God Is', *Musixmatch*, available at: https://www.musixmatch.com/lyrics/James-Cleveland-The-Southern-California-Community-Choir/God-Is, last accessed: February 25, 2020.

[259] Audio: Kanye West, 'Use This Gospel', *Youtube*, October 25, 2019, available at: https://www.youtube.com/watch?v=8yQVcGkbpAc&list=OLAK5uy_nG0R7GxWTXwhsxxi_cwx8QwZe0QI1tED8&index=10, last accessed: February 25, 2020; Lyrics: Kanye West, 'Use This Gospel', *Genius*, available at: https://genius.com/Kanye-west-use-this-gospel-lyrics, last accessed: February 25, 2020.

[260] Audio: The Two Door Cinema, 'Costume Party', *Youtube*, November 14, 2009, available at: https://www.youtube.com/watch?v=sz3AL5w1Rfs, last accessed: February 25, 2020. Lyrics: The Two Door Cinema, 'Costume Party', *Genius*, available at: https://genius.com/Two-door-cinema-club-costume-party-lyrics, last accessed: February 25, 2020.

[261] Audio: Kanye West, 'Jesus Is Lord', *Youtube*, October 25, 2019, available at: https://www.youtube.com/watch?v=rns_n82HiMo&list=OLAK5uy_nG0R7GxWTXwhsxxi_cwx8QwZe0QI1tED8&index=11, last accessed: February 25, 2020; Lyrics: Kanye West, 'Jesus Is Lord', *Genius*, available at: https://genius.com/Kanye-west-jesus-is-lord-lyrics, last accessed: February 25, 2020.

[262] Audio: Claude Léveillée, *'Un Homme Dans La Nuit'*, *Youtube*, October 19, 2018, available at: https://www.youtube.com/watch?v=jVv2ummG7Xk, last accessed: February 25, 2020.

CONCLUSIONS:

- from the point of view of creating music heard and used for the first time in the world and written and released *only* by Kanye West, there is a lower level of originality and novelty brought in the music industry in comparison with Taylor Swift;
- from the point of view that the musical notes and lyrics from songs already known and awarded in the music industry and a mix of them (in any format) by Kanye West is novelty in the music industry, then Kanye West brought a high level of originality and novelty in the music industry;
- Kanye West has a high level of abilities to mix different songs in a way that few people can do it;
- Kanye West's power to create music resides in listening to other songs, then to mix these songs with close or sometimes different musical notes and lyrics that can be connected or have some meaning to the theme of the song he intends to create (if he sings a lyric on a different note, he needs a different lyric and the right musical note to match the sound of that lyric); there are many songs in Kanye West's catalogue where his (and other producers from his albums) intervention is the creation of a close sound around a sound used already by another artist;
- Kanye West might struggle to create his own titles of songs as he uses title of songs in his catalogue that belongs to other artist (either inspired from the title of a song or either from the lyrics of the songs that he sampled).

II.1.4 The Sources of the Samples

The list of songs in this table are not used to argue that Kanye West infringed the copyrights of other artists or to claim any wrongdoing from any point of view of music (Kanye West acknowledge the sources he sampled and the wider music community is well aware of, also there is a high number of artists that agreed (verbally and written) the use of their ideas in his music). This table is used *only* to *show* and *understand* the background narrative of creating the music.

II.1.4.1 Taylor Swift

I read the lyrics of the songs that used samples to find out if there is a connection between the original song and the song that sampled the original song.

TABLE 9. THE SOURCES OF THE SAMPLES USED BY TAYLOR SWIFT		
NAME OF THE ALBUM	**NAME OF THE SONG**	**INSPIRATION**
Taylor Swift (Deluxe, 2006)	N/A	
Fearless (Platinum, 2008)	'Untouchable'	'Untouchable'
Speak Now (Deluxe, 2010)	N/A	
RED (Deluxe, 2010)	N/A	
1989 (Deluxe, 2014)	N/A	
reputation (2017)	'Look What You Made Me Do'	'I'm Too Sexy'
Lover (2019)	'The Archer'	'Humpty Dumpty'
	'London Boy'	'Cold War'
	'It's Nice to Have a Friend'	'Summer in the South'
folklore (Deluxe, 2020)	N/A	
Evermore (Deluxe, 2020)	N/A	
Fearless (Taylor's Version, 2021)	N/A	

CONCLUSIONS:

- Taylor Swift used a lower level of music instruments and lyrics from other songs;
- overall, the theme of the songs that Taylor Swift sampled is different than the songs released under her name and lyrics;
- in 2017 Taylor Swift changed the pattern of her songs by including samples, a feature that is highly visible on Kanye West's music catalogue and it is done on two albums: *reputation* and *Lover*, both being in close connection with Kanye West's albums: *My Beautiful Dark Twisted Fantasy* and *reputation* (dark theme) and *The Life of Saint Pablo* with *Lover* (personal perception about family, love, friends, and enemies).[263]

---

[263] See Casian Anton, *On the Famous Feud*.

II.1.4.2 Kanye West

In this table I added only the songs that I found to have some connection with Kanye West's titles and lyrics. I read the lyrics of the songs that used samples to find out the connection between the original song and the song that sampled the original song.

TABLE 10. THE SOURCES OF THE SAMPLES USED BY KANYE WEST		
NAME OF THE ALBUM	**NAME OF THE SONG**	**INSPIRATION**
The College Dropout (2004)	'All Falls Down'	'Mystery of Iniquity'
	'Spaceship'	'Distant Lover'
	'Jesus Walks'	'Walk with Me'; '(Don't Worry) If There's a Hell Below, We're All Going to Go';
	'Never Let Me Down'	'Maybe It's the Power of Love'
	'Slow Jamz'	'A House Is Not a Home'
	'School Spirit'	'Spirit in the Dark'
	'Two Words'	'Peace & Love (Amani Na Mapenzi) – Movement IV (Encounter)'
	'Through the Wire'	'Through the Fire'
	'Family Business'	'The Rainmaker' and 'Fonky Thang'
	'Last Call'	'Mr. Rockefeller' and 'She's Gone To Another'.
Late Registration (2005)	'Wake Up, Mr. West'	'Someone That I Used to Love'
	'Touch the Sky'	'Move On Up'
	'Gold Digger'	'I Got a Woman'
	'My Way Home'	'Home Is Where the Hatred Is'
	'Roses'	'Rosie'
	'Addiction'	'My Funny Valentine'
	'Diamonds From Sierra Leone'	'Diamonds Are Forever'
	'Gone'	'It's Too Late'
	'Late'	'I'll Erase Away Your Pain'
Graduation (2007)	'Champion'	'Kid Charlemagne'
	'Stronger'	'Harder, Better, Faster, Stronger'
	'I Wonder'	'My Song'
	'Good Life'	'P.Y.T. (Pretty Young Thing)'
88s & Heartbreak (2008)	'Bittersweet Poetry'	'Bittersweet'
	'Coldest Winter'	'Memories Fade'
My Beautiful Dark Twisted Fantasy (2010)	'Dark Fantasy'	'In High Places'
	'Power'	'It's Your Thing' and '21st Century Schizoid Man
	''So Appalled'	'You Are – I Am'

	'Who Will Survive in America'	'Comment No. 1'
Yeezus (2013)	'New Slaves'	'Gyöngyhajú lány'
	'Blood on the Leaves'	'Strange Fruit'
	'Guilt Trip'	'Chief Rocka'
	'Send it Up'	'Memories'
	'Bound 2'	'Bound'
The Life of Pablo (2016)	'Father Stretch My Hands'	'Father I Stretch My Hands'
	'Pt 2'	'Panda'
	'Famous'	'Do What You Gotta Do', 'Bam Bam' and 'Mi Sono Svegliato E... Ho Chiuso Gli Occhi'
	'So Alive'	'So Alive (Acapella)'
	'FML'	'Hit'
	'Real Friends'	'Friends'
	'30 Hours'	'Answers Me'
	'No More Parties in LA'	'Give Me My Love'
	'Facts (Charlie Version)'	'Dirt and Grime' and 'Jumpman'
	'Fade'	'(I Know) I'm Losing You', 'Mystery of Love', 'Deep Inside' and 'Rock the Boat'
	'Saint Pablo'	'Where I'm From'
Ye (2018)	'Ghost Town' from 'Take Me for a Little While'	'Take Me for a Little While'
Jesus is King (2019)	'Follow God'	'Can You Lose By Following God'
	'Water'	'We're All Water'
	'God is'	'God Is'

CONCLUSIONS:

- Kanye West's samples used in his music can generously be added in the following categories:

  o **the title of the song**: used the original title of the song that he was inspired from; modified the original title with his own idea, but with close/strong meaning with the original title that he sampled; used a part of the original title as a full title for his song; the title of his song was inspired and contains lyrics from the original song sampled in his song;

  o **lyrics**: is on four levels: **a.** some lyrics; **b.** more lyrics; **c.** a combination of his lyrics with other artists lyrics; **d.** rich lyrics from other songs;

- o **theme of the songs/albums**: follows the same pattern as lyrics, but with three levels: **a.** some connection; **b.** good connection; **c.** strong connection with the song that he sampled (lyrics, instrumentals and order of chorus, verse, intro, outro and a mix between them);
- o **the structure of a song**: sometimes he used the same musical structure of the song (first intro, verses, chorus, bridge, hook, outro, and so forth) that he sampled; modified and changed the position of a part of the song (for example chorus became Intro or Outro and so forth).

II.1.5 The Fame of the Samples

In this subchapter I investigated the fame of the samples used by both artists. The reason behind this investigation is to see if the samples used were already awarded and appreciated by the wider music community and the general public and to what degree.

II.1.5.1 The Fame of the Samples Used by Taylor Swift

The following table has only the songs that I could find information about their fame, it might be more songs which are not included here.

TABLE 11. THE FAME OF THE SAMPLES USED BY TAYLOR SWIFT		
NAME OF THE ALBUM	**NAME OF THE SONG**	**TOP CHARTS & AWARDS**
Taylor Swift (Deluxe, 2006)		N/A
Fearless (Platinum, 2008)	'Untouchable'	All Music rated the album 'Luna Halo' where the song was included with 3.5 out of 5 stars.[264]
Speak Now (Deluxe, 2010)		N/A
RED (Deluxe, 2010)		N/A
1989 (Deluxe, 2014)		N/A

---

[264] Jared Johnson, 'Luna Halo', All Music, available at: https://www.allmusic.com/album/luna-halo-mw0000582485, last accessed February 27, 2020.

reputation (2017)	'I'm Too Sexy'	'Is the debut song by British group *Right Said Fred*. The single peaked at number two on the UK Singles Chart. Outside the United Kingdom, 'I'm Too Sexy' topped the charts in six countries, including Australia, Ireland, and the United States. The song was nominated for an Ivor Novello Award for Best Selling 'A' Side. In April 2008, the song was rated No. 49 on 'The 50 Worst Songs Ever! Watch, Listen and Cringe!' by Blender. In June 2007, the song was voted No. 80 on VH1's 100 Greatest Songs of the '90s. In April 2011, it was voted No. 2 on VH1's 40 Greatest One-Hit Wonders of the '90s.'[265]
Lover (2019)	'Humpty Dumpty'	Humpty Dumpty is a character in an English nursery rhyme and one of the best known in the English-speaking world. The first recorded versions of the rhyme date from late eighteenth-century England and the tune from 1870 in James William Elliott's National Nursery Rhymes and Nursery Songs. The character of Humpty Dumpty was popularised in the United States on Broadway by actor George L. Fox, where his show ran from 1868 to 1869, for a total of 483 performances, becoming the longest-running Broadway show until it was passed in 1881. As a character and literary allusion, he has appeared or been referred to in many works of literature and popular culture, particularly English author Lewis Carroll's 1871 book *Through the Looking-Glass*, in which he was described as an egg.'[266]
	'Cold War'	I did not find information about the charts and awards for this song
	'Summer in the South'	It was created by a group of students from Toronto-based Regent Park School of Music.
folklore (Deluxe, 2020)		N/A
Evermore (Deluxe, 2020)		N/A
Fearless (Taylor's Version, 2021)		N/A

---

[265] I'm Too sexy, *Wikipedia*, available at: https://en.wikipedia.org/wiki/I%27m_Too_Sexy, last accessed: February 27, 2020.
[266] Humpty Dumpty, *Wikipedia*, available at: https://en.wikipedia.org/wiki/Humpty_Dumpty, last accessed: February 27, 2020.

CONCLUSIONS:

- the inspiration from other songs is too small to create a satisfactory argument that Taylor Swift's musical career is because of the samples that she used in her music, and without the samples she would not exist today as a global pop artist;
- if the title of 'the greatest artist of all time' is based on writing your own lyrics and musical notes, Taylor Swift is naturally one of the greatest artists of all time.

II.1.5.2 The Fame of the Sample Used by Kanye West

The following table has only the songs that I could find information about their fame, it might be more songs which are not included here.

TABLE 12. THE FAME OF THE SAMPLES USED BY KANYE WEST		
NAME OF THE ALBUM	**NAME OF THE SONG**	**TOP CHARTS & AWARDS**
The College Dropout (2004)	'Mystery of Iniquity'	Was nominated at the 45th Grammy Awards for Best Female Rap Solo Performance.'[267]
	'Distant Lover'	'The 1974 live version of 'Distant Lover' has been regarded as one of the greatest live performances of all time.'[268]
	'(Don't Worry) If There's a Hell Below, We're All Going to Go'	'The song earned U.S. Billboard Hot Soul Singles number 3. Also the song meant to serve as a warning regarding the state of race relations and the tempest growing in America's inner cities.'[269]
	'A House Is Not a Home'	'Despite its modest initial success, the song went on to achieve

---

[267] MTV Unplugged, *Wikipedia*, available at: https://en.wikipedia.org/wiki/MTV_Unplugged_No._2.0, last accessed: February 27, 2020.

[268] Distant Lover, *Wikipedia*, available at: https://en.wikipedia.org/wiki/Distant_Lover, last accessed: February 27, 2020.

[269] (Don't Worry) If There's a Hell Below, We're All Going to Go, *Wikipedia*, available at: https://en.wikipedia.org/wiki/(Don%27t_Worry)_If_There%27s_a_Hell_Below,_We%27re_All_Going_t o_Go, last accessed: February 27, 2020.

		greater renown through frequent recordings by other artists.'[270]
	'Spirit in the Dark'	'The song reached number 3 on the U.S. R&B chart and number 23 on the Billboard Hot 100 in 1970.'[271]
	'Through the Fire'	Is a song recorded by Chaka Khan from her sixth studio album, *I Feel for You* (1984). The David Foster-produced track was the third single from the album and reached number 60 on the US Billboard Hot 100 chart and number 15 on the Hot R&B/Hip-Hop Songs charts.[272]
Late Registration (2005)	'Someone That I Used to Love'	Also peaked at number 21 on the Billboard R&B chart, however, it was a single hit.'[273]
	'Move On Up'	'The song became a soul music classic over the years.'[274]
	'I Got a Woman'	'The song would be one of the prototypes for what later became termed as 'soul music' after Charles released 'What'd I Say' nearly five years later. It was a hit—Charles' first—climbing quickly to #1 R&B in January 1955. It was later ranked No. 239 on Rolling Stone's list of the 500 Greatest Songs of All Time.'[275]
	'Wildflower'	'It became a huge soul hit before breaking out nationally and crossing over to the pop charts. Eventually 'Wildflower' spent 21 weeks on the Billboard pop chart. [...] The song proved to be extremely popular in Canada as well; it ultimately peaked at number 10 on the RPM Top Singles chart, and number 1 on the Adult

[270] A House is Not a Home, *Wikipedia*, available at: https://en.wikipedia.org/wiki/A_House_Is_Not_a_Home_(song), last accessed: February 27, 2020.

[271] Aretha Franklin, 'Spirit in the Dark', *Music CVF*, available at: https://musicvf.com/song.php?id=2851&artist=Aretha+Franklin&title=Spirit+in+the+Dark, last accessed: February 27, 2020.

[272] Through the Fire, *Wikipedia*, available at: https://en.wikipedia.org/wiki/Through_the_Fire_(song), last accessed: February 27, 2020.

[273] Someone That I Used to Love, *Wikipedia*, available at: https://en.wikipedia.org/wiki/Someone_That_I_Used_to_Love, last accessed: February 27, 2020.

[274] Move On Up, *Wikipedia*, available at: https://en.wikipedia.org/wiki/Move_On_Up, last accessed: February 27, 2020.

[275] I Got a Woman, *Wikipedia*, available at: https://en.wikipedia.org/wiki/I_Got_a_Woman, last accessed: February 27, 2020.

		Contemporary chart. Total sales of the single exceeded one million copies.'[276]
	'My Funny Valentine'	'The song became a popular jazz standard, appearing on over 1300 albums performed by over 600 artists. The song first hit the charts in 1945, performed by Hal McIntyre with vocals by Ruth Gaylor. It only appeared for one week and hit #16.[277]
	'Diamonds Are Forever'	'It is the name of the one of the soundtracks of James Bond fim series, named 'Diamonds are Forever' (1971), which was a global commercial success.'[278]
	'It's Too Late'	'It reached #3 on the U.S. R&B chart in 1956.'[279]
	'Someone Saved My Life Tonight'	'It peaked on the Billboard Hot 100 chart in the U.S. at #4 and in Canada on the RPM Top Singles chart at #2. The song concludes side one of the album's narrative, chronicling the early history of John and lyricist, Bernie Taupin, and their struggles to find their place within the music industry. [280]
	'Kid Charlemagne'	'Reached number 82 in the Billboard charts. The guitar solo by jazz fusion guitarist Larry Carlton was ranked #80 in the list of the 100 greatest guitar songs by Rolling Stone.[281]
		This version won a Grammy Award for Best Dance Recording in 2009.

---

[276] Wildflower (Skylark song), *Wikipedia*, available at: https://en.wikipedia.org/wiki/Wildflower_(Skylark_song); Skylark Review Wildflower, https://books.google.co.uk/books?id=CQkEAAAAMBAJ&pg=PA17&dq=skylark+review+wildflower&num=100&client=firefox-a&redir_esc=y#v=onepage&q&f=true, last accessed: February 27, 2020.
[277] My Funny Valentine, *Wikipedia*, available at: https://en.wikipedia.org/wiki/My_Funny_Valentine, last accessed: February 27, 2020.
[278] Diamonds Are Forever (Film), *Wikipedia*, available at: https://en.wikipedia.org/wiki/Diamonds_Are_Forever_(film), last accessed: February 27, 2020; Diamonds Are Forever (soundtrack), Wikipedia, available at: https://en.wikipedia.org/wiki/Diamonds_Are_Forever_(soundtrack), last accessed: February 27, 2020.
[279] It's Too Late (Chuck Willis song), *Wikipedia*, available at: https://en.wikipedia.org/wiki/It%27s_Too_Late_(Chuck_Willis_song), last accessed: February 27, 2020.
[280] Someone Saved My Life Tonight, *Wikipedia*, available at: https://en.wikipedia.org/wiki/Someone_Saved_My_Life_Tonight, last accessed: February 27, 2020.
[281] Kid Charlemagne, *Wikipedia*, available at: https://en.wikipedia.org/wiki/Kid_Charlemagne, last accessed: February 27, 2020.

Graduation (2007)	'Harder, Better, Faster, Stronger'	In October 2011, NME placed it at number 132 on its list '150 Best Tracks of the Past 15 Years'. The song is built around a 'bouncy' keyboard riff sampled from the 1979 track 'Cola Bottle Baby' [which Kanye West used in one of his songs] by the funk musician Edwin Birdsong. Kanye West's song 'Stronger' from the album Graduation prominently features a sample of 'Harder, Better, Faster, Stronger'. Two actors who wore the robotic Daft Punk costumes in the film Daft Punk's Electroma appear in the music video for 'Stronger'. It was performed live at the 2008 Grammy Awards with Daft Punk in their trademark pyramid while Kanye West was on stage rapping. Daft Punk member Guy-Manuel de Homem-Christo said that 'Stronger' was 'not a collaboration in the studio, but the vibe of the music we do separately connected in what [Kanye West] did with the song'. He later clarified that the live version was 'truly a collaboration from the start. We really did it all hand in hand.'[282]
	'P.Y.T. (Pretty Young Thing)'	'The single charted at no. 10 on the Billboard Hot 100 and no. 46 on the Hot Black Singles chart, becoming the sixth Top 10 hit from Thriller. In the United Kingdom, the song reached a peak position of 11.'[283]
	'Bring the Noise'	'The single reached No. 56 on the Billboard Hot R&B/Hip-Hop Songs chart. It was included on the soundtrack of the 1987 film Less Than Zero.
	'Save the Country'	The most successful version was performed by The 5th Dimension. It reached #10 on the U.S. adult contemporary chart, #24 in Canada,

[282] Harder, Better, Faster, Stronger, *Wikipedia*, available at:
https://en.wikipedia.org/wiki/Harder,_Better,_Faster,_Stronger, last accessed: February 27, 2020.
[283] P.Y.T (Pretty Young Thing), *Wikipedia*, available at:
https://en.wikipedia.org/wiki/P.Y.T._(Pretty_Young_Thing), last accessed: February 27, 2020.

		#27 on the Billboard Hot 100, and #79 in Australia in 1970.'[284]
	'Wake the Town'	'It was U-Roy's first big hit and one of the songs that established U-Roy as the grandfather of the modern deejay phenomenon. It also helped created dancehall style in Jamaica, helped create the deejay sound.'[285]
808s & Heartbreak (2008)	'Sea Lion Woman'	'It charted through digital downloads on the Canadian Hot 100 under the title "Sea Lion Woman" and peaked #94 on the Billboard Canadian Hot 100 Chart.'[286]
	'In High Places'	'On the occasion of Virgin Records founder Richard Branson's launch of the then-largest hot-air balloon ever made, the song was released as a single in 1987 in the UK and Spain.'[287]
	'You Showed Me'	'The song was the group's last big hit in the U.S, U.S. Record World Weekly Chart: 1, U.S. Cash Box Top 100, weekly chart: 4.'[288]
	'It's Your Thing'[289]	'The song quickly rose to the top of both the Billboard pop and R&B singles charts, peaking at #2 [...] and marking their first #1 hit in the latter. In February 1970 the [authors of the song] became the first former Motown act to win a Grammy Award for Best R&B Vocal Performance by a Duo or Group. The song is ranked #420 on the Rolling Stone magazine's list of The 500 Greatest Songs of All Time.'[290]

---

[284] Save the Country, *Music CVF*, available at: https://www.musicvf.com/song.php?title=Save+the+Country+by+The+5th+Dimension&id=426, last accessed: February 27, 2020.

[285] Wake the Town, *Wikipedia*, available at: https://en.wikipedia.org/wiki/Wake_the_Town, last accessed: February 27, 2020.

[286] Feist, 'Sea Lion Woman', *Billboard Canadian Hot 100 Chart*, April 26, 2008, available at: https://www.billboard.com/charts/canadian-hot-100/2008-04-26, last accessed: February 27, 2020.

[287] In High Places, *Wikipedia*, available at: https://en.wikipedia.org/wiki/In_High_Places_(song), last accessed: February 27, 2020.

[288] You Showed Me, *Wikipedia*, available at: https://en.wikipedia.org/wiki/You_Showed_Me, last accessed: February 27, 2020.

[289] It's Your Thing, *Wikipedia*, available at: https://en.wikipedia.org/wiki/It%27s_Your_Thing, last accessed: February 27, 2020.

[290] It's Your Thing, *Wikipedia*, available at: https://en.wikipedia.org/wiki/It%27s_Your_Thing, last accessed: February 27, 2020.

My Beautiful Dark Twisted Fantasy (2010)	'21st Century Schizoid Man'	'The song encompasses the heavy metal, jazz-rock and progressive rock genres, and is considered to be an influence on the development of progressive metal. The atonal solo was rated number 82 in Guitar World's list of the Top 100 Greatest Guitar Solos in 2008. Louder Sound ranked the solo at no. 56 in its '100 greatest guitar solos in rock' poll.'[291]
	'Will You Love Me Tomorrow'	'It was originally recorded in 1960 by the Shirelles, who took their single to number one on the Billboard Hot 100 chart. The song is also notable for being the first song by a black all-girl group to reach number one in the United States. It was ranked at #126 among Rolling Stone's list of The 500 Greatest Songs of All Time. Billboard named the song #3 on their list of 100 Greatest Girl Group Songs of All Time.'[292]
	'Iron Man'	'The song won spot number 317 in Rolling Stone's list of the 500 Greatest Songs of All Time as of 2004. VH1 ranked the song as the greatest heavy metal song of all time.'[293]
	'Soul Makossa'	'The song also became an international hit leading to even more cover versions by various groups around the world.'[294]
	'Think (About It)'	The song is very popular for its raw drumbeat dressed with tambourine and multiple background vocals, which suggest the song was recorded altogether in one take. It peaked at No. 9 on the Billboard Best Selling Soul Singles chart and No. 66 on the Hot 100. Owing to the composition, it became a fan

[291] 21st Century Schizoid Man, *Wikipedia*, available at: https://en.wikipedia.org/wiki/21st_Century_Schizoid_Man, last accessed: February 27, 2020.
[292] Will You Love Me Tomorrow, *Wikipedia*, available at: https://en.wikipedia.org/wiki/Will_You_Love_Me_Tomorrow, last accessed: February 27, 2020.
[293] Iron Man, *Wikipedia*, available at: https://en.wikipedia.org/wiki/Iron_Man_(song) , last accessed: February 27, 2020.
[294] Soul Makossa, *Wikipedia*, available at: https://en.wikipedia.org/wiki/Soul_Makossa, last accessed: February 27, 2020.

		favourite and has been featured on various compilation albums posthumously.'[295]
Yeezus (2013)	'Gyöngyhajú lány'	'The song was very popular in many countries, including Germany, Great Britain, France, Poland, Romania, Czechoslovakia, Yugoslavia and Bulgaria.'[296]
	'Strange Fruit'	'The song protested American racism, particularly the lynching of African Americans. The song was highly regarded; the 1939 recording eventually sold a million copies, in time becoming Holiday's biggest-selling recording.'[297]
	'Chief Rocka'	'It peaked at #55 on the Billboard 200, the group's highest appearance on that chart, and went to #1 on the Hot Rap Singles.'[298]
	'Sweet Nothin's'	' 'It peaked at No. 4 on the Billboard Hot 100 and No. 12 on the Hot R&B Sides chart, in 1960. The song (as Sweet Nuthin's) also charted on the UK Singles Chart in 1960, peaking at No. 4.'[299]
	'Panda'	'The single received a nomination for Best Rap Performance at the 59th Annual Grammy Awards. A music video was released on May 10, 2016. It was nominated for Best Hip Hop Video at the 2016 MTV Video Music Awards. Rolling Stone named 'Panda' one of the 30 best songs of the first half of 2016. Billboard ranked 'Panda' at number 24 on their '100 Best Pop Songs of 2016', Pitchfork listed 'Panda' on their ranking of the 100 best songs of 2016 at number 56.'[300]

---

[295] Think (About It), *Wikipedia*, available at: https://en.wikipedia.org/wiki/Think_(About_It), last accessed: February 27, 2020.

[296] Gyöngyhajú lány, *Wikipedia*, available at: https://en.wikipedia.org/wiki/Gyöngyhajú_lány, last accessed: February 27, 2020.

[297] Strange Fruit, *Wikipedia*, available at: https://en.wikipedia.org/wiki/Strange_Fruit, last accessed: February 27, 2020.

[298] Chief Rocka, *Wikipedia*, available at: https://en.wikipedia.org/wiki/Chief_Rocka, last accessed: February 27, 2020.

[299] Sweet Nothin's, *Wikipedia*, available at: https://en.wikipedia.org/wiki/Sweet_Nothin%27s, last accessed: February 27, 2020.

[300] Panda (song), *Wikipedia*, available at: https://en.wikipedia.org/wiki/Panda_(song), last accessed: February 27, 2020.

	'Human'	Reached number 87 on the UK Singles Chart.[301]
The Life of Pablo (2016)	'Bam Bam'	'The song has been labeled as a 'well-known reggae anthem' arguably, one of the most sampled reggae songs ever.' [302]
	'Hot in Herre'	"Hot in Herre' was the inaugural winner of the Grammy Award for Best Male Rap Solo Performance at the 45th Annual Grammy Awards on February 23, 2003.'[303]
	'EI'	'It peaked at number 11 on the UK Singles Chart and 16 on the U.S. Billboard Hot 100.'[304]
	'Jumpman'	'Jumpman peaked at number 12 on the US Billboard Hot 100 chart in the week of November 7, 2015, prior to being released as a single. The song was eventually certified quadruple platinum by the Recording Industry Association of America for combined sales and streaming units of over four millions units.'[305]
	'(I Know) I'm Losing You'	"(I Know) I'm Losing You' was a No. 1 hit on the Billboard R&B singles chart, and reached No. 8 on the Billboard Pop Singles chart. In Canada the song reached No.21.'[306]
	'Rock the Boat'	'Rock the Boat' charted as an 'album cut' and peaked at number 14 on the Billboard Hot 100 in the week of January 5. The song stayed on the chart for twenty-five weeks. 'Rock the Boat' was nominated for Best Female R&B Vocal

[301] Human (Goldfrapp song), *Wikipedia*, available at: https://en.wikipedia.org/wiki/Human_(Goldfrapp_song), last accessed: February 27, 2020.

[302] Bam Bam (song), *Wikipedia*, available at: https://en.wikipedia.org/wiki/Bam_Bam_(song), last accessed: February 27, 2020.

[303] Hot in Herre, *Wikipedia*, available at: https://en.wikipedia.org/wiki/Hot_in_Herre, last accessed: February 27, 2020.

[304] E.I. (song), *Wikipedia*, available at: https://en.wikipedia.org/wiki/E.I._(song), last accessed: February 27, 2020.

[305] Jumpman, *Wikipedia*, available at: https://en.wikipedia.org/wiki/Jumpman_(song), last accessed: February 27, 2020.

[306] I Know I'm Losing You, *Wikipedia*, available at: https://en.wikipedia.org/wiki/(I_Know)_I%27m_Losing_You, last accessed: February 27, 2020.

		Performance at the 44th Annual Grammy Awards.'[307]
Ye (2018)	'Hey Young World'	'Hey Young World' was written and produced by Slick Rick. It was number 42 on the Hot Black Singles chart and number 17 on the Hot Rap Singles.[308]
	'Take Me For a Little While'	'Take Me For a Little While': according with a Reddit post: Kanye West sampled 75% of the original song.[309]
Jesus is King (2019)	'Oh My God'	'Oh My God' is a song from the album Midnight Marauders, an album included on various 'best of' lists by music writers.[310]

CONCLUSIONS:

- the inspiration from other songs is at good levels and can create at least a satisfactory argument that Kanye West's musical career is because of the samples that he used in his music and without samples he would not exist today as a global artist;
- Kanye West linked himself and used the instruments of songs that were highly awarded, topped the charts and were considered by critics the best songs of all time;
- if the title of 'the greatest artist of all time' is based on writing your own lyrics and musical notes, Kanye West (in comparison with Taylor Swift) is not the greatest artist of all time; if the title of 'the greatest artist of all time' is based on mixing other songs, titles (used in any formats) and lyrics that were created and belong to other artists, then Kanye West is one of the greatest artists of all time, and higher than Taylor Swift;
- Kanye West used sounds and lyrics well known in the music industry;

---

[307] Rock the Boat (Aaliyah song), *Wikipedia*, available at:
https://en.wikipedia.org/wiki/Rock_the_Boat_(Aaliyah_song), last accessed: February 27, 2020.
[308] Hey Young World, *Wikipedia*, available at: https://en.wikipedia.org/wiki/Hey_Young_World, last accessed: February 25, 2020.
[309] U/hobbbz, 'Kanye's "Ghost Town" is 75% a cover of "Take Me for a little While" whose author now makes racist albums', *Reddit*, available at:
https://www.reddit.com/r/hiphopheads/comments/8r25ju/kanyes_ghost_town_is_75_a_cover_of_tak e_me_for_a/, last accessed: July 31, 2022.
[310] See the list here: Midnight Marauders, *Wikipedia*, available at:
https://en.wikipedia.org/wiki/Midnight_Marauders, last accessed: February 25, 2020.

- Kanye West brought to life music lost in the past to a new generation that few to no people ever listened to the songs used in his music;
- Kanye West successfully managed to give glory to songs that were not awarded or received less appreciation than what he thinks the songs should;
- Kanye West successfully united music from various artists and genres.

Same road: Taylor Swift (for *Lover* album in 2019) used samples from 'Humpty Dumpty' which is a character in an English nursery rhyme and one of the best known in the English-speaking world; Kanye West used sample in the song 'Bad News' (from the album *808s & Heartbreak*, 2008) from 'Sea Lion Woman' which is a traditional African American folk song originally used as a children's playground song.[311]

II.1.6 The Race of the Samples

II.1.6.1 The Race of the Samples Used by Taylor Swift

TABLE 13. THE RACE OF THE SAMPLES USED BY TAYLOR SWIFT		
NAME OF THE ALBUM	**BLACK MALE ARTISTS**	**BLACK FEMALE ARTISTS**
Taylor Swift (Deluxe, 2006)	N/A	
Fearless (Platinum, 2008)	N/A	
Speak Now (Deluxe, 2010)	N/A	
RED (Deluxe, 2010)	N/A	
1989 (Deluxe, 2014)	N/A	
reputation (2017)	N/A	
Lover (2019)	2	0
folklore (Deluxe, 2020)	N/A	
Evermore (Deluxe, 2020)	N/A	
Fearless (Taylor's Version, 2021)	N/A	
TOTAL: 2 Black Male Artists + A group of students from Regent Park School of Music[312]		

---

[311] Sea Lion Woman, *Wikipedia*, available at: https://en.wikipedia.org/wiki/Sea_Lion_Woman, last accessed: February 25, 2020.

[312] I did not include a number of the students involved in making the sound that Taylor Swift used in her song as I did not find a verified information regarding the number of students and their ethnic background.

CONCLUSIONS:

- Taylor Swift's music contains extremely small number of black artists in her music to build at least a satisfactory argument that she is famous because she sampled songs created by black artists and she is taking advantage of them;
- the use of samples of music created by black artists can help to promote black artists at a global level and to millions of people.

II.1.6.2 The Race of the Samples Used by Kanye West

TABLE 14. THE RACE OF THE SAMPLES USED BY KANYE WEST		
NAME OF THE ALBUM	**WHITE MALE ARTISTS**	**WHITE FEMALE ARTISTS**
The College Dropout (2004)	7 out of 15	2 out of 6
Late Registration (2005)	N/A	
Graduation (2007)	5 out of 20	1 out of 1
88s & Heartbreak (2008)	2 out of 3	N/A
My Beautiful Dark Twisted Fantasy (2010)	21 out of 25	1 out of 1
Yeezus (2013)	2 out of 25	1 out of 2
The Life of Pablo (2016)	8 out o 64	2
Ye (2018)	3 out of 6	N/A
Jesus is King (2019)	5 out of 14	N/A
TOTAL	**53 out of 172**	**7 out of 10**
TOTAL IN PERCENTAGE	**31%**	**70%**

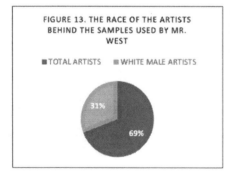

FIGURE 13. THE RACE OF THE ARTISTS BEHIND THE SAMPLES USED BY MR. WEST

■ TOTAL ARTISTS   ■ WHITE MALE ARTISTS

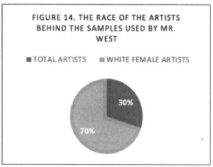

FIGURE 14. THE RACE OF THE ARTISTS BEHIND THE SAMPLES USED BY MR. WEST

■ TOTAL ARTISTS   ■ WHITE FEMALE ARTISTS

CONCLUSIONS:

- Kanye West's music contains 31% white artists in his music and there is evidence to build an argument that he is famous because he sampled songs created by white artists already known on the musical market and maybe by the general public; however, this report cannot prove that Kanye West is taking advantage of the white artists music as the white artists allowed (to what I read and in the time of writing this report Kanye West is not involved in any copyrights lawsuit about the use of unauthorized samples in his songs) Kanye West to use their music in the format that he wanted;
- the high number of white artists in the music of a black artist shows a high level of intellectual abilities of Kanye West to create music based on various lyrics, instruments and genres;
- the use of samples of music created by white artists was a new strategy of global promotion of their songs and their early success continued also with Kanye West and his version of their songs.

II.1.7 The Length of Songs

In this section of the chapter I investigated the length of songs released by Kanye West and Taylor Swift to show which artist has a higher number of minutes of music based purely on their own musical ear and writing abilities.

II.1.7.1 The Length of Songs as Sole Lyricist: Taylor Swift

TABLE 15. THE LENGTH OF SONGS AS SOLE LYRICIST TAYLOR SWIFT[313]		
NAME OF THE ALBUM	NAME OF THE SONG	LENGTH (MINUTES)
Taylor Swift (Deluxe, 2006)	The Outside	3:27
	Should've Said No	4:02
	Our Song	3:21
	Total: 10:50 minutes	
	Jump Then Fall: 3:57	3:57
	Forever & Always (piano version)	4:27

---

[313] On *Wikipedia* the songs have with 2 to 4 seconds more than on *Tidal*.

71

	The Other Side of the Door	3:58
Fearless (Platinum, 2008)	Fifteen	4:54
	Love Story	3:55
	Hey Stephen	4:14
	You're Not Sorry	4:22
	Forever & Always	3:45
	The Best Day	4:05
	Change	4:41
	Total: 42:18 minutes	
	Mine	3:50
	Sparks Fly	4:20
	Back to December	4:53
	Speak Now	4:00
	Dear John	6:53
	. Mean	3:57
	The Story of Us	4:25
	Never Grow Up	4:50
Speak Now (Deluxe, 2010)[314]	Enchanted	5:52
	Better than Revenge	3:37
	Innocent	5:02
	Haunted	4:02
	Last Kiss	6:07
	Long Live	5:17
	Ours	3:58
	Superman	4:36
	Total: 75:29 minutes	
	State of Grace	4:55
	Red	3:43
	I Almost Do	4:04
	Stay Stay Stay	3:25
	Holy Ground	3:22
RED (Deluxe, 2012)	Sad Beautiful Tragic	4:44
	The Lucky One	4:00
	Starlight	3:40
	Begin Again	3:59
	The Moment I Knew	4:46
	Girl at Home	3:40
	Total: 44:18 minutes	
1989 (Deluxe, 2014)	This Love	4:10
	Total: 4:10 minutes	
reputation (2017)	N/A	
	Lover	3:41
Lover (2019)	Cornelia Street	4:47
	Daylight	4:53
	Total: 13:21 minutes	

---

[314] The length of the songs *Our Song* and *Superman* was taken from Wikipedia.
https://en.wikipedia.org/wiki/Fearless_(Taylor_Swift_album)#Track_listing, last accessed: February 25, 2020.

folklore (Deluxe, 2020)	My Tears Ricochet	4:16
	Total: 4:16 minutes	
Evermore (Deluxe, 2020)	No Body, No Crime	3:35
	Total: 3:35 minutes	
	Today Was a Fairytale	4:01
Fearless (Taylor's Version, 2021)	Mr. Perfectly Fine	4:37
	Total: 8:38 minutes	
Total (songs/length)	**Songs: 48; Length: 206:55 minutes**	

II.1.7.2 The Length of Songs as Sole Lyricists: Kanye West

TABLE 16. THE LENGTH OF SONGS AS SOLE LYRICIST BY KANYE WEST		
NAME OF THE ALBUM	**NAME OF THE SONG**	**LENGTH (MINUTES)**
	Intro (Skit)	0:19
	Workout Plan (Skit)	0:46
	School Spirit (Skit 1)	1:18
The College Dropout (2004)	School Spirit (Skit 2)	0:43
	Lil Jimmy (Skit)	0:53
	Family Business	4:38
	Total: 8:57 minutes	
Late Registration (2005)	Celebration	3:18
	Total: 3:18 minutes	
Graduation (2007)	N/A	
808s & Heartbreak (2008)	Pinocchio Story	6:01
	Total: 6:01 minutes	
My Beautiful Dark Twisted Fantasy (2010)	N/A	
Yeezus (2013)	N/A	
The Life of Pablo (2016)	N/A	
Ye (2018)	N/A	
Jesus is King (2019)	N/A	
	Songs: With *Intro and Skit*: 8; Without *Intro and Skit*: 3	
Total (songs/length)	**Minutes**: With *Intro and Skit*: 18:16; Without *Intro and Skit*: 13:57	

TABLE 17. THE LENGTH OF SONGS AS SOLE LYRICIST	
TAYLOR SWIFT	**KANYE WEST**
Taylor Swift (Deluxe, 2006): 10:50 out of 51:14 minutes	The College Dropout (2004): 8:57 out of 76:11 minutes
Fearless (Platinum, 2008): 42:18 out of 79:32 minutes	Late Registration (2005): 3:18 out of 73:52 minutes
Speak Now (Deluxe, 2010): 75:29 out of 79:23 minutes	Graduation (2007): 0 out of 54:30 minutes
RED (Deluxe, 2012): 44:18 out of 77:27 minutes	88s & Heartbreak (2008): 6:01 out of 52:05 minutes

1989 (Deluxe, 2014): 4:10 out of 61:11 minutes	My Beautiful Dark Twisted Fantasy (2010): 0 out of 68:44 minutes
reputation (2017): 0 out of 55:44 minutes	Yeezus (2013): 0 out of 40:03 minutes
Lover (2019): 13:21 out of 61:48 minutes	The Life of Pablo (2016): 0 out of 66:01 minutes
folklore (Deluxe, 2020): 4:16 out of 67:01 minutes	Ye (2018): 0 out of 23:45 minutes
Evermore (Deluxe, 2020): 3:35 out of 69:08 minutes	Jesus is King (2019): 0 out of 27:04 minutes
Fearless (Taylor's Version, 2021): 8:38 out of 23:00 minutes	
Total minutes: 206:55 out of 625:37 minutes	*Total minutes: 18:16 out of 492:03 minutes (With Intro & Skit); 13:57 out of 492:03 minutes (Without Intro & Skit)*

CONCLUSIONS:

- Taylor Swift wrote alone at least 11 times (includes Intro & Skit by Kanye West) and at least 14 times (without Intro & Outro by Kanye West) more minutes of music than Kanye West;
- Taylor Swift wrote at least 6 (includes *Intro & Outro* by Kanye West) and 16 times (does not include *Intro & Outro* by Kanye West) more songs than Kanye West.

II.1.7.3 The Length of Songs with Two Lyricists (Taylor Swift included)

TABLE 18. THE LENGTH OF SONGS WITH TWO LYRICISTS (TAYLOR SWIFT INCLUDED)		
NAME OF THE ALBUM	**NAME OF THE SONG**	**LENGTH (MINUTES)**
Taylor Swift (Deluxe, 2006)	Tim McGraw	3:54
	Picture to Burn	2:55
	Teardrops on my Guitar	3:55
	Cold as You	4:01
	Tied Together with a Smile	4:11
	Stay Beautiful	3:58
	Invisible	3:26
	Total: 26:20 minutes	
Fearless (Platinum, 2008)	White Horse	3:54
	You Belong with Me	3:51
	Breathe	4:23
	Tell Me Why	3:20
	The Way I Loved You	4:04

	Come in the Rain	3:58
	Superstar	3:26
	Total: 27:51 minutes	
Speak Now (Deluxe, 2010)[315]	If This Was a Movie	3:54
	Total: 3:54 minutes	
	Treacherous	4:02
	All Too Well	5:29
RED (Deluxe, 2012)	Everything Has Changed	4:05
	Come Back ... Be Here	3:42
	Total: 17:18 minutes	
	Welcome to New York	3:32
	Out of the Woods	3:55
	All You Had To Do Was Stay	3:13
	I Wish You Would	3:27
1989 (Deluxe, 2014)	I Know Places	3:15
	Clean	4:30
	You Are In Love	4:27
	Total: 26:19 minutes	
	Getaway Car	3:53
	Dress	3:50
reputation (2017)	This is Why We Can't Have Nice Things	3:27
	Call It What You Want	3:23
	New Year's Day	3:55
	Total: 18:28 minutes	
	The Man	3:10
	The Archer	3:31
	I Think He Knows	2:53
	Miss Americana & The Heartbreak Prince	3:54
Lover (2019)	Paper Rings	3:42
	Death by a Thousand Cuts	3:19
	Soon You'll Get Better	3:22
	False God	3:20
	You Need To Calm Down	2:51
	Total: 30:02 minutes	
	the 1	3:30
	cardigan	3:59
	the last great American dynasty	3:51
	my tears ricochet	4:15
	mirrorball	3:29
	seven	3:28
	august	4:21
folklore (Deluxe, 2020)	this is me trying	3:15
	illicit affairs	3:10

---

[315] The length of the songs *Our Song* and *Superman* was taken from Wikipedia. https://en.wikipedia.org/wiki/Fearless_(Taylor_Swift_album)#Track_listing, last accessed: February 25, 2020.

	invisible string	4:12
	mad woman	3:57
	epiphany	4:49
	betty	4:54
	peace	3:54
	hoax	3:40
	Total: 58:44 minutes	
Evermore (Deluxe, 2020)	Willow	3:34
	Champagne Problems	4:04
	Gold Rush	3:05
	Tis the Damn Season	3:49
	Tolerate It	4:05
	Happiness	5:15
	Dorothea	3:45
	Cowboy Like Me	4:35
	Long Story Short	3:35
	Marjorie	4:17
	Closure	3:00
	Right Were You Left Me	4:05
	It's Time to Go	4:15
	Total: 51:24 minutes	
Fearless (Taylor's Version, 2021)	You All Over Me	3:40
	We Were Happy	4:04
	Don't You	3:28
	Bye Bye Baby	4:02
	Total: 15:14 minutes	
Total (songs/length)	***Songs: 72; Length: 275:34 minutes***	

II.1.7.4 The Length of Songs with Two Lyricists (Kanye West included)

TABLE 19. THE LENGTH OF SONGS WITH TWO LYRICISTS (KANYE WEST INCLUDED)		
NAME OF THE ALBUM	**NAME OF THE SONG**	**LENGTH (MINUTES)**
The College Dropout (2004)	'All Falls Down'	3:43
	'Breathe In Breathe Out'	4:06
	'School Spirit'	3:02
	Total: 10:51 minutes	
Late Registration (2005)	'Roses': 4:05	'Roses': 4:05
	'Bring Me Down': 3:18	'Bring Me Down': 3:18
	'Hey Mama': 5:05	'Hey Mama': 5:05
	Total: 12:28 minutes	
Graduation (2007)	'I Wonder'	4:03
	'Can't Tell Me Nothing'	4:31
	'Flashing Lights'	3:57
	'Big Brother'	4:47
	Total: 17:18 minutes	

808s & Heartbreak (2008)	'Bad News'	3:58
	Total: 3:58 minutes	
My Beautiful Dark Twisted Fantasy (2010)	N/A	
Yeezus (2013)	N/A	
The Life of Pablo (2016)	N/A	
Ye (2018)	N/A	
Jesus is King (2019)	N/A	
Total (songs/length)	**Songs: 11; Length: 44:35 minutes.**	

TABLE 20. THE LENGTH OF SONGS WITH TWO LYRICISTS	
TAYLOR SWIFT	**KANYE WEST**
Taylor Swift (Deluxe, 2006): 26:20 out of 51:14 minutes	The College Dropout (2004): 10:51 out of 76:11 minutes
Fearless (Platinum, 2008): 27:51 out of 79:32 minutes	Late Registration (2005): 12:28 out of 73:52 minutes
Speak Now (Deluxe, 2010): 3:54 out of 79:23 minutes	Graduation (2007): 17:18 out of 54:30 minutes
RED (Deluxe, 2012): 17:18 out of 77:27 minutes	88s & Heartbreak (2008): 3:58 out of 61:53 minutes
1989 (Deluxe, 2014): 26:19 out of 61:11 minutes	My Beautiful Dark Twisted Fantasy (2010): 0 out of 68:44 minutes
reputation (2017): 18:28 out of 55:44 minutes	Yeezus (2013): 0 out of 40:03 minutes
Lover (2019): 30:02 out of 61:48 minutes	The Life of Pablo (2016): 0 out of 66:01 minutes
folklore (Deluxe, 2020): 58:44 out of 67:01 minutes	Ye (2018): 0 out of 23:45 minutes
Evermore (Deluxe, 2020): 51:24 out of 69:08 minutes	Jesus is King (2019): 0 out of 27:04 minutes
Fearless (Taylor's Version, 2021): 15:14 out of 23:00 minutes	
Total length: 275:34 out of 625:37 minutes	**Total length: 44:35 out of 492:03 minutes**

CONCLUSION:

- Taylor Swift has written at least 6 times more songs with the help of a second writer than Kanye West, and 6 times more minutes of music than Kanye West.

II.1.7.5 Number of Songs Produced Only by Kanye West

TABLE 21. NUMBER OF SONGS PRODUCED ONLY BY KANYE WEST
The College Dropout (2004): 19 out of 22
Late Registration (2005): 4 out of 22
Graduation (2007): 3 out of 14
88s & Heartbreak (2008): 3 out of 12
My Beautiful Dark Twisted Fantasy (2010): 0 out of 14
Watch the Throne Deluxe (2011): 1 out of 16
Cruel Summer (2012): 0 out of 12
Yeezus (2013): 0 out of 10
The Life of Pablo (2016): 0 out of 20
Ye (2018): 0 out of 7
Kids See Ghosts (2018): 0 out of 7
Jesus is King (2019): 0 out of 11
Total songs: 30 out of 167

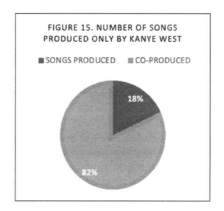

FIGURE 15. NUMBER OF SONGS PRODUCED ONLY BY KANYE WEST

■ SONGS PRODUCED   ■ CO-PRODUCED

18%

82%

CONCLUSIONS:

- Kanye West sole production is 18% of his songs, and Taylor Swift 0%;
- Kanye West's abilities are limited when he has to actually use the live piano and guitar; Taylor Swift, on the other hand, has good, maybe advanced, skills in using musical instruments such as piano and guitar, and also plays live using both instruments successfully with positive praise.

II.1.7.6 Length of Music Produced Only by Kanye West

TABLE 22. LENGTH OF MUSIC PRODUCED ONLY BY KANYE WEST
The College Dropout (2004): 8:57 out of 76:11 minutes
Late Registration (2005): 3:18 out of 73:52 minutes
Graduation (2007): 0 out of 54:30 minutes
88s & Heartbreak (2008): 6:01 out of 52:05 minutes
My Beautiful Dark Twisted Fantasy (2010): 0 out of 68:44 minutes
Watch the Throne Deluxe (2011): 0 out of 64:50 minutes
Cruel Summer (2012): 0 out of 54:34 minutes[316]
Yeezus (2013): 0 out of 40:03 minutes
The Life of Pablo (2016): 0 out of 66:01 minutes
Ye (2018): 0 out of 23:45 minutes
Kids See Ghosts (2018): 0 out of 23:53 minutes[317]
Jesus is King (2019): 0 out of 27:04 minutes
Total lengths: 18:16 out of 536:49 minutes (around 3.1%)

II.1.8 The Rabbit Hat: Fame, Originality and Creativity After VMA 2009

In this section of the chapter I investigated the roots of the new album released a year after the MTV scene[318] that is the music released by both artists in the autumn of 2010, first Taylor Swift then Kanye West.

TABLE 23. THE RABBIT'S HAT: TAYLOR SWIFT AND KANYE WEST		
CATEGORY	TAYLOR SWIFT: *SPEAK NOW (DELUXE, 2010)*	KANYE WEST: *MY BEAUTIFUL DARK TWISTED FANTASY (2010)*
FIRST WEEK SALES	HIGH INCREASE	HIGH DECREASE
OVERALL ALBUM SALES	HIGH NUMBER OF SALES ON LONG TERM	MODERATE NUMBER OF SALES WITH TRACKS OF SLOW SALES ON LONG TERM
USE OF SAMPLE	0%	10 OUT OF 14 SONGS
ORIGINAL SONGS WITH NO SAMPLE	17 SONGS (100%)	4 OUT OF 14 SONGS
ORIGINAL SONG AS SOLE LYRICIST	16 OUT OF 17 SONGS	0 SONGS (0%)
ORIGINAL SONG WITH TWO LYRICISTS	1 OUT OF 17 SONGS	0 OUT OF 14 SONGS (0%)
ORIGINAL SONG WITH THREE LYRICISTS	0 SONGS	1 OUT OF 14 SONGS
ORIGINAL SONG WITH AT LEAST FOUR LYRICICTS	0 SONGS	13 OUT OF 14 SONGS
DIRECT INSPIRATION FROM OTHER SONGS	NO	YES
TOP CHARTS & AWARDS OF THE SONG SAMPLED	NO	YES

---

[316] Kanye West, 'Kanye West Presents Good Music Cruel Summer', *Tidal,* available alt: https://listen.tidal.com/album/17078868, last accessed: February 20, 2020.
[317] Kanye West, 'Kids See Ghosts Credits', *Tidal*, available at: https://listen.tidal.com/album/90151605, last accessed: February 20, 2020.
[318] See Casian Anton, *On the Famous Feud*.

DIRECT WHITE MALE INSPIRATION	N/A	21 OUT OF 25
DIRECT WHITE FEMALE INSPIRATION	N/A	1 OUT OF 1
DIRECT BLACK MALE INSPIRATION	N/A	4 out of 25
DIRECT BLACK FEMALE INSPIRATION	N/A	
METACRITIC RATING	77	94
LENGTH OF SONG AS SOLE LYRICIST	75:29 MINUTES	0 MINUTES
LENGTH OF SONG WITH TWO LYRICISTS	3:54	0 MINUTES (THERE IS A HIGHER NUMBER OF MINUTES ONLY TO SONGS WITH AT LEAST 4 SONGWRITERS)
LYRICS	OWN LYRICS	LYRICS FROM OTHER ARTISTS
THE ORIGINS OF TITLE SONGS	OWN TITLES	FROM OTHER TITLE SONGS AND LYRICS OF SONGS SAMPLED IN HIS MUSIC
PATTERN OF MUSIC RELEASE	2006: October 24 2008: November 11 2010: October 25	2004: February 10 2005: August 30 2007: September 11 2008: November 24 2010: November 22
	The following date are written to observe the full pattern of music release of both artists.	
	2012: October 22 2014: October 27 2017: November 10 2019: August 23 2020: July 24 2020: December 11	2013: June 18 2016: February 14 2018: June 1 2019: October 25

CONCLUSIONS:

- *Taylor Swift*:

    o came with traces of global success;

    o came with her lyrics and musical instruments;

    o released an album with original songs never heard in the music industry;

    o the length of the music written by herself for *Standard Edition* is 100% of the album, for *Deluxe Edition* she has one song written in partnership with another lyricist; Kanye West has 0% as sole lyricist;

    o released the music following October – November pattern;

    o behind the lyrics of her songs is Taylor Swift.

- *Kanye West*:

○ came with lyrics written by other artists and instruments already created and used by other artists in the music industry;

○ 13 out of 14 songs were written by at least 4 lyricists, compared to Taylor Swift who wrote all the songs on her own (Standard Edition) and sold at least 50% more albums in one week than him;

○ it is inspired by the music written by white male artists, 21 out of 25 male artists;

○ overall, his album was rated on Metacritic with higher grade than Taylor Swift, 94, while for Taylor Swift is 77;

○ changed the pattern of music release and interfered for a second time in Taylor Swift's pattern of album release: one album in each year for two years and in total for four albums: the first two albums: 2004 and 2005, the next two albums: 2007 and 2008; since 2008 Kanye West changed the season and released his album in the same month as Taylor Swift, but two weeks later: Taylor Swift on November 11, 2008 and Kanye West on November 24; in 2010: Taylor Swift released the album on October 25 (she released her first album in October 24, 2006), then Kanye West later in November 22, keeping the release date connected with the last release, which is the first and last time when Kanye West follows this release pattern; the following albums will be released in different seasons, only to change it to October 25, 2019 with *Jesus is King*, the same date that Taylor Swift released *Speak Now* in 2010;

○ behind the lyrics of his music is him but also many lyricists and producers.

- **Album reviews**: Kanye West received higher reviews and grades than Taylor Swift, but given the sources of his songs, the following questions arise: do the reviews also include an analysis of his voice? Online critics argue that his singing skills are either weak or he does not know how to sing[319], did the reviewers perform a genuine analysis of his voice? If this argument is true, how did he manage to get such a high score? Moreover, Kanye West used samples (title, lyrics, instrumental music) from other artists, basically what is Kanye West's original contribution in his album? Are the reviews and grades received based only on his work or the final song that contains samples? Are reviewers able to make the difference between Kanye West's original part and the samples part? If we take the samples from Kanye's album, what remains written and produced by him alone is worth grades 9 and 10? Taylor Swift got the grades based on her own lyrics and 50% participation as producer of her album and were 7 and 8 in the eyes of the reviewers, Kanye got the grades 9 and 10 with the help of more lyricists and producers than Taylor Swift, but we do not know for sure how much is Kanye's contribution in the lyrics of the songs and production. Are the reviews real or have they been exaggerated to the detriment of the music industry, but also of the white artist Taylor Swift to prove that black artists have better music than white artists and Kanye West was right to point out that Taylor Swift did not deserve the award from 2009?

II.1.9 Producers and Lyricists

In the following pages I created figures with the number of producers and lyricists used by both artists. The conclusion is that Taylor Swift needed less producers and lyricists to create and sell millions of songs and albums than Kanye West.

---

[319] *Quora*, 'How Well Does Kanye West Really Sing', available at: https://www.quora.com/How-well-does-Kanye-West-really-sing, last accessed: February 25, 2020; 'Why is Kanye West considered to be a great artist? I have listened to his music, and it sounds like every other song on the radio. Am I missing something?', available at: https://www.quora.com/Why-is-Kanye-West-considered-to-be-a-great-artist-I-have-listened-to-his-music-and-it-sounds-like-every-other-song-on-the-radio-Am-I-missing-something, last accessed: February 25, 2020; 'David Crosby: Kanye West can neither sing, nor write, nor play', *The Guardian*, October 28, 2016, available at: https://www.theguardian.com/music/2016/oct/28/david-crosby-kanye-west, last accessed: February 25, 2020.

II.1.9.1 Number of Producers: Kanye West and Taylor Swift

Figure 16 is used to compare the number of producers at the start of the career of both artists.

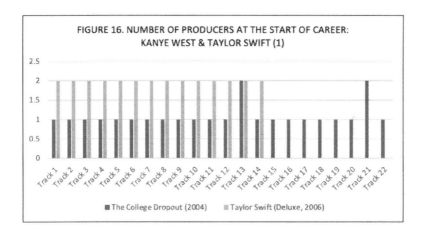

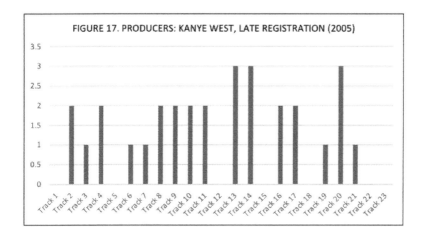

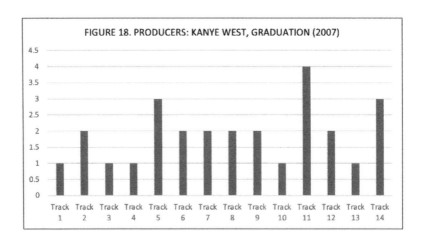

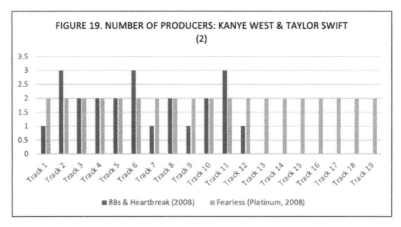

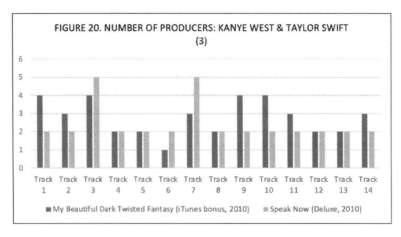

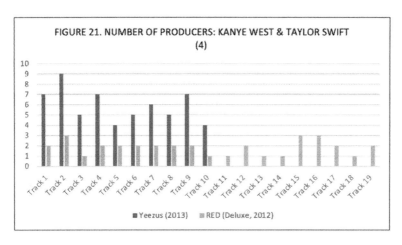

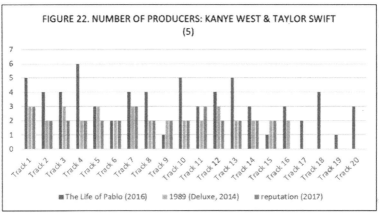

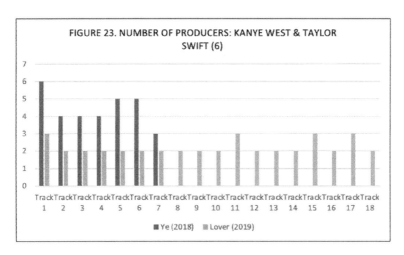

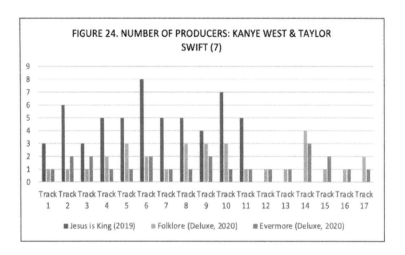

II.1.9.2 *Number of Lyricists: Kanye West and Taylor Swift.*

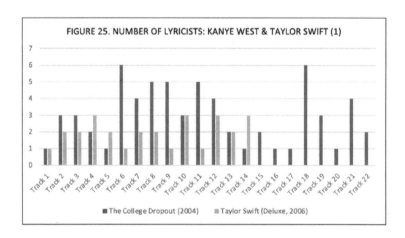

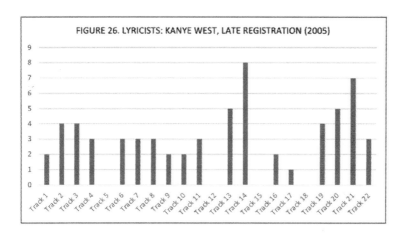

FIGURE 26. LYRICISTS: KANYE WEST, LATE REGISTRATION (2005)

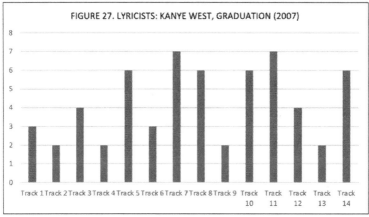

FIGURE 27. LYRICISTS: KANYE WEST, GRADUATION (2007)

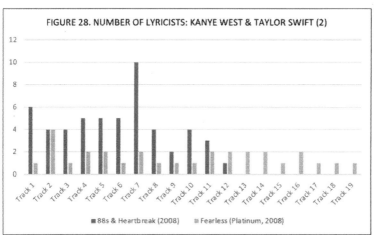

FIGURE 28. NUMBER OF LYRICISTS: KANYE WEST & TAYLOR SWIFT (2)

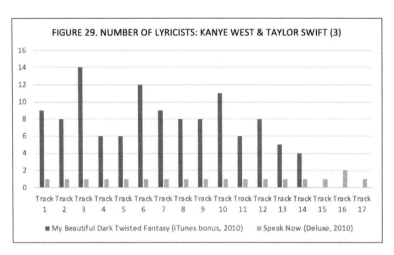

FIGURE 29. NUMBER OF LYRICISTS: KANYE WEST & TAYLOR SWIFT (3)

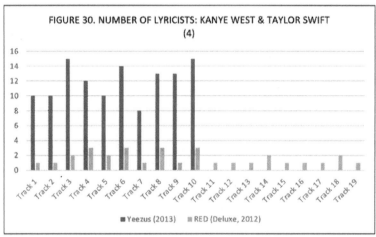

FIGURE 30. NUMBER OF LYRICISTS: KANYE WEST & TAYLOR SWIFT (4)

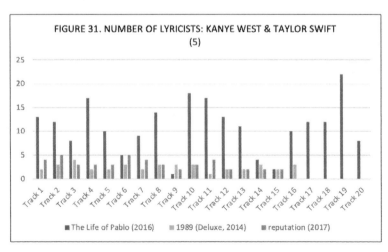

FIGURE 31. NUMBER OF LYRICISTS: KANYE WEST & TAYLOR SWIFT (5)

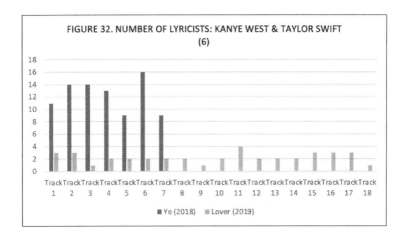

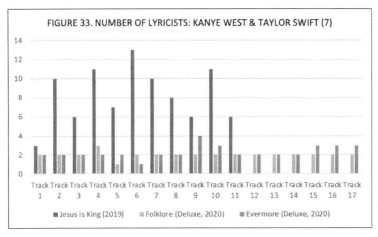

II.1.10 The Rating on Metacritic

TABLE 24. THE ALBUM RATINGS ON METACRITIC	
TAYLOR SWIFT[320]	**KANYE WEST**[321]
Taylor Swift (Deluxe, 2006): not on Metacritic	The College Dropout (2004): 87
Fearless (Platinum, 2008): 73	Late Registration (2005): 85
Speak Now (Deluxe, 2010): 77	Graduation (2007): 79
RED (Deluxe, 2012): 77	88s & Heartbreak (2008): 75

---

[320] Taylor Swift, *Metacritic*, available at: https://www.metacritic.com/person/taylor-swift, last accessed: July 1, 2021.
[321] Kanye West, *Metacritic*, available at: https://www.metacritic.com/person/kanye-west?filter-options=music&sort_options=date&num_items=30, last accessed: July 1, 2021.

1989 (Deluxe, 2014): 76	My Beautiful Dark Twisted Fantasy (2010): 94
reputation (2017): 71	Yeezus (2013): 84
Lover (2019): 79	The Life of Pablo (2016): 75
folklore (Deluxe, 2020): 88	Ye (2018): 64
Evermore (Deluxe, 2020): 85	Jesus is King (2019): 55
Fearless (Taylor's Version, 2021): 82	
Total average: 78.66	*Total average: 77.55*

CONCLUSIONS:

- *Taylor Swfit*:

    o the notes received for each album are based on the work and the ideas of the artist, but also to a considerable extent of other artists and producers she worked with (see the producers of *folklore* and *Evermore*, most of them is one producer: Aaron Dessner);

    o male producers are the constant base of her musical career;

    o compared to Kanye West and Metacritic, the grades received is close to 8, where they increase and decrease over the years;

    o a significant percentage of the grade received is based purely on her ability to write and compose unheard songs; also, to write lyrics to various instruments that she listened for the first time; in her music catalogue there are songs that were written shortly after she heard the instruments and were included in various charts for long term;

    o Metacritic does not include all the reviews written about her albums, there are reviews with higher and lower grades which are not included; it is highly possible that the final grade to be over 80.

- *Kanye West*:

    o the notes received for each album are based on the work and the ideas of the artist, but also to a considerable extent of other artists from whom he abundantly sampled;

90

also, for lyricists and producers who contributed to his songs;

o   compared to Taylor Swift (the grades increased and before the age 30 she has the highest awarded album in her life, *folklore*), he received a high grade, 87 and then decreased (for 3 albums), then raised to the highest grade (94) and since then is continuously decreasing, the last album receiving grade 55;

o   parts of his grades belong to white artists as well;

o   Metacritic does not include all the reviews written about his albums, there are reviews with higher and lower grades which are not included; it is highly possible that the final grade to be over 80.

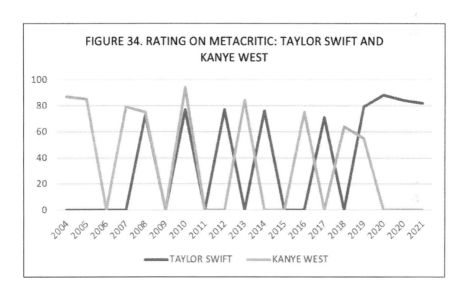

FIGURE 34. RATING ON METACRITIC: TAYLOR SWIFT AND KANYE WEST

II.2 *Beyoncé* and *Kendrick Lamar*

In the following section of chapter II, I investigated the music released by Beyoncé (black woman) and Kendrick Lamar (black man). I applied the research methods used for Kanye West and Taylor Swift.

The idea of this chapter is to see similarities between the black artists. In the first chapter I investigated Kanye West.

The information from this chapter will be used to compare the black artists (Beyoncé and Kendrick Lamar) with the white artists (Adele, Beck, Taylor Swift and Macklemore & Ryan).

II.2.1 Samples

II.2.1.1 Use of Sample

TABLE 25. USE OF SAMPLE	
BEYONCÉ	**KENDRICK LAMAR**
Dangerously in Love (2003): 8 out of 16[322]	Section.80 (2011): 8 out of 16[323]
B'Day (Deluxe, 2006): 3 out of 17[324]	good kid, m.A.A.d. City (Deluxe, 2012): 8 out of 17[325]
I am...Sasha Fierce (Platinum, 2008): 0 out of 20[326]	To Pimp a Butterfly (2015): 6 out of 16[327]

[322] Beyoncé, 'Dangerously In Love Credits', 2003, *Tidal*, available at: https://listen.tidal.com/album/2859862, last accessed: July 1, 2021.
[323] Kendrick Lamar, 'Section.80', 2011, *Tidal*, available at: https://listen.tidal.com/album/114492492, last accessed: July 1, 2021.
[324] Beyoncé, 'B'Day (Deluxe Edition) Credits', 2006, *Tidal*, available at: https://listen.tidal.com/album/3347090, from Volume 2 only Amor Gitano is included as the rest of the songs are Spanish (one song is mixed with Spanish and English) and remixes of songs from volume 1; last accessed: July 1, 2021.
[325] Kendrick Lamar, 'good kid, m.A.A.d. city (Deluxe Edition) Credits', 2012, *Tidal* available at: https://listen.tidal.com/album/20556792, last accessed: July 1, 2021.
[326] Beyoncé, 'I am...Sasha Fierce (Platinum Edition) Credits', *Tidal*, available at: https://listen.tidal.com/album/3147463, last accessed: July 1, 2021.
[327] Kendrick Lamar, 'To Pimp a Butterfly', 2015, *Tidal*, available at: https://listen.tidal.com/album/77703636, last accessed: July 1, 2021.

4 (2011): 4 out of 14[328]	Damn (2017): 10 out of 14[329]
Beyoncé (Platinum, 2013): 3 out of 16[330]	
Lemonade (2016): 7 out of 12[331]	
Total: 25 out of 95 songs (26%)	***Total: 32 out of 63 songs (51%)***

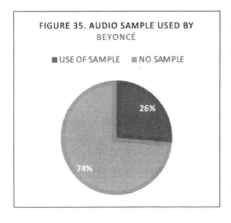

FIGURE 35. AUDIO SAMPLE USED BY BEYONCÉ

USE OF SAMPLE   NO SAMPLE

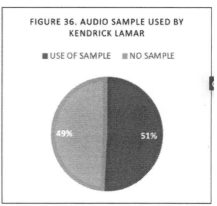

FIGURE 36. AUDIO SAMPLE USED BY KENDRICK LAMAR

USE OF SAMPLE   NO SAMPLE

II.2.1.2 No Use of Sample

TABLE 26. NO USE OF SAMPLE	
BEYONCÉ	**KENDRICK LAMAR**
Dangerously in Love (2003): 8 out of 16	Section.80 (2011): 8 out of 16
B'Day (Deluxe, 2006): 13 out of 17	good kid, m.A.A.d. City (Deluxe, 2012): 9 out of 17
I am...Sasha Fierce (Platinum, 2008): 20 out of 20	To Pimp a Butterfly (2015): 10 out of 16
4 (2011): 10 out of 14	Damn (2017): 4 out of 14
Beyoncé (Platinum, 2013): 13 out of 16	
Lemonade (2016): 5 out of 12	
Total: 69 out of 95 songs (73%)	***Total: 31 out of 63 songs (closed to 50%)***

---

[328] Beyoncé, '4 Credits', 2011, *Tidal*, available at: https://listen.tidal.com/album/19646520, last accessed: July 1, 2021.

[329] Kendrick Lamar, 'Damn Credits', 2017, *Tidal*, available at: https://listen.tidal.com/album/72694579, last accessed: July 1, 2021.

[330] Beyoncé, 'Beyoncé (Platinum Edition) Credits', 2014, *Tidal*, available at: https://listen.tidal.com/album/37936030, last accessed: July 1, 2021.

[331] Beyoncé, 'Lemonade Credits', 2016, *Tidal,* available at: https://listen.tidal.com/album/108043414. Track 'Sorry' (Original Demo) is not listed in this table, last accessed: July 1, 2021.

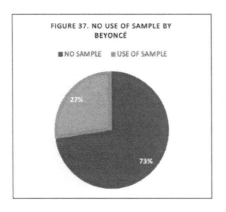

FIGURE 37. NO USE OF SAMPLE BY BEYONCÉ

■ NO SAMPLE   ■ USE OF SAMPLE

27%

73%

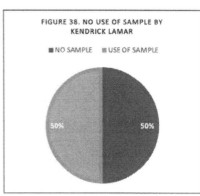

FIGURE 38. NO USE OF SAMPLE BY KENDRICK LAMAR

■ NO SAMPLE   ■ USE OF SAMPLE

50%   50%

II.2.2 Lyricists

II.2.2.1 Sole Lyricist

TABLE 27. ORIGINAL SONG AS SOLE LYRICIST	
BEYONCÉ	**KENDRICK LAMAR**
Dangerously in Love (2003): 1 out of 16	Section.80 (2011): 0 out of 16
B'Day (Deluxe, 2006): 0 out of 17	good kid, m.A.A.d. City (Deluxe, 2012): 0 out of 17
I am...Sasha Fierce (Platinum, 2008): 0 out of 20	To Pimp a Butterfly (2015): 0 out of 16
4 (2011): 0 out of 14	Damn (2017): 0 out of 14
Beyoncé (Platinum, 2013): 0 out of 16	
Lemonade (2016): 0 out of 12	
Total: 1 out of 95 songs (less than 1%)	*Total: 0 out of 63 songs (0%)*

94

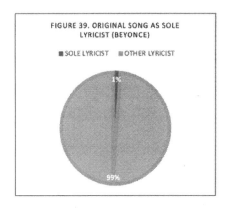

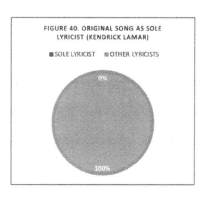

II.2.2.2 Two Lyricists

TABLE 28. ORIGINAL SONG WITH TWO LYRICISTS	
BEYONCÉ	**KENDRICK LAMAR**
Dangerously in Love (2003): 4 out of 16	Section.80 (2011): 10 out of 16
B'Day (Deluxe, 2006): 0 out of 17	good kid, m.A.A.d. City (Deluxe, 2012): 4 out of 17
I am...Sasha Fierce (Platinum, 2008): 0 out of 20	To Pimp a Butterfly (2015): 1 out of 16
4 (2011): 0 out of 14	Damn (2017): 4 out of 14
Beyoncé (Platinum, 2013): 3 out of 16	
Lemonade (2016): 1 out of 12	
Total: 8 out of 95 songs (8%)	*Total: 19 out of 63 songs (30%)*

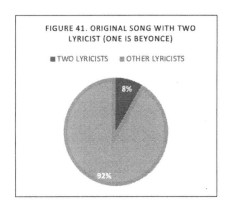

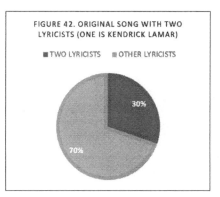

CONCLUSION:

- Beyoncé has fewer original songs written with two lyricists (herself included) than Kendrick Lamar.

II.2.2.3 Three Lyricists

TABLE 29. ORIGINAL SONG WITH THREE LYRICISTS	
BEYONCÉ	**KENDRICK LAMAR**
Dangerously in Love (2003): 3 out of 16	Section.80 (2011): 6 out of 16
B'Day (Deluxe, 2006): 4 out of 17	good kid, m.A.A.d. City (Deluxe, 2012): 5 out of 17
I am...Sasha Fierce (Platinum, 2008): 6 out of 20	To Pimp a Butterfly (2015): 3 out of 16
4 (2011): 8 out of 14	Damn (2017): 1 out of 14
Beyoncé (Platinum, 2013): 5 out of 16	
Lemonade (2016): 3 out of 12	
Total: 29 out of 95 songs (31%)	*Total: 15 out of 63 songs (24%)*

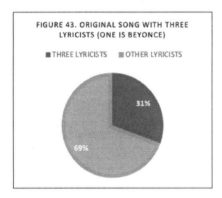

FIGURE 43. ORIGINAL SONG WITH THREE LYRICISTS (ONE IS BEYONCE)

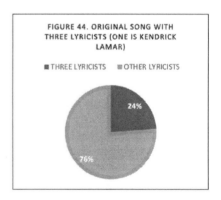

FIGURE 44. ORIGINAL SONG WITH THREE LYRICISTS (ONE IS KENDRICK LAMAR)

II.2.2.4 At Least Four Lyricists

TABLE 30. ORIGINAL SONG WITH AT LEAST FOUR LYRICISTS	
BEYONCÉ	**KENDRICK LAMAR**
Dangerously in Love (2003): 8 out of 16	Section.80 (2011): 0 out of 16

B'Day (Deluxe, 2006): 13 out of 17	good kid, m.A.A.d. City (2Deluxe, 012): 8 out of 17
I am...Sasha Fierce (Platinum, 2008): 13 out of 20	To Pimp a Butterfly (2015): 12 out of 16
4 (2011): 5 out of 14	Damn (2017): 9 out of 14
Beyoncé (Platinum, 2013): 8 out of 16	
Lemonade (2016): 8 out of 12	
Total: 55 out of 95 songs (58%)	*Total: 29 out of 63 songs (46%)*

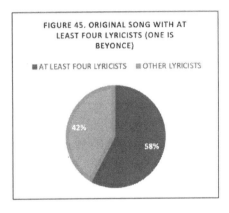

FIGURE 45. ORIGINAL SONG WITH AT LEAST FOUR LYRICISTS (ONE IS BEYONCE)

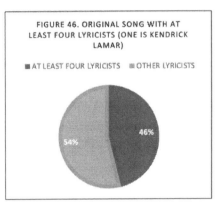

FIGURE 46. ORIGINAL SONG WITH AT LEAST FOUR LYRICISTS (ONE IS KENDRICK LAMAR)

CONCLUSION:

- both artists use at least four writers, Beyoncé 12% more than Kendrick Lamar.

II.2.3 The List of Samples

II.2.3.1 The List of Samples Used by Beyoncé

TABLE 31. THE LIST OF SAMPLES USED BY BEYONCÉ	
NAME OF THE ALBUM	**SAMPLES**
Dangerously in Love (2003)	1. 'Crazy in Love' samples 'Are You My Woman (Tell Me So)' (1970) by the Chi-Lites 2. 'Naughty Girl' contains interpolations from 'Love to Love You Baby' (1975) by Donna Summer 3. 'Baby Boy' contains interpolations from 'Hot Stepper' (1990) by Ini Kamoze.

	4. 'Be with You' samples 'Ain't Nothing I Can Do' (1979) Tyrone Davis and contains interpolations from 'I'd Rather Be with You' (1976) by Bootsy's Rubber Band and 'Strawberry Letter 23' (1977) by the Brothers Johnson. 5. 'That's How You Like It' contains interpolations from 'I Like It' (1982) by DeBarge 6. 'Gift from Virgo' samples 'Rainy Day' (1974) by Shuggie Otis. 7. '03 Bonnie & Clyde' contains interpolations from 'If I Was Your Girlfriend' (1987) by Prince and samples of 'Me and My Girlfriend' (1996) by 2Pac. 8. 'What's It Gonna Be' samples 'Do It Roger' (1981) by Roger Troutman.
B'Day (Deluxe, 2006)	1. 'Suga Mama' samples 'Searching for Soul' by Jake Wade and the Soul Searchers. 2. 'Upgrade U' samples 'Girls Can't Do What the Guys Do' by Betty Wright. 3. 'Resentment' samples 'Think (Instrumental)' by Curtis Mayfield.
I Am... Sasha Fierce (Platinum, 2008)	N/A
4 (2011)	1. 'Party' contains a sample of 'La Di Da Di' as performed by Doug E. Fresh and the Get Fresh Crew featuring MC Ricky D. and written by Douglas Davis and Ricky Walters. 2. 'Countdown' contains a sample of 'Uhh Ahh' as performed by Boyz II Men and written by Michael Bivins, Nathan Morris and Wanya Morris. 3. 'End of Time' contains an uncredited sample of 'BTSTU' as performed and written by Jai Paul. 4. 'Run the World (Girls)' contains a sample 'Pon de Floor' as performed by Major Lazer and written by Afrojack, Vybz Cartel, Diplo and Switch.
4 (2011)	N/A
Beyoncé (Platinum, 2013)	1. 'Partition' contains an interpolation of the French-dubbed version of the 1998 film *The Big Lebowski*, performed by Hajiba Fahmy. 2. 'Flawless' contains portions of the speech 'We should all be feminists', written and delivered by Chimamanda Ngozi Adichie. 3. 'Heaven' contains portions of 'The Lord's Prayer' in Spanish, performed by Melissa Vargas.
	1. 'Hold Up'[332] contains elements of 'Can't Get Used to Losing You'[333], written by Doc Pomus and Mort Shuman,

[332] Audio: Beyoncé, 'Hold Up', *Youtube*, September 4, 2016, available at: https://www.youtube.com/watch?v=PeonBmeFR8o&list=OLAK5uy_m9dO997hqyquaE-xTYmZUqhm2pyKbQj-k&index=2, last accessed February 26, 2020; Lyrics: Beyoncé, 'Hold Up', *Genius*, available at: https://genius.com/BEYONCÉ-hold-up-lyrics, last accessed: February 26, 2020.
[333] Audio: Andy, Williams, 'Can't Get Used To Losing You', *Youtube*, May 25, 2013, available at: https://www.youtube.com/watch?v=kO_vKrVxGJM, last accessed: February 26, 2020. Lyrics: *Genius*, available at: https://genius.com/Andy-williams-cant-get-used-to-losing-you-lyrics, last accessed: February 26, 2020.

Lemonade (2016)	performed by Andy Williams; portions of 'Turn My Swag On'[334], written and performed by Soulja Boy, Antonio Randolph, Kelvin McConnell and elements of 'Maps'[335], written and performed by Yeah Yeah Yeahs (Brian Chase, Karen O and Nick Zinner). 2. 'Don't Hurt Yourself'[336] contains samples of 'When the Levee Breaks'[337], written by Memphis Minnie and Led Zeppelin, performed by Led Zeppelin (Jimmy Page, Robert Plant, John Paul Jones, John Bonham). 3. '6 Inch'[338] contains samples of 'Walk On By'[339], written by Burt Bacharach and Hal David, performed by Isaac Hayes; and an interpolation of 'My Girls'[340], written by Avey Tare (Dave Portner), Panda Bear (Noah Lennox) and Geologist (Brian Weitz), performed by Animal Collective. 4. 'Freedom'[341] contains samples of 'Yeah'[342] performed by Jojo Simmons; also contains samples of 'Let Me Try'[343],

[334] Soulja Boy Tell'em, 'Turn My Swag On', *Youtube*, December 14, 2009, available at: https://www.youtube.com/watch?v=9yRme0C2pmI, last accessed: last accessed: February 26, 2020; Lyrics: Soulja Boy Tell'em, 'Turn My Swag On', *Genius*, available at: https://genius.com/Soulja-boy-tell-em-turn-my-swag-on-lyrics, last accessed: February 26, 2020.

[335] Yeah, Yeah, Yeahs, 'Maps', *Youtube*, June 17, 2009, available at: https://www.youtube.com/watch?v=oIIxlgcuQRU, last accessed: February 26, 2020; Lyrics: Yeah, Yeah, Yeahs, 'Maps', *Genius*, available at: https://genius.com/Yeah-yeah-yeahs-maps-lyrics, last accessed: February 26, 2020.

[336] Audio: Beyoncé, 'Don't Hurt Yourself', *Youtube*, April 22, 2019, available at: https://www.youtube.com/watch?v=xnMnZURoztQ&list=OLAK5uy_m9dO997hqyquaE-xTYmZUqhm2pyKbQj-k&index=3, last accessed February 26, 2020; Lyrics: Beyoncé, 'Don't Hurt Yourself', *Genius*, available at: https://genius.com/BEYONCÉ-dont-hurt-yourself-lyrics, last accessed: February 26, 2020.

[337] Audio: Led Zeppelin, 'When the Levee Breaks', *Youtube*, January 25, 2017, available at: https://www.youtube.com/watch?v=uwiTs60VoTM, last accessed: last accessed: February 26, 2020. Lyrics: Led Zeppelin, 'When the Levee Breaks', *Genius*, available at: https://genius.com/Led-zeppelin-when-the-levee-breaks-lyrics, last accessed: February 26, 2020.

[338] Audio: Beyoncé, '6 Inch', *Youtube*, April 22, 2019, available at: https://www.youtube.com/watch?v=UKMmfBkrhtY&list=OLAK5uy_m9dO997hqyquaE-xTYmZUqhm2pyKbQj-k&index=5, last accessed February 26, 2020; Lyrics: Beyoncé, '6 Inch', *Genius*, available at: https://genius.com/BEYONCÉ-6-inch-lyrics, last accessed: February 26, 2020.

[339] Audio: Isaac Hayes, 'Walk On By', *Youtube*, December 30, 2010, available at: https://www.youtube.com/watch?v=iqR4CZj0mJQ, last accessed: February 26, 2020. Lyrics: Isaac Hayes, 'Walk On By', *Genius*, available at: https://genius.com/Isaac-hayes-walk-on-by-lyrics, last accessed: February 26, 2020.

[340] Audio: Animal Collective, 'My Girls', January 14, 2009, *Youtube*, available at: https://www.youtube.com/watch?v=zol2MJf6XNE, last accessed: February 26, 2020. Lyrics: Animal Collective, 'My Girls', *Genius*, available at: https://genius.com/Animal-collective-my-girls-lyrics, last accessed: February 26, 2020.

[341] Audio: Beyoncé, 'Freedom', *Youtube*, April 22, 2019, available at: https://www.youtube.com/watch?v=7FWF9375hUA&list=OLAK5uy_m9dO997hqyquaE-xTYmZUqhm2pyKbQj-k&index=10, last accessed: February 26, 2020; Lyrics: Beyoncé, 'Freedom', *Genius*, available at: https://genius.com/BEYONCÉ-freedom-lyrics, last accessed: February 26, 2020.

[342] I have not found the audio and the lyrics.

[343] Audio: Kaleidoscope, 'Let me try', *Youtube*, January 15, 2020, available at: https://www.youtube.com/watch?v=KhyDmEb1L_Y, last accessed: February 26, 2020; Kaleidoscope, 'Let Me Try (BEYONCÉ - Freedom *Story Behind the Beat*)', *Youtube*, available at:

	written by Frank Tirado, performed by Kaleidoscope; samples of 'Collection Speech/Unidentified Lining Hymn'[344], recorded by Alan Lomax in 1959, performed by Reverend R.C. Crenshaw; and samples of 'Stewball'[345], recorded by Alan Lomax and John Lomax, Sr. in 1947, performed by Prisoner '22' at Mississippi State Penitentiary at Parchman. 5. 'All Night'[346] contains a sample of 'SpottieOttieDopaliscious'[347], written by OutKast (André Benjamin, Antwan Patton) and Sleepy Brown (Patrick Brown), performed by OutKast. 6. 'Lemonade' contains a sample of 'The Court of the Crimson King'[348], performed by King Crimson, written by Ian McDonald and Peter Sinfield. 7. 'Sorry (Original Demo)'[349] interpolates 'Young, Wild & Free'[350], as performed by Snoop Dogg, Wiz Khalifa and Bruno Mars.

II.2.3.2 The List of Sample Used by Kendrick Lamar

TABLE 32. THE LIST OF SAMPLES USED BY KENDRICK LAMAR	
NAME OF THE ALBUM	**SAMPLE**

---

https://www.youtube.com/watch?v=9BdTjPSV0p8Lyrics: Kaleidoscope, 'Let me try', *Genius*, available at: https://genius.com/Kaleidoscope-let-me-try-lyrics, last accessed: February 26, 2020.

[344] Audio: Alan Lomax, 'Collection Speech/Unidentified Lining Hymn', *Youtube*, April 25, 2016, available at: https://www.youtube.com/watch?v=f2dRRkUjVnw, last accessed: February 26, 2020.

[345] Audio: Alan Lomax and John Lomax, 'Stewball', (recorded in 1947), *Youtube*, November 7, 2009, available at: https://www.youtube.com/watch?v=SYq0EPX8mS0, last accessed: February 26, 2020.

[346] Audio: Beyoncé, 'All Night', *Youtube*, November 30, 2016, available at: https://www.youtube.com/watch?v=gM89Q5Eng_M&list=OLAK5uy_m9dO997hqyquaE-xTYmZUqhm2pyKbQj-k&index=11, last accessed February 26, 2020; Lyrics: Beyoncé, 'All Night', *Genius*, available at: https://genius.com/BEYONCÉ-all-night-lyrics, last accessed: February 26, 2020.

[347] Audio: OutKast, 'SpottieOttieDopaliscious', *Youtube*, January 1, 2008, available at: https://www.youtube.com/watch?v=vXmqauitBkM, last accessed: February 26, 2020. Lyrics: OutKast, 'SpottieOttieDopaliscious', *Genius*, available at: https://genius.com/Outkast-spottieottiedopaliscious-lyrics, last accessed: February 26, 2020.

[348] The Court of the Crimson King, *Wikipedia*, available at: https://en.wikipedia.org/wiki/The_Court_of_the_Crimson_King, last accessed: February 26, 2020.

[349] Audio: Beyoncé, 'Sorry (Original Demo), *Youtube*, April 22, 2019, available at: https://www.youtube.com/watch?v=c8hhQHnJWzE&list=OLAK5uy_m9dO997hqyquaE-xTYmZUqhm2pyKbQj-k&index=13, last accessed February 26, 2020; Lyrics: Beyoncé, 'Sorry (Original Demo), *Genius*, available at: https://genius.com/BEYONCÉ-sorry-original-demo-lyrics, last accessed: February 26, 2020.

[350] Audio: Snoop Dogg, Wiz Khalifa, Bruno Mars, 'Young, Wild & Free', *Youtube*, available at: https://www.youtube.com/watch?v=Wa5B22KAkEk, last accessed: February 26, 2020. Lyrics: Snoop Dogg, Wiz Khalifa, Bruno Mars, 'Young, Wild & Free', *Genius*, available at: https://genius.com/Snoop-dogg-and-wiz-khalifa-young-wild-and-free-lyrics, last accessed: February 26, 2020.

Section.80 (2011)	1. 'Hol' Up' contains a sample of 'Shifting Sands of Sound', as performed by Dick Walter. 2. 'Tammy's Song (Her Evils)' contains a sample of 'Alfie', as performed by Dick Hyman. 3. 'Chapter Six' contains a sample of 'Hey', as performed by King. 4. 'Poe Mans Dreams (His Vice)' contains a sample of 'Peace Go With You, Brother', as performed by Gil Scott-Heron. 5. 'The Spiteful Chant' contains a sample of 'Iron', as performed by Woodkid. 6. 'Keisha's Song (Her Pain)' contains a sample of 'Old and Wise', as performed by The Alan Parsons Project. 7. 'Rigamortis' contains a sample of 'The Thorn', as performed by Willie Jones III. 8. 'Blow My High (Members Only)' contains samples of '4 Page Letter', as performed by Aaliyah; 'Voyager', as performed by Dexter Wansel; and 'Big Pimpin'', as performed by Jay-Z featuring UGK.
	1. 'Bitch, Don't Kill My Vibe'[351] contains portions of 'Tiden Flyver'[352], as performed by Boom Clap Bachelors. 2. 'Backseat Freestyle'[353] contains a sample of 'Yo Soy Cubano'[354], as performed by The Chakachas. 3. 'The Art of Peer Pressure'[355] contains a sample of 'Helt Alene'[356], as performed by Suspekt.

[351] Audio: Kendrick Lamar, 'Bitch, Don't Kill My Vibe', *Youtube*, May 13, 2013, available at: https://www.youtube.com/watch?v=GF8aaTu2kg0&list=OLAK5uy_mhYMgh1v0LpLuS0FqC693tfVkyVZK 9WSQ&index=2, last accessed February 26, 2020; Lyrics: Kendrick Lamar, 'Bitch, Don't Kill My Vibe', *Genius*, available at: https://genius.com/Kendrick-lamar-bitch-dont-kill-my-vibe-lyrics, last accessed: February 26, 2020.

[352] Audio: Boom Clap Bachelors, 'Tiden Flyver', *Youtube*, November 3, 2013, available at: https://www.youtube.com/watch?v=ZrHNIRLh-ps, last accessed: February 26, 2020. Lyrics: Boom Clap Bachelors, 'Tiden Flyver', *Genius*, available at: https://genius.com/Boom-clap-bachelors-tiden-flyver-lyrics, last accessed: February 26, 2020.

[353] Audio: Kendrick Lamar, 'Backseat Freestyle', *Youtube*, January 7, 2013, available at: https://www.youtube.com/watch?v=EZW7et3tPuQ&list=OLAK5uy_mhYMgh1v0LpLuS0FqC693tfVkyVZK 9WSQ&index=3, last accessed February 26, 2020; Lyrics: Kendrick Lamar, Backseat Freestyle', *Genius*, available at: https://genius.com/Kendrick-lamar-backseat-freestyle-lyrics, last accessed: February 26, 2020.

[354] Audio: The Chakachas, 'Yo Soy Cubano', *Youtube*, February 21, 2015, available at: https://www.youtube.com/watch?v=mNTH-isTTiU, last accessed: February 26, 2020. Lyrics: The Chakachas, 'Yo Soy Cubano', *Metrolyrics*, available at: https://www.metrolyrics.com/yo-soy-cubano-lyrics-chakachas.html, last accessed: February 26, 2020.

[355] Audio: Kendrick Lamar, 'The Art of Peer Pressure', *Youtube*, July 26, 2018, available at: https://www.youtube.com/watch?v=t93uK0DKvEk&list=OLAK5uy_mhYMgh1v0LpLuS0FqC693tfVkyVZK 9WSQ&index=4, last accessed February 26, 2020; Lyrics: Kendrick Lamar, 'The Art of Peer Pressure', *Genius*, available at: https://genius.com/Kendrick-lamar-the-art-of-peer-pressure-lyrics, last accessed: February 26, 2020.

[356] Audio: Suspekt, Tina Dickow, 'Helt Alene', *Youtube*, January 23, 2012, available at: https://www.youtube.com/watch?v=Oj7F14vlTFk, last accessed: February 26, 2020. Lyrics: Suspekt, 'Helt Alene', *Genius*, available at: https://genius.com/Suspekt-helt-alene-lyrics, last accessed: February 26, 2020.

good kid, m.A.A.d. City (Deluxe, 2012)	4. 'Money Trees'[357] contains a sample of 'Silver Soul'[358], as performed by Beach House. 5. 'Poetic Justice'[359] contains excerpts from 'Any Time, Any Place'[360], as performed by Janet Jackson. 6. 'm.A.A.d city'[361] contains samples of 'Don't Change Your Love'[362], as performed by The Five Stairsteps; 'Funky Worm'[363], as performed by Ohio Players; 'A Bird In The Hand'[364] as performed by Ice Cube; 7. 'Sing About Me, I'm Dying of Thirst'[365] contains a sample of 'Maybe Tomorrow'[366], as performed by Grant Green; 'I'm

[357] Audio: Kendrick Lamar, 'Money Trees', *Youtube*, July 26, 2018, available at: https://www.youtube.com/watch?v=Iy-dJwHVX84&list=OLAK5uy_mhYMgh1v0LpLuS0FqC693tfVkyVZK9WSQ&index=5, last accessed: February 26, 2020; Lyrics: Kendrick Lamar, 'Money Trees', *Genius*, available at: https://genius.com/Kendrick-lamar-money-trees-lyrics, last accessed: .

[358] Audio: Beach House, 'Silver Soul', *Youtube*, March 4, 2010, available at: https://www.youtube.com/watch?v=njbmwfndFH4, last accessed: February 26, 2020. Lyrics: Beach House, 'Silver Soul', *Genius*, available at: https://genius.com/Beach-house-silver-soul-lyrics, last accessed: February 26, 2020.

[359] Audio: Kendrick Lamar, 'Poetic Justice', *Youtube*, February 22, 2013, available at: https://www.youtube.com/watch?v=yyr2gEouEMM&list=OLAK5uy_mhYMgh1v0LpLuS0FqC693tfVkyVZ K9WSQ&index=6, last accessed February 26, 2020; Lyrics: Kendrick Lamar, 'Poetic Justice', *Genius*, available at: https://genius.com/Kendrick-lamar-poetic-justice-lyrics, last accessed: February 26, 2020.

[360] Audio: Janet Jackson, 'Any Time, Any Place', *Youtube*, November, 16, 2010, available at: https://www.youtube.com/watch?v=3HO9H1VMMOk, last accessed: February 26, 2020. Lyrics: Janet Jackson, 'Any Time, Any Place', *Genius*, available at: https://genius.com/Janet-jackson-any-time-any-place-lyrics, last accessed: February 26, 2020.

[361] Audio: Kendrick Lamar, 'm.A.A.d city', *Youtube*, July 24, 2018, available at: https://www.youtube.com/watch?v=KKCSwOVudMo, last accessed February 26, 2020; Lyrics: Kendrick Lamar, 'm.A.A.d. city', *Genius*, available at: https://genius.com/Kendrick-lamar-maad-city-lyrics, last accessed: February 26, 2020.

[362] Audio: The Five Stairsteps, 'Don't Change Your Love', *Youtube*, March 13, 2011, available at: https://www.youtube.com/watch?v=zzLfR2Cn56s, last accessed: February 26, 2020. Lyrics: The Five Stairsteps, 'Don't Change Your Love', *Genius*, available at: https://genius.com/Ice-cube-a-bird-in-the-hand-lyrics, last accessed: February 26, 2020.

[363] Audio: Ohio Players, 'Funky Worm', *Youtube*, November 21, 2009, available at: https://www.youtube.com/watch?v=bSlb4T5vu9E, last accessed: February 26, 2020. Lyrics: Ohio Players, 'Funky Worm', *Genius*, available at: https://genius.com/Ohio-players-funky-worm-lyrics, last accessed: February 26, 2020.

[364] Audio: Ice Cube, 'A Bird In The Hand', *Youtube*, June 28, 2012, available at: https://www.youtube.com/watch?v=QQU8lazOsKc, last accessed: February 26, 2020. Lyrics: Ice Cube, 'A Bird In The Hand', *Genius*, available at: https://genius.com/Ice-cube-a-bird-in-the-hand-lyrics, last accessed: February 26, 2020.

[365] Audio: Kendrick Lamar, 'Sing About Me, I'm Dying Of Thirst', *Youtube*, July 26, 2018, available at: https://www.youtube.com/watch?v=75wmW7xjyog&list=OLAK5uy_mhYMgh1v0LpLuS0FqC693tfVkyVZ K9WSQ&index=10, last accessed February 26, 2020; Lyrics: Kendrick Lamar, 'Sing About Me, I'm Dying Of Thirst', *Genius*, available at: https://genius.com/Kendrick-lamar-sing-about-me-im-dying-of-thirst-lyrics, last accessed: February 26, 2020.

[366] Audio: Grant Green, 'Maybe Tomorrow', *Youtube*, September 10, 2007, available at: https://www.youtube.com/watch?v=k9oNHowrg4w, last accessed: February 26, 2020. Lyrics: Grant Green, 'Maybe Tomorrow', *Genius*, available at: https://genius.com/Grant-green-maybe-tomorrow-lyrics, last accessed: February 26, 2020.

	Glad Your Mine'[367], as performed by Al Green; sampled 'Use Me'[368], as performed by Bill Whither; sampled 'My Romance'[369], as performed by The Singers Unlimited. 8. 'Compton'[370] contains excerpts from 'What's This World Coming To'[371], as performed by Formula IV. 9. 'The Recipe'[372] contains a sample of 'Meet the Frownies'[373], as performed by Twin Sister.
	1. 'Wesley's Theory'[374] contains elements of 'Every Nigger is a Star'[375], written and performed by Boris Gardiner. 2. 'King Kunta'[376] contains interpolations of 'Get Nekkid'[377], written by Johnny Burns and performed by Mausberg;

[367] Audio: Al Green, 'I'm Glad Your Mine', *Youtube*, February 16, 2010, available at: https://www.youtube.com/watch?v=QzAL59zslSM, last accessed: February 26, 2020. Lyrics: Al Green, 'I'm Glad Your Mine', *Genius*, available at: https://genius.com/Al-green-im-glad-youre-mine-lyrics, last accessed: February 26, 2020.

[368] Audio: Bill Whiters, 'Use Me', *Youtube*, February 17, 2008, available at: https://www.youtube.com/watch?v=g3hBYTkI-sE, last accessed: February 26, 2020. Lyrics: Bill Whiters, 'Use Me', *Genius*, available at: https://genius.com/Bill-withers-use-me-lyrics, last accessed: February 26, 2020.

[369] Audio: The Singers Unlimited, 'My Romance', *Youtube*, January 29, 2014, available at: https://www.youtube.com/watch?v=DOQCsLsyTBU, last accessed: February 26, 2020. Lyrics: The Singers Unlimited, 'My Romance', *Flashlyrics*, available at: https://www.flashlyrics.com/lyrics/the-singers-unlimited/my-romance-23, last accessed: February 26, 2020.

[370] Audio: Kendrick Lamar, 'Compton', *Youtube*, July 26, 2018, available at: https://www.youtube.com/watch?v=9PovU-C2osU&list=OLAK5uy_mhYMgh1v0LpLuS0FqC693tfVkyVZK9WSQ&index=12, last accessed February 26, 2020; Lyrics: Kendrick Lamar, 'Compton', *Genius*, available at: https://genius.com/Kendrick-lamar-compton-lyrics, last accessed: February 26, 2020.

[371] Audio: Formula IV, 'What's This World Coming To', *Youtube*, October, 24, 2012, available at: https://www.youtube.com/watch?v=JyEFODrogjo, last accessed: February 26, 2020.

[372] Audio: Kendrick Lamar, 'The Recipe', *Youtube*, April 23, 2012, available at: https://www.youtube.com/watch?v=YpugKORpEaU, last accessed February 26, 2020; Lyrics: Kendrick Lamar, 'The Recipe', *Genius*, available at: https://genius.com/Kendrick-lamar-the-recipe-lyrics, last accessed: February 26, 2020.

[373] Audio: Twin Sister, 'Meet The Frownies', *Youtube*, October 13, 2010, available at: https://www.youtube.com/watch?v=P-F7AS-Xhus, last accessed: February 26, 2020. Lyrics: Twin Sister, 'Meet The Frownies', *Genius*, available at: https://genius.com/Boris-gardiner-every-nigger-is-a-star-lyrics, last accessed: February 26, 2020.

[374] Audio: Kendrick Lamar, 'Wesley's Theory', *Youtube*, December 12, 2018, available at: https://www.youtube.com/watch?v=l9fN-8NjrvI&list=OLAK5uy_n_dmtzA0IWImBN3fbUBUl_WgD-YSaMZal, last accessed February 26, 2020; Lyrics: Kendrick Lamar, 'Wesley's Theory', *Genius*, available at: https://genius.com/Kendrick-lamar-wesleys-theory-lyrics, last accessed: February 26, 2020.

[375] Audio: Boris Gardiner, 'Every Nigger Is A Star', *Youtube*, January 21, 2011, available at: https://www.youtube.com/watch?v=mYnenIWZjwE, last accessed: February 26, 2020. Lyrics: Boris Gardiner, 'Every Nigger Is A Star', *Genius*, available at: https://genius.com/Boris-gardiner-every-nigger-is-a-star-lyrics, last accessed: February 26, 2020.

[376] Audio: Kendrick Lamar, 'King Kunta', *Youtube*, April 1, 2015, available at: https://www.youtube.com/watch?v=hRK7PVJFbS8&list=OLAK5uy_n_dmtzA0IWImBN3fbUBUl_WgD-YSaMZal&index=3, last accessed February 26, 2020; Lyrics: Kendrick Lamar, 'King Kunta', *Genius*, available at: https://genius.com/Kendrick-lamar-king-kunta-lyrics, last accessed: February 26, 2020.

[377] Audio: Mausberg, 'Get Nekkid', *Youtube*, April 10, 2011, available at: https://www.youtube.com/watch?v=cvZCs27gg70, last accessed: February 26, 2020. Lyrics: Mausberg,

To Pimp a Butterfly (2015)	resung lyrics from 'Smooth Criminal'[378], written and performed by Michael Jackson; elements of 'The Payback'[379], written by James Brown, Fred Wesley and John Starks, and performed by James Brown; and samples of 'We Want the Funk'[380], written and performed by Ahmad Lewis. 3. 'Momma'[381] contains elements of 'Wishful Thinkin'[382] written by Sylvester Stone and performed by Sly and the Family Stone; and elements of 'On Your Own'[383], written and performed by Lalah Hathaway; sampled 'So[rt]'[384], by Knxwledge; sampled 'Control (HOF)'[385], as performed by Big Sean, Kendrick Lamar and Jay Electronica. 4. 'Hood Politics'[386] contains a sample of 'All for Myself'[387], written and performed by Sufjan Stevens.

'Get Nekkid', *Genius*, available at: https://genius.com/Mausberg-get-nekkid-lyrics, last accessed: February 26, 2020.

[378] Audio: Michael Jackson, 'Smooth Criminal', *Youtube*, November 19, 2010, available at: https://www.youtube.com/watch?v=h_D3VFfhvs4, last accessed: February 26, 2020. Lyrics: Michael Jackson, 'Smooth Criminal', *Genius*, available at: https://genius.com/Michael-jackson-smooth-criminal-lyrics, last accessed: February 26, 2020.

[379] Audio: James Brown, 'The Payback', *Youtube*, May 2, 2011, available at: https://www.youtube.com/watch?v=istJXUJJP0g, last accessed: February 26, 2020. Lyrics: James Brown, 'The Payback', *Genius*, available at: https://genius.com/James-brown-the-payback-lyrics, last accessed: February 26, 2020.

[380] Audio: Ahmad Lewis, 'We Want The Funk', *Youtube*, November 6, 2010, available at: https://www.youtube.com/watch?v=NyaP1B1AypE, last accessed: February 26, 2020. Lyrics: Ahmed Lewis, 'We Want The Funk', *Metrolyrics*, available at: https://www.metrolyrics.com/we-want-the-funk-lyrics-ahmad.html, last accessed: February 26, 2020.

[381] Audio: Kendrick Lamar, 'Momma', *Youtube*, December 12, 2018, available at: https://www.youtube.com/watch?v=q1AOP6NtGuc&list=OLAK5uy_n_dmtzA0IWImBN3fbUBUI_WgD-YSaMZaI&index=9, last accessed February 26, 2020; Lyrics: Kendrick Lamar, 'Momma', *Genius*, available at: https://genius.com/Kendrick-lamar-momma-lyrics, last accessed: February 26, 2020.

[382] Audio: Sly & The Family Stone, 'Wishful Thinkin'', *Youtube*, November 8, 2014, available at: https://www.youtube.com/watch?v=HUICXLAKUX4, last accessed: February 26, 2020. Lyrics: Sly & The Family Stone, 'Wishful Thinkin'', *Genius*, available at: https://genius.com/Sly-and-the-family-stone-wishful-thinkin-lyrics, last accessed: February 26, 2020.

[383] Audio: Lalah Hathaway, 'On Your Own', *Youtube*, July 26, 2018, available at: https://www.youtube.com/watch?v=jhZ6nuO5uos, last accessed: February 26, 2020. Lyrics: Lalah Hathaway, 'On Your Own', *Genius*, available at: https://genius.com/Lalah-hathaway-on-your-own-lyrics, last accessed: February 26, 2020.

[384] Audio: Knxwledge, 'So[rt]', *Youtube*, December 12, 2017, available at: https://www.youtube.com/watch?v=fPaZTF1kJrs, last accessed: February 26, 2020.

[385] Audio: Big Sean, Kendrick Lamar, Jay Electronica, 'Control', *Youtube*, August 13, 2013, available at: https://www.youtube.com/watch?v=xufJHc2EdBA, last accessed: February 26, 2020. Lyrics: Big Sean, Kendrick Lamar, Jay Electronica, 'Control', *Genius*, available at: https://genius.com/Big-sean-control-lyrics, last accessed: February 26, 2020.

[386] Audio: Kendrick Lamar, 'Hood Politics', *Youtube*, December 12, 2018, available at: https://www.youtube.com/watch?v=iIsHg3BHpB0&list=OLAK5uy_n_dmtzA0IWImBN3fbUBUI_WgD-YSaMZaI&index=10, last accessed February 26, 2020; Lyrics: Kendrick Lamar, 'Hard Politics', *Genius*, available at: https://genius.com/Kendrick-lamar-hood-politics-lyrics, last accessed: February 26, 2020.

[387] Audio: Sufjan Stevens, 'All For Myself', *Youtube*, September 10, 2010, available at: https://www.youtube.com/watch?v=5zlxFUIRgdg, last accessed: February 26, 2020. Lyrics: Sufjan Stevens, 'All For Myself', *Genius*, available at: https://genius.com/Sufjan-stevens-all-for-myself-lyrics, last accessed: February 26, 2020.

	5. 'i'[388] contains a sample of 'That Lady'[389], written by Ronald Isley, O'Kelly Isley, Jr., Ernie Isley, Marvin Isley, Rudolph Isley and Christopher Jasper, and performed by The Isley Brothers. 6. 'Mortal Man'[390] contains excerpts from 'I No Get Eye for Back'[391], written by Fela Anikulapo Kuti and performed by Houston Person; and a sample of music journalist Mats Nileskar's November 1994 interview with Tupac Shakur for P3 Soul Broadcasting Corporation.
Damn (2017)	1. 'Blood' and 'DNA' contain elements of Fox News commentators Eric Bolling, Kimberly Guilfoyle and Geraldo Rivera criticizing Lamar's 2015 BET Awards performance' 'DNA' also contains a sample from a live recording of 'Mary Jane', as written and performed by Rick James, from the album Come Get It!. 2. 'Yah' contains elements from 'How Good Is Your Game', performed by Billy Paul. 3. 'Element' contains pieces from 'Ha', as written by Terius Gray and Byron O. Thomas, and performed by Juvenile, from the album 400 Degreez. 4. 'Feel' contains a sample of 'Stormy', as written and performed by O. C. Smith, from the album For Once in My Life; and an interpolation from 'Don't Let Me Down', as written and performed by Fleurie, from the album Love and War. 5. 'Loyalty' contains samples of '24K Magic', as written by Bruno Mars, Christopher Brody Brown and Philip Lawrence, and performed by Bruno Mars, from the album 24K Magic; 'Shimmy Shimmy Ya', as written by Russell Jones and Robert Diggs, and performed by Ol' Dirty Bastard, from the album Return to the 36 Chambers: The Dirty Version; and 'Get Your Mind Right Mami', as written by Shawn Carter, Cordozar Calvin Broadus, Jr., Gerrell Gaddis and Malik Cox, and performed by Jay-Z featuring Snoop Dogg, Rell and Memphis Bleek, from the album The Dynasty: Roc La Familia.

[388] Audio: Kendrick Lamar, 'i', *Youtube*, December 12, 2018, available at: https://www.youtube.com/watch?v=tt2-GsPA9kk&list=OLAK5uy_n_dmtzA0IWImBN3fbUBUl_WgD-YSaMZaI&index=15, last accessed February 26, 2020; Lyrics: Kendrick Lamar, 'i', *Genius*, available at: https://genius.com/Kendrick-lamar-i-album-version-lyrics, last accessed: February 26, 2020.

[389] Audio: The Isley Brothers, 'That Lady', *Youtube*, July 31, 2015, available at: https://www.youtube.com/watch?v=S1Mvy3E8P2U, last accessed: February 26, 2020. Lyrics: The Isley Brothers, 'That Lady', *Genius*, available at: https://genius.com/The-isley-brothers-that-lady-pt-1-and-2-lyrics, last accessed: February 26, 2020.

[390] Audio: Kendrick Lamar, 'Mortal Man', *Youtube*, December 12, 2018, available at: https://www.youtube.com/watch?v=axwpgn3GRMs&list=OLAK5uy_n_dmtzA0IWImBN3fbUBUl_WgD-YSaMZaI&index=16, last accessed February 26, 2020; Lyrics: Kendrick Lamar, 'Mortal Man', *Genius*, available at: https://genius.com/Kendrick-lamar-mortal-man-lyrics, last accessed: February 26, 2020.

[391] Audio: Houston Person, 'I No get Eye For Back', *Youtube*, December 5, 2011, available at: https://www.youtube.com/watch?v=DhClaL03Ec4, last accessed: February 26, 2020.

	6. 'Lust' contains a sample of 'Knock Knock Knock', as written and performed by Rat Boy, from the album Neighbourhood Watch. 7. 'Fear' contains a sample of 'Poverty's Paradise', as written by Dale Warren and performed by 24-Carat Black, from the album Ghetto: Misfortune's Wealth. 8. 'XXX' contains samples of 'Get Up Offa That Thing', as written by Deanna Brown, Diedra Brown and Yamma Brown, and performed by James Brown, from the album Get Up Offa' That Thing; 'Fugue', as written and performed by Foals, from the album Total Life Forever; and 'Wah Wah Man', performed by Young-Holt Unlimited. 9. 'God' contains a sample of 'End of the World', as written and performed by Illmind, from the album #BoomTrap Vol. 2. 10. 'Duckworth' contains samples of 'Atari', as written by Nai Palm and performed by Hiatus Kaiyote; 'Be Ever Wonderful', as written by Don Robey and Joe Scott, and performed by Ted Taylor, from the album Keepin' My Head Above Water; 'Ostavi Trag', as written by September, from the album Zadnja Avantura; and 'Let the Drums Speak', as written by Bill Curtis and performed by the Fatback Band, from the album Yum Yum.

II.2.4 The Sources of the Samples

I read the lyrics of the songs that used samples to find out the connection between the original song and the song that sampled the original song.

TABLE 33. THE SOURCES OF THE SAMPLES USED BY BEYONCÉ AND KENDRICK LAMAR		
NAME OF THE ALBUM	**NAME OF THE SONG**	**INSPIRATION**
	'Hold Up'	Good connection with the theme of the song (relationships, cheating, losing someone) 'Can't Get Used to Losing You' and use of lyrics from 'Turn My Swag On' and 'Maps'. Some lyrics of this song 'Can't Get Used to Losing You' are being used to create a visual representation in the music video, which is also genuine similar with the video of the Swiss visual artist Pipilotti

106

Beyoncé (Lemonade, 2016)		Rist's project 'Ever Is Over All'.[392] On the album *Aquemini* (contains the word 'aque' acronymous for 'aqua' which translates as 'water' (which is one of the main themes and visuals of the album *Lemonade*), from which Beyoncé samples the song 'SpottieOttieDopaliscious', has the introductory song named 'Hold On, Be Strong.'[393]
	'Don't Hurt Yourself'	'When the Levee Breaks': good connection with the song's theme and use of lyrics. The song is a reflection of the experience during the upheaval caused by the Great Mississippi Flood of 1927, which is linked with Beyoncé's visual album with floods (water) in Formation and other videos which represents the real world and the negative side effects of tornadoes, hurricanes from the USA.
	'6 Inch'	Title and lyrics connection with 'My Girls'.
	'Freedom'	Some connection with 'Let Me Try'.
	'All Night'	Some connection with the theme of the song (events from a night) 'SpottieOttieDopaliscious'. However, there is strong connection between the whole album of Lemonade (visual and lyrics themes) and the whole album named Aquemini ('SpottieOttieDopaliscious' is one of the songs included in this album), released in 1998 by the hip-hop duo Outkast. Lyrically, much of Aquemini features introspection about the desolation of the human condition (strong theme in Lemonade), which include precarious relationships (Lemonade: between her and her husband, Jay Z), freedom from self-inflicted struggles (Lemonade: between her and her husband, Jay Z), also one of Beyoncé songs from Lemonade is named Freedom. If Aquemini is about a shift between science – fiction inspired topics

---

[392] Phil Maphela, 'Here We Go Again BEYONCÉ Accused of Stealing Hold Up Music Video B Scott lovebscottcom', *Youtube*, May 3, 2016, https://www.youtube.com/watch?v=2V7tQwnJQEo, last accessed: February 26, 2020.
[393] Aquemini, *Wikipedia*, available at: https://en.wikipedia.org/wiki/Aquemini, last accessed: February 27, 2020.

		combined with the harsh reality of urban life, Lemonade is showing in her videos the harsh reality of the country and urban life of black people. In the end, the similarity between the two albums is the experimentation of delivery styles on the record, using relaxed, hyper, distorted, speedy and conversational presentations.'[394]
	'Sorry (Original Demo)'	Use of lyrics from the title 'Young, Wild & Free' and chorus.
good kid, m.A.A.d City (Deluxe, 2012)	*'m.A.A.d. City'*	Some connection with 'Don't Change Your Love' and 'A Bird In The Hand.'
	'The Art of Peer Pressure'	'Helt Alene': it was the main sample for this track.
	'Poetic Justice'	'It used heavily sample from the song 'Any Time, Any Place' co-written and performed by Janet Jackson.'
	'The Receipe'	Some lyrics from 'Meet the Frownies.'
To Pimp a Butterfly (2015)	'Wesley's Theory'	Lyrics from 'Every Nigger is a Star.'
	'King Kunta'	Lyrics from 'Smooth Criminal' and 'We Want the Funk.'
	'Momma'	Some connection with 'On Your Own' and some lyrics from 'Control (HOF).'

II.2.5 The Fame of the Samples

TABLE 34. THE FAME OF THE SAMPLES USED BY BEYONCÉ AND KENDRICK LAMAR		
NAME OF THE ALBUM	**NAME OF THE SONGS**	**TOP CHARTS & AWARDS**
	'Can't Get Used to Losing You' (1963)	'The song was number 2 in both the US and the UK'. [395]
		'The song was US Rap Songs (Billboard) weekly charts number 3, US Pop 100 (Billboard) weekly charts number 39, US Hot R&B/Hip Hop Songs (Billboard) weekly charts number 3.'[396] 'The music video received extensive play on MTV, it reached number 9 on Billboard's Alternative Songs chart and was

---

[394] *Ibidem.*
[395] Can't get Used to Losing You, *Wikipedia*, available at:
https://en.wikipedia.org/wiki/Can%27t_Get_Used_to_Losing_You, last accessed: February 27, 2020.
[396] Turn My Swag On, *Wikipedia*, available at: https://en.wikipedia.org/wiki/Turn_My_Swag_On, last accessed: February 27, 2020.

	'Maps' (2004)	included in popular video game Rock Band.' Other success includes: 'NME best alternative love song in 2009; number 6 on Pitchfork Media's top 500 songs of the 2000s; Roling Stone ranked it number 386 on their list of the 500 Greatest Songs of All Time; in 2011 NME placed the song at number 55 on its list '150 Best Tracks of the Past 150 Years'; NME ranked the song at number 1 on their list of 'Indie Weddings Songs: 20 Tracks Perfect For Your First Dance'.[397]
Beyoncé (Lemonade, 2016)	'When the Levee Breaks' (1929)	'It is a wide loved country blue song'.[398]
	'My Girls' (2009)	'The lyrics of the song are about the desire of the artist on a basic level to own my own place and kind of provide a safe house for my family and the people I care about.' Other success include: Pitchfork named the song number 1 of 2009 and also number 9 on their Top 500 Tracks of the 2000s; NME named the 5th best song of 2009; Slant Magazine named the best song of 2009; The Village Voice name the third best song of 2009; NME in 2011 place it at number 91 on their list '150 Best Tracks of the Past 15 Years'; NME in 2014 named the 248th best song of all time.'[399]
	'Walk On By' (1963)	'The song peacked at number 6 on the US Billboard Hot 100 and number 1 on the Cash Box Rhythm and Blues Chart in June 1964; also, it was nominated for a 1965 Grammy Award for the Best Rhythm and Blues Recording.'[400]
		'It is a song from the album *Aquemini* which is the third studio

[397] Maps (Yeah, Yeah, Yeah), *Wikipedia*, available at: https://en.wikipedia.org/wiki/Maps_(Yeah_Yeah_Yeahs_song), last accessed: February 27, 2020.

[398] When the Levee Breaks, *Wikipedia*, available at: https://en.wikipedia.org/wiki/When_the_Levee_Breaks#Led_Zeppelin_version, last accessed: February 27, 2020.

[399] My Girls (Animal Collective Song), *Wikipedia*, available at: https://en.wikipedia.org/wiki/My_Girls_(Animal_Collective_song), last accessed: February 27, 2020.

[400] Walk On By, *Wikipedia*, available at: https://en.wikipedia.org/wiki/Walk_On_By_(song), last accessed: February 27, 2020.

II. **black** and **white** music

	'SpottieOttieDopaliscious'	album of the American hip hop duo Outkast. Aquemini received highly widespread acclaim from critics with most the grade being one 3,5 out of 4 stars from USA Today and Chicago Sun-Times, to 5 out of 5 stars from Q, to A- from Christgau's Consumer Guide, to A from Entertainment Weekly. Los Angeles Times gave 4 stars out of 4, Rolling Stone 4 out of 5 stars. In the end the album was included in several publication's best album lists such as: in 2003 Rolling Stone ranked it on their 500 Greatest Albums of All Time and number 11 on the list '100 best Albums of the Nineties'; Paste called it 'the best Atlanta hip-hop album of all time'; Pitchfork ranked it number 50 on their 'Top 100 Albums of the 1990s'; Spin ranked it number 35 on the '90 Greatest Albums of the '90'' and number 3 on the 'Top 20 Albums of '98''; the lead single 'Rosa Park' was nominated in the category Grammy Award for Best Rap Performance by a Duo or Group at the 1999 Grammy Awards; in the end the song 'SpottieOttieDopaliscious' was ranked at number 16 on Pitchfork Media's list of the top 200 tracks of the 1990s.' The legacy of this album is virtuosic masterpiece, a landmark hip-hop, artistic success, brilliant, avant-garde, sonic ideas, new sounds, ravenous as ever which is in direct line with the reviews received by Beyoncé for *Lemonade*, her highest rated album yet.[401]
	'Don't Change Your Love'	Album inspiration from *Aquemini*: record production and aesthetic.[402]
good kid, m.A.A.d City (Deluxe, 2012)	'Any Time, Any Place'	'The song reached number 2 on the US Billboard Hot 100 and became an R&B chart-topper. Also, it held the number-one position on the Billboard Hot R&B/Hip-Hop Songs

---

[401] Aquemini.
[402] ibidem.

110

		for ten weeks and was Janet Jackson's biggest hit on the chart.'[403]
	'Smooth Criminal'	'The song was number 7 on the Billboard Hot 100, number 2 on the Billboard Hot Black Singles chart.'[404]
To Pimp a Butterfly (2015)	*'The Payback'*	'Samples from this song was heavily used in popular games and movies.'[405]
	'That Lady'	'The song is ranked number 357 on Rolling Stone's list of the 500 Greatest Songs of All Time.'[406]

II.2.6 The Rating on Metacritic

TABLE 35. THE ALBUM RATINGS	
BEYONCÉ	**KENDRICK LAMAR**
Dangerously in Love (2003): 63	Section.80 (2011): 80
B'Day (Deluxe, 2006): 70	good kid, m.A.A.d. City (Deluxe, 2012): 91
I am...Sasha Fierce (Platinum, 2008): 62	To Pimp a Butterfly (2015): 96
4 (2011): 73	Damn (2017): 95
Beyoncé (Platinum, 2013): 85	
Lemonade (2016): 92	
Total average: 74.16	*Total average: 90.5*

---

[403] Any Time, Any Place, *Wikipedia*, available at: https://en.wikipedia.org/wiki/Any_Time,_Any_Place, last accessed: February 27, 2020.

[404] Smooth Criminal, *Wikipedia*, available at: https://en.wikipedia.org/wiki/Smooth_Criminal, last accessed: February 27, 2020.

[405] The Payback, *Wikipedia*, available at: https://en.wikipedia.org/wiki/The_Payback_(song), last accessed: February 27, 2020.

[406] That Lady (song), *Wikipedia*, available at: https://en.wikipedia.org/wiki/That_Lady_(song), last accessed: February 27, 2020.

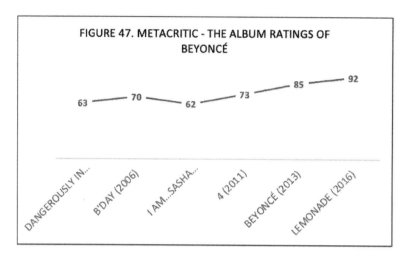

FIGURE 47. METACRITIC - THE ALBUM RATINGS OF BEYONCÉ

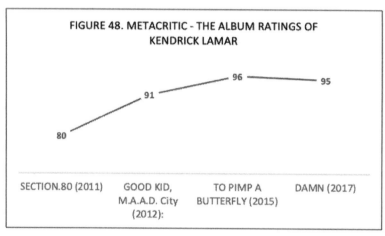

FIGURE 48. METACRITIC - THE ALBUM RATINGS OF KENDRICK LAMAR

II.3 Beyoncé versus Taylor Swift

In this part of the chapter I used the information presented in the last pages about both artists with no recitation.

II.3.1 Use of Sample

TABLE 36. USE OF SAMPLE	
TAYLOR SWIFT	**BEYONCÉ**
Taylor Swift (Deluxe, 2006): 0 out of 14	Dangerously in Love (2003): 8 out of 16
Fearless (Platinum, 2008): 1 out of 19	B'Day (Deluxe, 2006): 3 out of 17
Speak Now (Deluxe, 2010): 0 out of 17	I am...Sasha Fierce (Platinum, 2008): 0 out of 20
RED (Deluxe, 2012): 0 out of 19	4 (2011): 4 out of 14
1989 (Deluxe, 2013): 0 out of 16	Beyoncé (Platinum, 2013): 3 out of 16
reputation (2017): 1 out of 15	Lemonade (2016): 7 out of 12
Lover (2019): 3 out of 18	
folklore (Deluxe, 2020): 0 out of 17	
Evermore (Deluxe, 2020): 0 out of 17	
Fearless (Taylor's Version, 2021): 0 out of 7	
Total: 5 out of 159 songs (3%)	**Total: 25 out of 95 songs (26%)**

CONCLUSION:

- Beyoncé used 5 times more samples in her songs than Taylor Swift.

II.3.2 No Use of Sample

TABLE 37. NO USE OF SAMPLE	
TAYLOR SWIFT	**BEYONCÉ**
Taylor Swift (Deluxe, 2006): 14 out of 14	Dangerously in Love (2003): 8 out of 16
Fearless (Platinum, 2008): 18 out of 19	B'Day (Deluxe, 2006): 13 out of 17
Speak Now (Deluxe, 2010): 17 out of 17	I am...Sasha Fierce (Platinum, 2008): 20 out of 20
RED (Deluxe, 2012): 19 out of 19	4 (2011): 10 out of 14

1989 (Deluxe, 2014): 16 out of 16	Beyoncé (Platinum, 2013): 13 out of 16
reputation (2017): 14 out of 15	Lemonade (2016): 5 out of 12
Lover (2019): 15 out of 18	
folklore (Deluxe, 2020): 17 out of 17	
Evermore (Deluxe): 17 out of 17	
Fearless (Taylor's Version, 2021): 7 out of 7	
Total: 154 out of 159 songs (97%)	*Total: 69 out of 95 songs (73%)*

II.3.3 Original Song as Sole Lyricist

TABLE 38. ORIGINAL SONG AS SOLE LYRICIST	
TAYLOR SWIFT	**BEYONCÉ**
Taylor Swift (Deluxe, 2006): 3 out of 14	Dangerously in Love (2003): 1 out of 16
Fearless (Platinum, 2008): 10 out of 19	B'Day (Deluxe, 2006): 0 out of 17
Speak Now (Deluxe, 2010): 16 out of 17	I am...Sasha Fierce (Platinum, 2008): 0 out of 20
RED (Deluxe, 2012): 11 out of 19	4 (2011): 0 out of 14
1989 (Deluxe, 2014): 1 out of 16	Beyoncé (Platinum, 2013): 0 out of 16
reputation (2017): 0 out of 15	Lemonade (2016): 0 out of 12
Lover (2019): 3 out of 18	
folklore (Deluxe, 2020): 1 out of 17	
Evermore (Deluxe, 2020): 1 out of 17	
Fearless (Taylor's Version, 2021): 2 out of 7	
Total: 48 out of 159 (30%)	*Total: 1 out of 95 songs (less than 1%)*

CONCLUSION:

- Taylor has written 48 times more songs as sole lyricists than Beyoncé.

II.3.4 The Length of Original Song as Sole Lyricist

TABLE 39. THE LENGTH OF ORIGINAL SONG AS SOLE LYRICIST
TAYLOR SWIFT: 206:55 minutes
BEYONCÉ: 16 seconds

CONCLUSION:

- Taylor Swift single-handedly wrote 775.93 times more seconds of music than Beyoncé.

II.3.5 Original Song with Two Lyricists

TABLE 40. ORIGINAL SONGS WITH TWO LYRICISTS	
TAYLOR SWIFT	**BEYONCÉ**
Taylor Swift (Deluxe, 2006): 7 out of 14	Dangerously in Love (2003): 4 out of 16
Fearless (Platinum, 2008): 7 out of 19	B'Day (Deluxe, 2006): 0 out of 17
Speak Now (Deluxe, 2010): 1 out of 17	I am...Sasha Fierce (Platinum, 2008): 0 out of 20
RED (Deluxe, 2012): 4 out of 19	4 (2011): 0 out of 14
1989 (Deluxe, 2014): 7 out of 16	Beyoncé (Platinum, 2013): 3 out of 16
reputation (2017): 5 out of 15	Lemonade (2016): 1 out of 12
Lover (2019): 9 out of 18	
folklore (Deluxe, 2020): 15 out of 17	
Evermore (Deluxe, 2020): 13 out of 17	
Fearless (Taylor's Version, 2021): 4 out of 7	
Total: 72 out of 159 songs (45%)	***Total: 8 out of 95 songs (8%)***

CONCLUSION:

- Taylor Swift has written 9 times more songs with the help of a second songwriter than Beyoncé.

II.3.6 Original Song with Three Lyricists

TABLE 41. ORIGINAL SONGS WITH THREE LYRICISTS	
TAYLOR SWIFT	**BEYONCÉ**
Taylor Swift (Deluxe, 2006): 4 out of 14	Dangerously in Love (2003): 3 out of 16
Fearless (Platinum, 2008): 1 out of 19	B'Day (Deluxe, 2006): 4 out of 17
Speak Now (Deluxe, 2010): 0 out of 17	I am...Sasha Fierce (Platinum, 2008): 6 out of 20
RED (Deluxe, 2012): 4 out of 19	4 (2011): 8 out of 14
1989 (Deluxe, 2014): 7 out of 16	Beyoncé (Platinum, 2013): 5 out of 16
reputation (2017): 5 out of 15	Lemonade (2016): 3 out of 12
Lover (2019): 5 out of 18	
folklore (Deluxe, 2020): 1 out of 17	
Evermore (Deluxe, 2020): 2 out of 17	

Fearless (Taylor's Version, 2021): 1 out of 7	
Total: 30 out of 159 songs (19%)	**Total: 29 out of 95 songs (31%)**

II.3.7 Original Song with Four or More Lyricists

TABLE 42. ORIGINAL SONGS WITH FOUR OR MORE LYRICISTS	
TAYLOR SWIFT	**BEYONCÉ**
Taylor Swift (Deluxe, 2006): 0 out of 14	Dangerously in Love (2003): 8 out of 16
Fearless (Platinum, 2008): 1 out of 19	B'Day (Deluxe, 2006): 13 out of 17
Speak Now (Deluxe, 2010): 0 out of 17	I am...Sasha Fierce (Platinum, 2008): 13 out of 20
RED (Deluxe, 2012): 0 out of 19	4 (2011): 5 out of 14
1989 (Deluxe, 2014): 1 out of 16	Beyoncé (Platinum, 2013): 8 out of 16
reputation (2017): 5 out of 15	Lemonade (2016): 8 out of 12
Lover (2019): 1 out of 18	
folklore (Deluxe, 2020): 0 out of 16	
Evermore (Deluxe, 2020): 1 out of 17	
Fearless (Taylor's Version, 2021): 0 out of 7	
Total: 9 out of 159 songs (6%)	**Total: 55 out of 95 songs (58%)**

CONCLUSION:

- Beyoncé used at least 6 times more lyricists than Taylor Swift.

II.3.8 Number of Producers

The following figures show the number of producers and lyricists used by Beyoncé and Taylor Swift. The conclusion is: Taylor Swift used less producers and lyricists than Beyoncé.

116

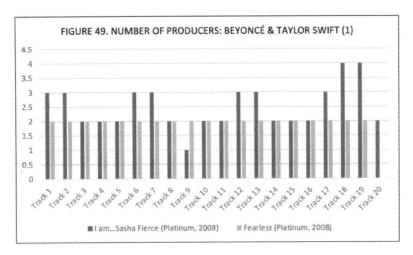

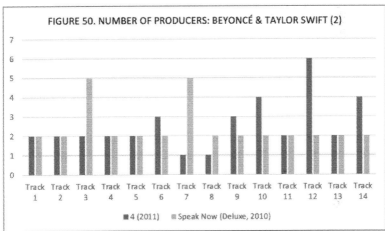

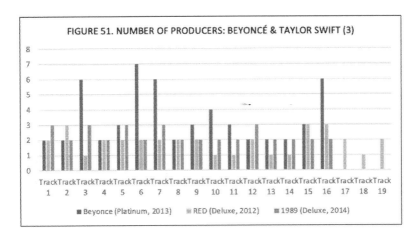

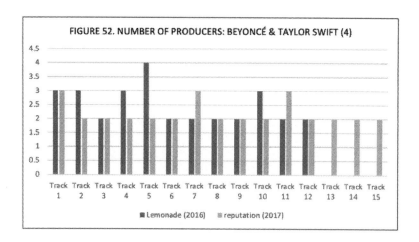

II.3.9 Number of Lyricists

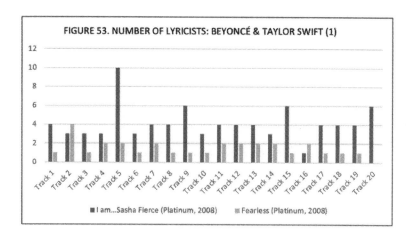

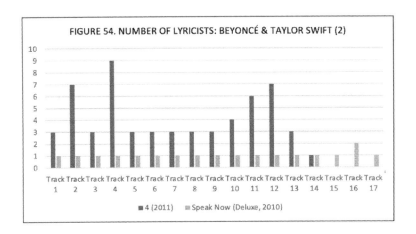

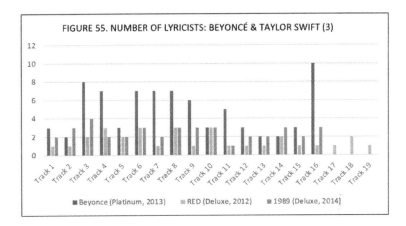

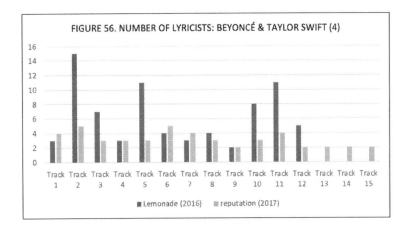

II.3.10 The Rating on Metacritic

From the point of view of linking the number of producers and lyricists with the grades received based on music review, there is the following conclusion: Beyoncé's grades increased after the involvement of more producers and lyricists; in contrast, Taylor Swift's grades increased with a low number of producers and lyricists.

| TABLE 43. THE RATING ON METACRITIC (BEYONCÉ & TAYLOR SWIFT) ||
BEYONCÉ	TAYLOR SWIFT
Dangerously in Love (2003): 63	Fearless (Platinum, 2008): 73
B'Day (Deluxe, 2006): 70	Speak Now (Deluxe, 2010): 77
I am...Sasha Fierce (Platinum, 2008): 62	RED (Deluxe, 2012): 77
4 (2011): 73	1989 (Deluxe, 2014): 76
Beyoncé (Platinum, 2013): 85	reputation (2017): 71
Lemonade (2016): 92	Lover (2019): 79
	folklore (Deluxe, 2020): 88
	Evermore (Deluxe, 2020): 85
	Fearless (Taylor's Version, 2021): 82
Total average: 74.16	*Total average: 78.66*

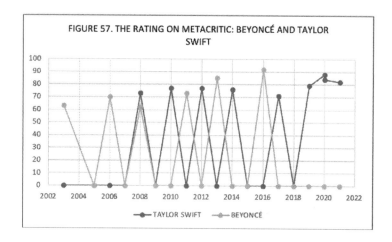

FIGURE 57. THE RATING ON METACRITIC: BEYONCÉ AND TAYLOR SWIFT

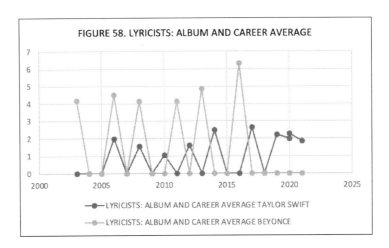

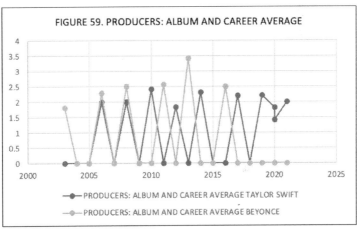

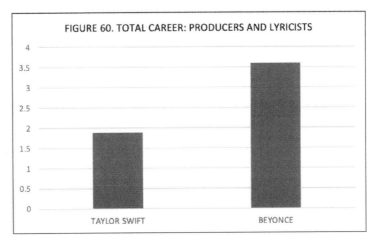

II.3.11 The Album Release

In this section of the chapter I explored the album release dates with the purpose to find patterns that might show new information about the album releases and how artists promote their music.

TABLE 44. THE ALBUM RELEASE: TAYLOR SWIFT AND BEYONCÉ		
ARTIST	**TAYLOR SWIFT**	**BEYONCÉ**
NAME OF THE ALBUM	*FEARLESS (PLATINUM, 2008)*	*I AM... SASHA FIERCE (2008)*
THEME	"This album is called *Fearless*, and I guess I'd like to clarify why we chose that as the title. To me, *Fearless* is not the absence of fear. It's not being completely unafraid. To me, *Fearless* is having fears, *Fearless* is having doubts. Lots of them. To me, *Fearless* is living in spite of those things that scare you to death. *Fearless* is falling madly in love again, even though you've been hurt before. *Fearless* is walking into your freshman year of high school at fifteen. *Fearless* is getting back up and fighting for what you want over and over again... even though every time you've tried before, you've lost. It's *Fearless* to have faith that someday things will change. *Fearless* is having the courage to say goodbye to someone who only hurts you, even though you can't breathe without them. I think it's *Fearless* to fall for your best friend, even though he's in love with someone else. And when someone apologizes to you enough times for things they'll never stop doing, I think it's *Fearless* to stop believing them. It's *Fearless* to say "you're NOT sorry". I think loving someone despite what people think is *Fearless*. I think allowing yourself to cry on the bathroom floor is	"I'm in a very good place right now. I'm very happy. I'm growing up, and I'm really comfortable with myself. I'm getting wiser and smarter. Hopefully my fans have grown with me, because some of the things that I loved, I don't love so much anymore, and I love new things. That's a part of life. I know that people see celebrities, and they seem like they're so perfect — they seem like their life is so great, and they have money and fame. But I'm a human being. I cry. I'm very passionate and sensitive. My feelings get hurt. I get scared and nervous like everyone else. And I wanted to show that about myself. It's about love. That's what this album is all about. It's about love." "You know, I'm a woman, I'm married, and this portion of my life is all in the album. It's a lot more personal. I'm very private and I don't talk about a lot of things, but there are certain songs that are on the album that are very personal. It's my diary. It's my story." "Young women listen to my album when they need encouragement, and when they are going through tough times,

	Fearless. Letting go is Fearless. Then, moving on and being alright... That's *Fearless* too. But no matter what love throws at you, you have to believe in it. You have to believe in love stories and prince charmings and happily ever after. That's why I write these songs. Because I think love is *Fearless*.[407]"	or when they need to forget about what their tough times are, and they just want to have fun and put on their sexy dresses and go dance with their friends, or when they need the strength to be out of a bad relationship, they listen to my album in the car. So I still have my album of fun songs.[408]"
RELEASE DATE USA	November 11, 2008	November 18, 2008
RELEASE DATE OTHER COUNTRIES	*November 11, 2008*: Canada; *November 15, 2008*: Australia; Platinum edition was announced on September 10, 2009 and released on October 26, 2009.	*November 12, 2008*: Japan *November 14, 2008*: Australia and Germany; *November 17, 2008*: France and United Kingdom; Platinum edition was released in September – October (depends on country) 2009.
METACRITIC	73	62
PATTERN OF MUSIC RELEASE	2006: October 24 2008: November 11, 15.	2003: June 17 2006: September 4 2008: November 12, 14, 17, 18
	The following dates are written to observe the full pattern of music release by both artists.	
	2010: October 25 2012: October 22 2014: October 27 2017: November 10 2019: August 23 2020: July 24 2020: December 11	2011: June 24 2013: December 13 2016: April 23
AWARDS	Winner of the Album of the Year at the 52nd Annual Grammy Awards. The most awarded album in the history of country music.	At the 52nd Annual Grammy Awards ceremony she was awarded with five Grammys with a lower grade from critics, and eventually collecting a record setting six wins—the most awards won in one night by a female artist.

---

[407] Taylor Swift, *Fearless* (Platinum Edition, 2009).
[408] I do not know if this is the good source to explain the theme of the album, but is the best information that I could find about Beyoncé and her message about her album.

CONCLUSIONS:

- Beyoncé's album release patterns are:

  fixed pattern: June 2003 and 2011;
  surprise pattern: 2013 and 2016 (here the album release dates interfered in Taylor Swift's narrative as it was released on her birthday, December 2013; and after Kanye West's song *Famous* in 2016, but this time Taylor has a negative image because of the lyrics of the *Famous* song and the line 'that bitch';

- on the contrary, Taylor Swift followed the *long term fixed pattern*: autumn for 6 albums; however, after *Lover* (2019) the pattern changed: *Lover* was released following a different pattern: August 23, 2019: two years since the announcement of the *reputation* album (2017), is like ending a cycle of two albums: *reputation* first part and *Lover* as second and final part; in the end, Taylor created a *surprise pattern* like Beyoncé: with two albums, *folklore* and *Evermore*;
- Taylor Swift: *folklore* and *Evermore* are two sister albums; Beyoncé: *I Am... Sasha Fierce*: an album with two discs: first disc name is *I Am...* while the second disc name is *Sasha Fierce*;
- Beyoncé album release (November 12, 2008 in Japan) is in the same month as Taylor Swift: November 11, which is the second day after Taylor Swift; however, the full release in the USA by Beyoncé is on next week, November 18, 2008, a week before Kanye West's album: November 24, 2008;
- *the strange element*: the keyword and theme of both artists is *fear*.

TABLE 45. THE ALBUM RELEASE: TAYLOR SWIFT, BEYONCÉ AND KANYE WEST			
ARTIST	**TAYLOR SWIFT**	**BEYONCÉ**	**KANYE WEST**
ALBUM	*FEARLESS (PLATINUM, 2008)*	*I AM... SASHA FIERCE (2008)*	*808s & HEARTHBREAK (2008)*
RELEASE DATE USA	November 11, 2008	November 18, 2008	November 24, 2008
PATTERN OF MUSIC RELEASE	2006: October 24 2008: November 11 2010: October 25 2012: October 22 2014: October 27 2017: November 10	2003: June 17 2006: September 4 2008: November 12 2011: June 24 2013: December 13 2016: April 23	2004: February 10 2005: August 30 2007: September 11 2008: November 24 2010: November 22 2013: June 18

	2019: August 23		2016: February 14
	2020: July 24		2018: June 1
	2020: December 11		2019: October 25

CONCLUSIONS:

- Beyoncé album release (November 12, 2008 in Japan) is in the same month as Taylor Swift: November 11, which is the second day after Taylor Swift; however, the full release in the USA by Beyoncé is on next week, November 18, 2008, a week before Kanye West's album: November 24, 2008;

- Kanye West changed the pattern of music release and interfered for a second time in Taylor Swift's pattern of album release: one album in each year for two years and in total for four albums: 2004 and 2005, the next two albums: 2007 and 2008; since 2008 Kanye West changed the season and released his album in the same month as Taylor Swift, but two weeks later: Taylor Swift on November 11, 2008 and Kanye West on November 24; in 2010: Taylor Swift released the album on October 25 (she released her first album in October 24, 2006), then Kanye West later in November 22, keeping the release date connected with the last release, which is the first and last time when Kanye West follows this release pattern; the following albums will be released in different seasons, only to change it to October 25, 2019 with *Jesus is King*, the same date that Taylor Swift released *Speak Now* in 2010;

- Kanye West (change of release pattern) and Beyoncé (fixed pattern: June 2003 and 2011; surprise pattern: 2013 and 2016) changed the album release date and both artists released their albums in the same month as Taylor Swift (fixed pattern until *Lover* album 2019), then for the next album Kanye West and Beyoncé will change the release month again; strangely a year later all the artists will find themselves (with the generous help of Kanye West) involved into one of the most famous feuds of all time in the music industry with the starting point at the MTV Music Awards for the Video Music Awards (September 13, 2009) based on the albums Taylor Swift and Beyoncé released in the same month of November 2008;

II. **black** and **white** music

- The MTV Video Music Awards were presented on September 13, 2009: the lucky number of Taylor Swift (or not so lucky for this day) where Kanye West showed his lack of manners in front of the entire world.

II.4 *Kendrick Lamar* versus *Taylor Swift*

In this section of the chapter I investigated the music released by Taylor Swift in 2014 (the album *1989*) and Kendrick Lamar (*To Pimp a Butterfly*) in 2015 and were in direct competition for the Album of the Year at the Grammy Awards in 2016 and for which Kanye West said that Kendrick Lamar should have won because his album is better.

II.4.1 No Use of Sample

TABLE 46. ORIGINAL SONGS WITH NO SAMPLES
TAYLOR SWIFT: 1989 (Deluxe, 2014): N/A
KENDRICK LAMAR: To Pimp a Butterfly (2015): 10 out of 16

II.4.2 Original Songs as Sole Lyricist

TABLE 47. ORIGINAL SONGS AS SOLE LYRICIST
TAYLOR SWIFT: 1989 (Deluxe, 2014): 1 out of 16
KENDRICK LAMAR: To Pimp a Butterfly (2015): 0 out of 16

II.4.3 The Length of Original Song as Sole Lyricist

TABLE 48. THE LENGTH OF SONGS AS SOLE LYRICIST
TAYLOR SWIFT: 1989 (Deluxe, 2014): This Love with 4:10 minutes
KENDRICK LAMAR: To Pimp a Butterfly (2015): 0 minutes

II.4.4 Original Songs with Two Lyricists

TABLE 49. ORIGINAL SONGS WITH TWO LYRICISTS. (ONE IS THE MAIN ARTIST)
TAYLOR SWIFT: 1989 (Deluxe, 2014): 7 out of 16
KENDRICK LAMAR: To Pimp a Butterfly (2015): 1 out of 16

II.4.5 The Length of Original Songs with Two Lyricists

TABLE 50. THE LENGTH OF ORIGINAL SONGS WITH TWO LYRICISTS (ONE IS THE MAIN ARTIST)
TAYLOR SWIFT: 1989 (Deluxe, 2014): 26:19 minutes
KENDRICK LAMAR: To Pimp a Butterfly (2015): 4:51

II.4.6 The Sources of the Samples

TABLE 51. SOURCES OF SAMPLES	
ARTIST & ALBUM	**SOURCE OF SAMPLES**
TAYLOR SWIFT: 1989 (Deluxe, 2014)	N/A: (Taylor Swift is in a case of a copyright issue regarding *Shake it off* song in the USA).
KENDRICK LAMAR: To Pimp a Butterfly (2015)	1. 'Wesley's Theory' contains elements of 'Every Nigger is a Star', written and performed by Boris Gardiner. 2. 'King Kunta' contains interpolations of 'Get Nekkid', written by Johnny Burns and performed by Mausberg; resung lyrics from 'Smooth Criminal', written and performed by Michael Jackson; elements of 'The Payback', written by James Brown, Fred Wesley and John Starks, and performed by James Brown; and samples of 'We Want the Funk', written and performed by Ahmad Lewis. 3. 'Momma' contains elements of 'Wishful Thinkin' written by Sylvester Stone and performed by Sly and the Family Stone; and elements of 'On Your Own', written and performed by Lalah Hathaway; sampled 'So[rt]', by Knxwledge; sampled 'Control (HOF)', as performed by Big Sean, Kendrick Lamar and Jay Electronica. 4. 'Hood Politics' contains a sample of 'All for Myself', written and performed by Sufjan Stevens. 5. 'i' contains a sample of 'That Lady', written by Ronald Isley, O'Kelly Isley, Jr., Ernie Isley, Marvin Isley, Rudolph Isley and Christopher Jasper, and performed by The Isley Brothers. 6. 'Mortal Man' contains excerpts from 'I No Get Eye for Back', written by Fela Anikulapo Kuti and performed by Houston Person; and a sample of music journalist Mats Nileskar's November 1994 interview with Tupac Shakur for P3 Soul Broadcasting Corporation.

II.4.7 The Fame of The Samples

TABLE 52. THE FAME OF THE SAMPLES	
TAYLOR SWIFT: 1989 (Deluxe, 2014)	N/A (there is no final court law decision regarding the originality of the song *Shake it off* by Taylor Swift)
KENDRICK LAMAR: To Pimp a Butterfly (2015)	1. 'Smooth Criminal': 'The song was number 7 on the Billboard Hot 100, number 2 on the Billboard Hot Black Singles chart.' 2. 'The Payback': 'Samples from this song was heavily used in popular games and movies.' 3. 'That Lady': 'The song is ranked number 357 on Rolling Stone's list of the 500 Greatest Songs of All Time.'

II.4.8 Producers and Lyricists

TABLE 53. PRODUCERS AND LYRICISTS
TAYLOR SWIFT: 1989 (Deluxe, 2014): *Producers*: Max Martin, Taylor Swift, Jack Antonoff, Nathan Chapman, Imogen Heap, Mattman & Robin, Ali Payami, Shellback, Ryan Tedder, Noel Zancanella. *Lyricists*: between one to four, most of the songs have two and three lyricists.
KENDRICK LAMAR: To Pimp a Butterfly (Deluxe, 2015): *Producers*: Boi-1da, Flippa, Flying Lotus, Knxwledge, KOZ, Larrance Dopson, LoveDragon, Pharrell Williams, Rahki, Sounwave, Tae Beast, Taz Arnold, Terrace Martin, Thundercat, Tommy Black, Whoarei. *Lyricists*: from two to eight.

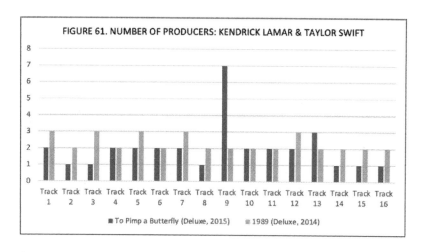

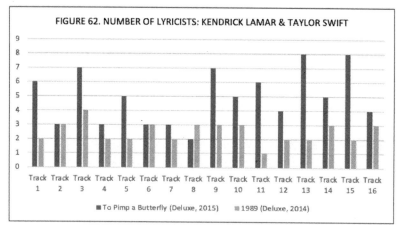

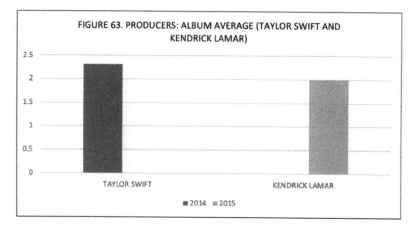

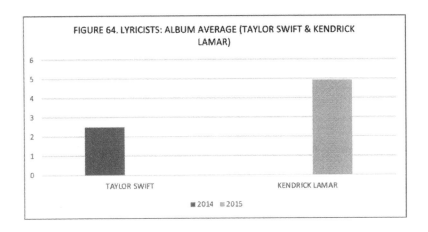

CONCLUSIONS:

- Taylor Swift used less lyricists to create the album and has a higher level of originality because her sounds and lyrics are not based on other songs as it happens with Kendrick Lamar;
- Taylor Swift is part of the producers, but Kendrick Lamar is not;
- perhaps because of these conclusions The Recording Academy decided that Taylor Swift has a more genuine ground than Kendrick Lamar to be awarded with the *Album of the Year* and less because she is white and her album sold millions of copies in the world in the last two years since the release of the album (2014) and the award ceremony (2016).

II.4.9 The Album Ratings

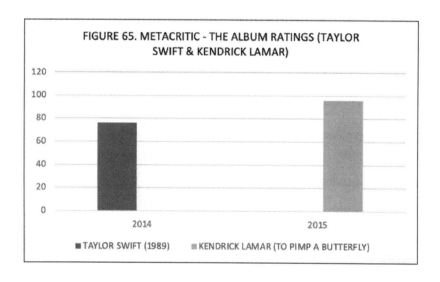

CONCLUSIONS:

- Taylor Swift's grades are based on her clean music, while Kendrick Lamar's grades are based also on the samples used;
- Taylor Swift used less lyricists than Kendrick Lamar, but a higher number of producers than Kendrick Lamar;
- Taylor Swift's album is clean and belongs to a greater extent to herself and the producers and lyricists and this might be the outstanding reason to be the winner of the *Album of the Year*, and not Kendrick Lamar.

II.5 Beyoncé versus Beck

In the next section of this chapter I investigated the album released by Beyoncé (black woman) in 2013 and Beck (white male) in 2014 to find why she lost the Album of the Year at the Grammy Awards.

II.5.1 No Use of Sample

TABLE 54. ORIGINAL SONGS WITH SAMPLE
BEYONCÉ: Beyoncé (Platinum, 2013): 3 out of 16
BECK: Morning Phase (2014): 0 out of 13[409]

II.5.2 Original Songs as Sole Lyricist

TABLE 55. ORIGINAL SONGS AS SOLE LYRICIST
BEYONCÉ: Beyoncé (Platinum, 2013): 0 out of 16
BECK: Morning Phase (2014): 13 out of 13

II.5.3 The Length of Songs as Sole Lyricists

TABLE 56. THE LENGTH OF SONGS AS SOLE LYRICIST
BEYONCÉ: Beyoncé (Platinum, 2013): 0 minutes
BECK: Morning Phase (2014): 47:03 minutes (100%)

---

[409] Beck, 'Morning Phase Credits', *Tidal,* 2014, available at:
https://listen.tidal.com/album/77668770/credits, last accessed: February 25, 2020. This source it is used for the rest of the section of this chapter.

II.5.4 The Sources of the Samples

TABLE 57. THE SOURCES OF THE SAMPLES	
BEYONCÉ: Beyoncé (Platinum, 2013):	*BECK*: Morning Phase (2014):
1. 'Partition' contains an interpolation of the French-dubbed version of the 1998 film The Big Lebowski, performed by Hajiba Fahmy.	own musical mind.
2. 'Flawless' contains portions of the speech 'We should all be feminists', written and delivered by Chimamanda Ngozi Adichie.	
3. 'Heaven' contains portions of 'The Lord's Prayer' in Spanish, performed by Melissa Vargas.	

II.5.5 The Fame of The Samples

TABLE 58. THE FAME OF THE SAMPLES	
NAME OF THE ALBUM	**SAMPLES**
BEYONCÉ: Beyoncé (Platinum, 2013)	1. *The Big Lebowski:* become a cult classic. An annual festival, Lebowski Fest, which expanded to several other cities and countries. Various publications included this film in different charts: Entertainment Weekly ranked it 8th on their Funniest Movies of the Past 25 Years list, also was ranked No. 34 on their list of 'The Top 50 Cult Films' and ranked No. 15 on the magazine's 'The Cult 25: The Essential Left-Field Movie Hits Since '83' list. The film was also nominated for the prestigious Grand Prix of the Belgian Film Critics Association. The Big Lebowski was voted as the 10th best film set in Los Angeles in the last 25 years by a group of Los Angeles Times writers and editors with two criteria: 'The movie had to communicate some inherent truth about the L.A. experience, and only one film per director was allowed on the list.' Roger Ebert added The Big Lebowski to his list of 'Great Movies' in March 2010.[410]
	2. *We Should All Be Feminists':* it was a speech that later was extended into a book 'which received overwhelmingly positive reviews.' Rupert Hawksley said: 'it just might be the most important book you read all year" in The Telegraph. The Independent selected it as a book of the year'.[411]

---

[410] The Big Lebowski, *Wikipedia*, available at: https://en.wikipedia.org/wiki/The_Big_Lebowski#Legacy, last accessed: February 25, 2020.

[411] We Should All Be Feminists, *Wikipedia*, available at: https://en.wikipedia.org/wiki/We_Should_All_Be_Feminists, last accessed: February 25, 2020.

	3. *'The Lord's Prayer'*, also called the *Our Father* (Latin: Pater Noster), is a central Christian prayer which, according to the New Testament, Jesus taught as the way to pray.
BECK: Morning Phase (2014)	N/A

II.5.6 Producers and Lyricists

TABLE 59. PRODUCERS AND LYRICISTS

BEYONCÉ: Beyoncé (Platinum, 2013):	BECK: Morning Phase (2014):
Producers: Beyoncé (also exec.) 40, Ammo Boots, Brian Soko, Caroline Polachek, Detail, Dre Moon, HazeBanga, Hit-Boy, J-Roc, Justin Timberlake, Key Wane, Majid Jordan, Mike Dean, Omen, Patrick Wimberly, Pharrell Williams, Rasool Ricardo Diaz, Rey Reel, Ryan Tedder, The-Dream, Timbaland. *Lyricists*: from two to ten.	*Producer*: Beck *Lyricist*: Beck

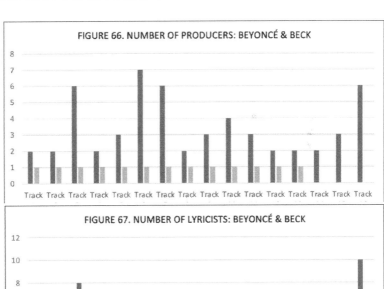

FIGURE 66. NUMBER OF PRODUCERS: BEYONCÉ & BECK

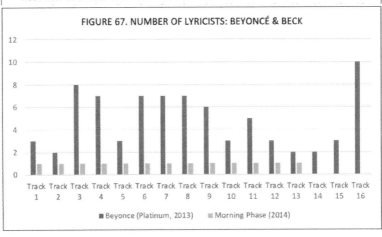

FIGURE 67. NUMBER OF LYRICISTS: BEYONCÉ & BECK

■ Beyonce (Platinum, 2013)   ■ Morning Phase (2014)

135

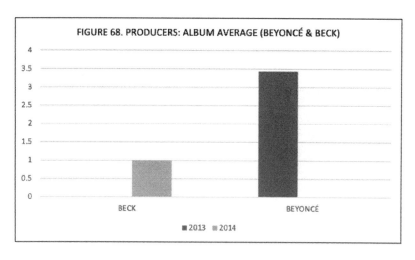

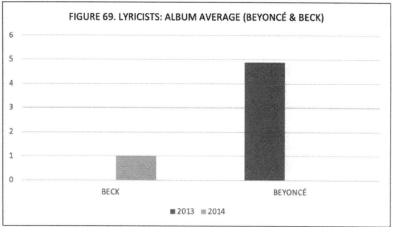

CONCLUSION:

- Beck is the sole producer and lyricist of his album and maybe this is a genuine argument for being the winner of the Album of the Year instead of Beyoncé and the producers and lyricists which contributed to her album. It seems that number 13 (also the lucky number of Taylor Swift) was a lucky number for Beck's number of songs (13), but bad luck for Beyoncé which released her self-titled album on December 13, 2013 (it is the birthday of Taylor Swift: December 13, 1989, and at that time she already won the *Album of the Year* in 2009 with *Fearless* and won again in 2016 for the album *1989* (the standard edition has 13 songs).

II.5.7 The Album Ratings

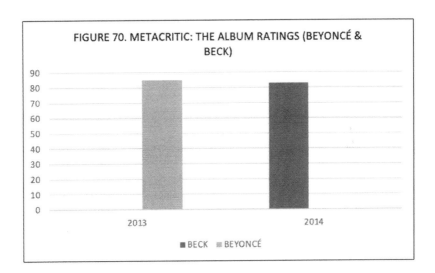

FIGURE 70. METACRITIC: THE ALBUM RATINGS (BEYONCÉ & BECK)

CONCLUSION:

- Beck's final review grade is based on his personal contribution, while Beyoncé's final review grade is based on her personal contribution, but to a considerable extent to other producers and lyricists.

II.6 *Beyoncé* versus *Adele*

In this subchapter I investigated the album released by Beyoncé (black woman) in 2016 and Adele (white woman) in 2015 to find why Beyoncé lost the Album of the Year at the Grammy Awards.

II.6.1 No Use of Sample

TABLE 60. ORIGINAL SONGS WITH NO SAMPLE
BEYONCÉ: Lemonade (2016): 5 out of 12
ADELE: 25 (Target, 2015): 14 out of 14[412]

II.6.2 Original Songs as Sole Lyricist

TABLE 61. ORIGINAL SONGS AS SOLE LYRICIST
BEYONCÉ: Lemonade (2016): 0 out of 12
ADELE: 25 (Target, 2015): 14 out of 14

Adele is credited on *Tidal* as sole lyricist, but on the *Composer Lyricists* her songs are credited with a second lyricist. In this report, I used only *Lyricist* as Adele (this is the raw version of the song, the main idea that later was transformed into a song).

II.6.3 The Length of the Original Songs as Sole Lyricist

TABLE 62. THE LENGTH OF THE ORIGINAL SONGS AS SOLE LYRICIST
BEYONCÉ: Lemonade (2016): 0 minutes

---

[412] Adele, '25 Credits', *Tidal*, 2015, available at: https://listen.tidal.com/album/62300892/credits, last accessed: February 25, 2020. The songs from the version *25 (Target Edition)* were taken from Wikipedia, available at: https://en.wikipedia.org/wiki/25_(Adele_album), last accessed: February 25, 2020. This source it is used for the rest of the section of this chapter.

ADELE: 25 (Target, 2015): 60:12 minutes

Adele is credited on *Tidal* as sole lyricist, but on the *Composer Lyricists* her songs are credited with a second lyricist. In this report, I used only *Lyricist* as Adele (this is the raw version of the song, the main idea that later was transformed into a song).

II.6.4 The Sources of the Samples

TABLE 63. THE SOURCES OF THE SAMPLES	
ARTIST & ALBUM	**SOURCE OF SAMPLES**
BEYONCÉ: Lemonade (2016)	1. *'Hold Up'*: Good connection with the theme of the song (relationships, cheating, losing someone) 'Can't Get Used to Losing You' and use of lyrics from 'Turn My Swag On' and 'Maps'. Some lyrics of this song 'Can't Get Used to Losing You' are being used to create a visual representation in the music video, which is also genuinely similar with the video of the Swiss visual artist Pipilotti Rist's project 'Ever Is Over All'. On the album Aquemini (contains the word 'aque' acronymous for 'aqua' which translates as 'water' (which is one of the main themes and visuals of the album Lemonade), from which Beyoncé samples the song 'SpottieOttieDopaliscious', has the introductory song named 'Hold On, Be Strong.' 2. *Don't Hurt Yourself*: 'When the Levee Breaks': good connection with the song's theme and use of lyrics. The song is a reflection of the experience during the upheaval caused by the Great Mississippi Flood of 1927, which is linked with Beyoncé's visual album with floods (water) in Formation and other videos which represents the real world and the negative side effects of tornadoes, hurricanes from the United States of America. 3. *'6 inch'*: Title and lyrics connection with 'My Girls'. 4. *'Freedom'*: Some connection with 'Let Me Try'. 5. *'All Night'*: Some connection with the theme of the song (events from a night) 'SpottieOttieDopaliscious'. However, there is strong connection between the whole album of Lemonade (visual and lyrics themes) and the whole album named Aquemini ('SpottieOttieDopaliscious' is one of the songs included in this album), released in 1998 by the hip-hop duo Outkast. Lyrically, much of Aquemini features introspection about the desolation of the human condition (strong theme in Lemonade), which include precarious relationships (Lemonade: between her and Mr. Carter), freedom from self-inflicted struggles (Lemonade: between her and Mr. Carter), also one of Beyoncé songs from Lemonade is named Freedom. If Aquemini is about a shift between science – fiction inspired topics combined with the harsh reality of urban life, Lemonade is showing in her videos the harsh reality of the country

139

	and urban life of black people. In the end, the similarity between the two albums is the experimentation of delivery styles on the record, using relaxed, hyper, distorted, speedy and conversational presentations.' 6. *'Sorry (Original Demo)'*: Use of lyrics from the title 'Young, Wild & Free' and chorus.
ADELE: 25 (Target, 2015)	N/A as she did not used samples in her music. Adele was accused of ripping off an artist from Turkey.[413]

II.6.5 The Fame of The Samples

TABLE 64. THE FAME OF THE SAMPLES USED	
ARTIST & ALBUM	**THE FAME OF THE SAMPLES**
BEYONCÉ: Lemonade (2016)	1. *'Turn My Swag On'*: 'The song was US Rap Songs (Billboard) weekly charts number 3, US Pop 100 (Billboard) weekly charts number 39, US Hot R&B/Hip Hop Songs (Billboard) weekly charts number 3.' 2. *'Maps'*: The music video received extensive play on MTV, it reached number 9 on Billboard's Alternative Songs chart and was included in popular video game Rock Band.' Other success includes: 'NME best alternative love song in 2009; number 6 on Pitchfork Media's top 500 songs of the 2000s; Rolling Stone ranked it number 386 on their list of the 500 Greatest Songs of All Time; in 2011 NME placed the song at number 55 on its list '150 Best Tracks of the Past 150 Years'; NME ranked the song at number 1 on their list of 'Indie Weddings Songs: 20 Tracks Perfect For Your First Dance' 3. *When the Levee Breaks'*: 'It is a wide loved country blue song'. 4. *'My Girls'*: 'The lyrics of the song is about the desire of the artist on a basic level to own my own place and kind of provide a safe house for my family and the people I care about.' Other success include: Pitchfork named the song number 1 of 2009 and also number 9 on their Top 500 Tracks of the 2000s; NME named the 5th best song of 2009; Slant Magazine named the best song of 2009; The Village Voice name the third best song of 2009; NME in 2011 place it at number 91 on their list '150 Best Tracks of the Past 15 Years'; NME in 2014 named the 248th best song of all time'. 5. *'Walk On By'*: 'The song peaked at number 6 on the US Billboard Hot 100 and number 1 on the Cash Box Rhythm and Blues Chart in June 1964; also, it was nominated for a 1965 Grammy Award for the Best Rhythm and Blues Recording.' 6. *'SpottieOttieDopaliscious'*: 'It is a song from the album Aquemini which is the third studio album of the American hip hop duo

[413] Paul Gallagher, 'Adele accused by 'stealing' Kuridsh singer's 1985 song for new album', *The Independent*, December 7, 2015, available at: https://www.independent.co.uk/arts-entertainment/music/news/adele-accused-of-stealing-kurdish-singer-s-1985-song-for-her-new-album-25-a6764041.html, last accessed: February 25, 2020.

	Outkast. Aquemini received highly widespread acclaim from critics with most the grade being one 3,5 out of 4 stars from USA Today and Chicago Sun-Times, to 5 out of 5 stars from Q, to A- from Christgau's Consumer Guide, to A from Entertainment Weekly. Los Angeles Times gave 4 stars out of 4, Rolling Stone 4 out of 5 stars. In the end the album was included in several publication's best album lists such as: in 2003, Rolling Stone ranked it on their 500 Greatest Albums of All Time and number 11 on the list '100 best Albums of the Nineties'; Paste called it 'the best Atlanta hip-hop album of all time'; Pitchfork ranked it number 50 on their 'Top 100 Albums of the 1990s'; Spin ranked it number 35 on the '90 Greatest Albums of the '90" and number 3 on the 'Top 20 Albums of '98"; the lead single 'Rosa Park' was nominated in the category Grammy Award for Best Rap Performance by a Duo or Group at the 1999 Grammy Awards; in the end the song 'SpottieOttieDopaliscious' was ranked at number 16 on Pitchfork Media's list of the top 200 tracks of the 1990s.' The legacy of this album is virtuosic masterpiece, a landmark hip-hop, artistic success, brilliant, avant-garde, sonic ideas, new sounds, ravenous as ever which is in direct line with the reviews received by Beyoncé for Lemonade, her highest rated album yet. *7. 'Young, Wild & Free'*: 'The song peaked at number 7 on the Billboard Hot 100. The song was praised for standing out stylistically from the rest of the soundtrack with hip-hop drums and a piano back. It was a commercial success and by April 16, 2013 was certified 3 times Platinum by the Recording Industry Association of America and before Lemonade release, around 4 times platinum. The song was nominated for Best Rap Song at the 2013 Grammy Awards'.
ADELE: 25 (Target, 2015)	N/A as she did not used samples in her music. Adele was accused of ripping off an artist from Turkey.[414]

II.6.6 Producers and Lyricists

25 (Target, 14 songs*)* has 3 songs more than the standard edition (11 songs), for Target Edition (extra 3 songs) I used Wikipedia as source for *Lyricists* and the number is 2 per song, however, considering *Tidal* credits for standard edition it is possible that the main *Lyricist* to be Adele, while the *Composer Lyricists* to be Adele and the second lyricist as it happens with the standard edition.

TABLE 65. PRODUCERS AND LYRICISTS	
BEYONCÉ: Lemonade (2016)	*ADELE*: 25 (Target, 2015):

[414] *Ibidem.*

Producers: Beyoncé (also exec.), Beyoncé, Diplo, Kevin Garret, Ezra Koenig, Jack White, MeLo-X, Dina Gordon, Boots, DannyBoyStyles, Mike Dean, Vincent Berry II, James Blake, Jonathan Coffer, Just Blaze, Mike Will Made It. **Lyricists**: between two to fifteen.	**Producers**: Danger Mouse, Samuel Dixon, Paul Epworth, Greg Kurstin, Max Martin, Linda Perry, Ariel Rechtshaid, Mark Ronson, Shellback, The Smeezingtons, Ryan Tedder. **Lyricists**: one, Adele (Composer Lyricist: most of the songs have two).

The average for *Producers* and *Lyricists* used in the figure is based on *25 (Target)* with 14 songs.

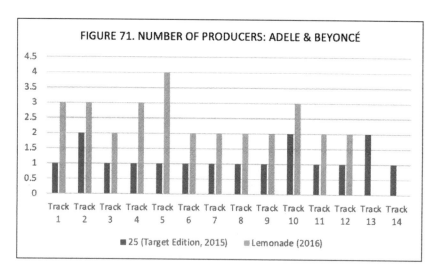

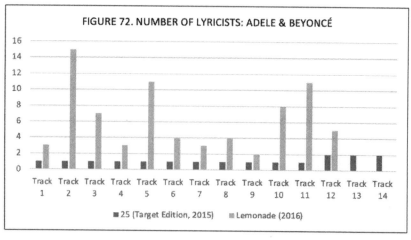

142

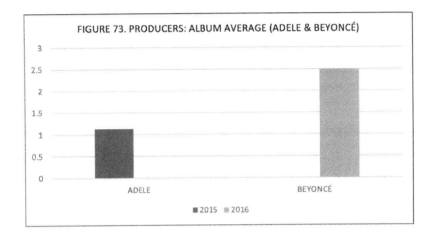

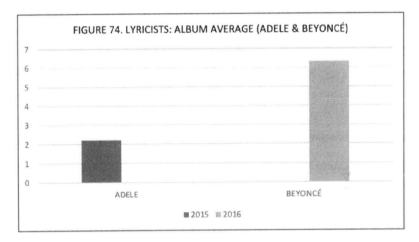

CONCLUSIONS:

- Adele used less producers and lyricists than Beyoncé which used a high level of producers, inspirations of sounds, themes and lyrics of other songs already known, included in charts and awarded in the music industry;
- Adele is the sole lyricist of her music, but with a second lyricist for *Composer Lyricist*;
- the figures available in this report reveal evidence to build a good argument that Adele has a better musical dossier of high personal

involvement in the making of her album and maybe this is the reason why she was awarded with the *Album of the Year*.

II.6.7 The Album Ratings

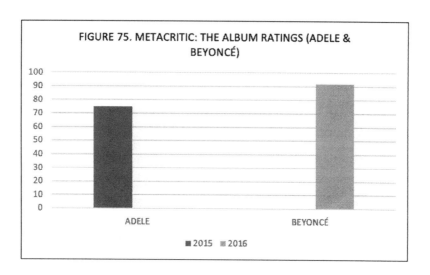

FIGURE 75. METACRITIC: THE ALBUM RATINGS (ADELE & BEYONCÉ)

CONCLUSION:

- Adele's final review grade is based on her personal contribution at high level, while Beyoncé's final review grade is based on her personal contribution, but to a considerable extent to other producers, lyricists, samples with music already included in charts and awarded.

II.7 Macklamore & Ryan versus Kendrick Lamar

On January 26, 2014, Macklamore & Ryan Lewis won the Grammy Award for Best Rap Album. According to K.B. Denis, "Macklemore & Ryan were criticised and a good number of people within the music industry felt that Kendrick Lamar was cheated. Strangely, Macklamore & Ryan Lewis considered Kendrick Lamar as the right winner and offered an apology; there were news which presented the award to Macklamor & Ryan Lewis as a controversial turn of events where Kendrick Lamar was seen as the right winner; another criticism was that Macklemore is white and his whiteness lift and granted them the Grammy which has also made a habit of over-rewarding white rappers; also Macklamore & Ryan Lewis are very much aware of their white privilege and how it is has given them advantages in life and career."[415]

In this section I investigated the origin of Macklamore & Ryan Lewis and Kendrick Lamar's music albums that were in direct competition for the Best Rap Album of the Year at the Grammy Awards in 2014.

II.7.1 Use of Sample

TABLE 66. ORIGINAL SONGS WITH NO SAMPLE
MACKLEMORE & RYAN LEWIS: The Heist (Deluxe, 2012): 0 out of 18[416]
KENDRICK LAMAR: good city, m.A.A.d. city (Deluxe, 2012): 9 out of 18

---

[415] I added the following source as also a reply to K.B. Denis's article. However, the idea of this paragraph existed before the publication of his article, but it was changed to contains more of the author intervention: K.B. Denis, 'Grammy Rewind: 6 Years Later, How Did Macklemore Beat Out Kendrick Lamar at the Grammys?', *Awardswatch*, July 10, 2020, available at: https://awardswatch.com/grammy-rewind-6-years-later-how-did-macklemore-beat-out-kendrick-lamar-at-the-grammys/, last accessed: July 11, 2020.

[416] Macklemore & Ryan, 'The Heist (Deluxe, 2021) Credits', *Tidal,* available at: https://listen.tidal.com/album/23374211/credits, last accessed: February 25, 2020. This source it is used for the rest of the section of this chapter.

II.7.2 Original Songs as Sole Lyricist

TABLE 67. ORIGINAL SONGS AS SOLE LYRICIST
MACKLEMORE & RYAN LEWIS: The Heist (Deluxe, 2012): 1 out of 18 (by Ryan Lewis)
KENDRICK LAMAR: good city, m.A.A.d. city (Deluxe, 2012): 0 out of 18

II.7.3 Original Songs with Two Lyricists

TABLE 68. ORIGINAL SONGS WITH TWO LYRICISTS
MACKLEMORE & RYAN LEWIS: The Heist (Deluxe, 2012): 5 out of 18 (Written by Macklemore & Ryan Lewis)
KENDRICK LAMAR: good city, m.A.A.d. city (Deluxe, 2012): 5 out of 18

CONCLUSION:

- both artist's albums contain songs with two lyricists, however, Macklemore & Ryan are the main artists in writing and singing their songs as a group.

II.7.4 The Length of Songs as Sole Lyricist

TABLE 69. THE LENGTH OF SONGS AS SOLE LYRICIST
MACKLEMORE & RYAN LEWIS: The Heist (Deluxe, 2012): 4:55 minutes out of 76:18 minutes
KENDRICK LAMAR: good city, m.A.A.d. city (Deluxe, 2012): 0 minutes out of 100:03 minutes

CONCLUSION:

- Ryan is the sole lyricist of a song included in the album, while all of Kendrick Lamar's songs are written in partnership with at least a second lyricist.

II.7.5 The Length of Songs with Two Lyricists

TABLE 70. THE LENGTH OF SONGS WITH TWO LYRICISTS
MACKLEMORE & RYAN LEWIS: The Heist (Deluxe, 2012): 19:49 minutes out of 76:18 minutes
KENDRICK LAMAR: good city, m.A.A.d. city (Deluxe, 2012): 23:49 minutes out of 100:03 minutes

II.7.6 The Sources of the Samples

TABLE 71. THE SOURCES OF THE SAMPLES	
MACKLEMORE & RYAN LEWIS: The Heist (Deluxe, 2012)	N/A as they did not use samples in their music.
KENDRICK LAMAR: good city, m.A.A.d. city (Deluxe, 2012)	While Kendrick Lamar used samples, I found these songs to be used more than the others: 1. 'The Art of Peer Pressure': 'Helt Alene': it was the main sample for this track. 2. 'Poetic Justice': 'It used heavily sample from the song 'Any Time, Any Place' co-written and performed by Janet Jackson.' 3. 'The Receipe': Some lyrics from 'Meet the Frownies.'

CONCLUSION:

- Kendrick Lamar's album has more samples from other songs than Macklemore & Ryan which opted for their own musical ear.

II.7.7 The Fame of the Sample

TABLE 72. THE FAME OF THE SAMPLES USED	
MACKLEMORE & RYAN LEWIS: The Heist (Deluxe, 2012)	N/A as they did not use samples in their music.
	1. 'Smooth Criminal': 'The song was number 7 on the Billboard Hot 100, number 2 on the Billboard Hot Black Singles chart.'

KENDRICK LAMAR: good city, m.A.A.d. city (Deluxe, 2012)	2. 'The Payback': 'Samples from this song was heavily used in popular games and movies.'
	3. 'That Lady': 'The song is ranked number 357 on Rolling Stone's list of the 500 Greatest Songs of All Time.'

CONCLUSION:

- the samples used by Kendrick Lamar were already included in charts, awarded and recognized in the music industry; Macklemore & Ryan came with their own album and got recognition, their songs were included in various charts and awarded for the first time in the music industry.

II.7.8 Producers and Lyricists

TABLE 73. PRODUCERS AND LYRICISTS	
MACKLEMORE & RYAN LEWIS: The Heist (Deluxe, 2012):	KENDRICK LAMAR: good city, m.A.A.d. city (Deluxe, 2012):
Producer: Ryan Lewis **Lyricists**: the average number of lyricists per song is 2.72; all songs are written by Macklemore & Ryan Lewis with support for a second and third lyricist.	**Producer**: DJ Dahi, Hit-Boy, Just Blaze, Like, Pharrell Williams, Rahki, Scoop DeVille, Skhye Hutch, Sounwave, T-Minus, Tabu, Terrace Martin, THC, Tha Bizness; most of the song is credited with one producer, however, Kendrick Lamar is not credited as producer for his songs. **Lyricists**: the average number of lyricists per song is 3.77.

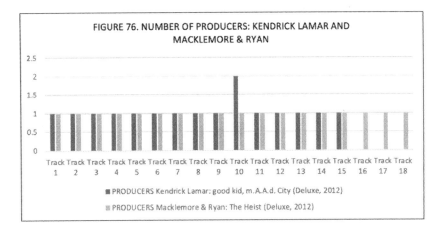

FIGURE 76. NUMBER OF PRODUCERS: KENDRICK LAMAR AND MACKLEMORE & RYAN

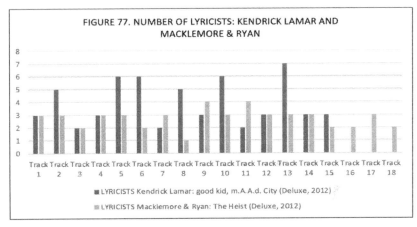

FIGURE 77. NUMBER OF LYRICISTS: KENDRICK LAMAR AND MACKLEMORE & RYAN

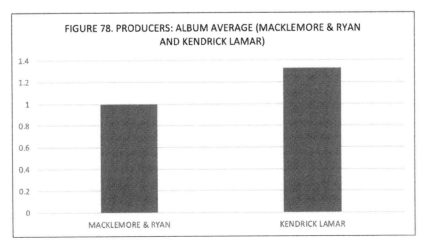

FIGURE 78. PRODUCERS: ALBUM AVERAGE (MACKLEMORE & RYAN AND KENDRICK LAMAR)

CONCLUSIONS:

- Ryan Lewis is the artist and the sole producer of his album;
- from the information that I had access: Kendrick Lamar has no credit as producer for this album;
- overall Macklamore & Ryan used less lyricists than Kendrick Lamar;
- Macklamore has one song written solely on his album, while Kendrick Lamar none;
- Macklemore & Ryan have a higher level of their own musical notes and lyrics, maybe they can rap faster than Kendrick Lamar and perhaps this is why they won the Best Rap Album.

II.7.9 The Album Ratings

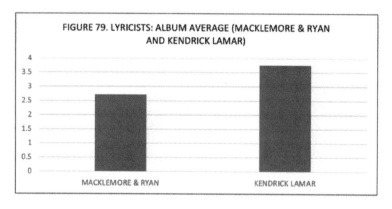

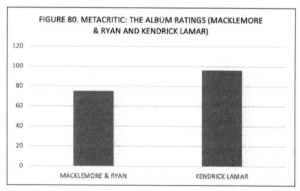

CONCLUSIONS:

- Macklemore & Ryan[417] final review grade is based on a higher personal contribution in their own album, while Kendrick Lamar's[418] final review grade is based on his personal contribution, but to a considerable extent to other producers, lyricists, samples with music already existent in the music industry, included in charts and awarded;
- Macklemore & Ryan have a higher level of their own musical notes and lyrics, maybe they can rap faster than Kendrick Lamar, and maybe these are the reasons to be awarded with the *Best Rap Album*.

---

[417] Macklemore & Ryan, 'The Heist (Deluxe, 2012)', *Metacritic*, available at:
https://www.metacritic.com/music/the-heist/ryan-lewis, last accessed: February 25, 2020.
[418] Kendrick Lamar, 'good kid, m.A.A.d. city (Deluxe, 2012)', *Metacritic*, available at:
https://www.metacritic.com/music/good-kid-maad-city/kendrick-lamar, last accessed: February 25, 2020.

II.8 Awards

II.8.1 Single Ladies *versus* You Belong with Me for MTV: Origins

In this section I investigated to find which artist is more original regarding the song and the video sent for consideration to MTV Music Video Awards for which Kanye West interrupted Taylor Swift during the ceremony of this event in 2009.

TABLE 74. SINGLE LADIES VERSUSS YOU BELONG WITH ME: ORIGINS		
ARTIST	**BEYONCÉ**	**TAYLOR SWIFT**
NAME OF THE SONG	*SINGLE LADIES (PUT A RING ON IT)*	*YOU BELONG WITH ME*
VIDEO INSPIRATION	From 1969 Bob Fosse routine entitled 'Mexican Breakfast' seen on The Ed Sullivan Show, which featured Fosse's wife, Gwen Verdon, dancing with two other women. The 'Mexican Breakfast' was an Internet viral sensation the previous summer after Unk's 'Walk It Out' was dubbed over the original mix. The choreography of 'Single Ladies' was liberally adapted from 'Mexican Breakfast'. Beyoncé said: 'I saw a video on YouTube [...] had a plain background and it was shot on the crane; it was 360 degrees, they could move around. And I said, 'This is genius.''[419]	Traditional love game: a girl likes a guy that she knows, but he is in a sort of complicated relationship with another girl and in the end, by remaining true to herself, she gets the guy. The video follows the traditional love scene of a girl who likes a guy who plays rugby, the popular game in the USA.
LYRICS	Beyoncé, Terius 'The-Dream' Nash, Thaddis 'Kuk' Harrell, and Christopher 'Tricky' Stewart	Taylor Swift & Liz Rose

---

[419] Beyoncé's Infectious Moves, *NPR*, , November 22, 2008, https://www.npr.org/templates/story/story.php?storyId=97356053&singlePage=true&t=15958684923 27, last accessed: February 26, 2020.

CONCLUSIONS:

- Taylor Swift wrote the song with another lyricist, while Beyoncé was in partnership with extra three lyricists;
- Taylor Swift released a song that truly was more hers than *Single Ladies* for Beyoncé;
- Beyoncé used the choreography of a song that was an internet sensation a year before her video release, while Taylor Swift used the traditional scene of a girl who likes a guy that plays rugby, which has no novelty as the scenes are set in already well-known environment; it could be novelty for Taylor Swift and her fans;
- perhaps the reason why more people considered that Taylor Swift's video was the best among all is because of the themes of the song: love, dreams and pain, while Beyoncé's dancing scenes are repetitive, boring and spin around for the whole video, and few people could see themselves/identify in her narrative?
- Taylor Swift's video is a love story that captures you in the narrative and leads you to the idea of whether she will finally be able to tell him how she feels about him and whether they will end up together; while Beyoncé's video makes you wonder how she did it, what kind of tricks she used to dance 360 degrees, and other people already knew that she used a choreography that was famous a year before her video;
- Taylor Swift used her own lyrics and musical notes in her video, while Beyoncé used another artist choreography in her video.

II.8.2 If I Were a Boy *versus* The Man: Origins

In 2019 Taylor Swift was accused of copying and ripping-off Beyoncé's music video *If I Were a Boy* with her new song *The Man* for the album *Lover*. In this section I investigated this allegation.

TABLE 75. IF I WERE A BOY VERSUS THE MAN: ORIGINS		
ARTIST	**BEYONCÉ**	**TAYLOR SWIFT**
NAME OF THE SONG	**IF I WERE A BOY**	**THE MAN**
	The song was not written by Beyoncé but by BC Jean and	

	Toby Gad, 'who also handled its production alongside Beyoncé. [...] The song was initially recorded by Jean, whose record company rejected it, then later Beyoncé recorded her own version. Jean was upset when she learned that Beyoncé was releasing it as a single, but eventually, they reached an agreement'.[420]	Personal experience.
VIDEO INSPIRATION		
LYRICS	BC Jean & Toby Gad	Taylor Swift & Joel Little

CONCLUSIONS:

- Taylor Swift wrote the song with another lyricist, while Beyoncé had no role in writing the song;
- Taylor Swift's song contains her own view about being a man with lyrics and musical instruments of her own vision for which she is credited for lyrics and as producer; Beyoncé's song is the view of a different artist that had the bad luck to be rejected by her company producer which offered a chance to Beyoncé;
- Taylor Swift did not copied or ripped-off Beyoncé's song as she is not the artists that composed the song in the first place, the core idea belonged to another artist; also BC Jean, then Beyoncé through her song, is not the first female in the world to imagine herself as a man: this association is a hundred if not thousands of years old in the minds of women around the planet, it is nothing new and no intellectual property to get permission to use; women don't need BC Jean, Beyoncé, Taylor Swift or other artists to inspire them to imagine their lives from a man's point of view.

II.8.3 Grammy Awards

In the last section I investigated the overall origin of the music released only by Taylor Swift, Kendrick Lamar, Kanye West and Beyoncé as this

---

[420] *If I Were a Boy*, Wikipedia, available at: https://en.wikipedia.org/wiki/If_I_Were_a_Boy, last accessed: February 26, 2020.

group of artists are more on the news and I already have the right information collected for their whole career. Overall, the information from this section show that Taylor Swift has a higher level of originality and own lyrics than the artists from this section and report.

Before moving on the comparison between the artists, let's see the reason of being the winner of the *Album of the Year* according to the 54th Annual Grammy Awards description guide:

"For albums containing at least 51% playing time of new vocal or instrumental recordings. Award to Artist(s) and to Featured Artist(s), Songwriter(s) of new material, Producer(s), Recording Engineer(s), Mixer(s) and Mastering Engineer(s) credited with at least 33% playing time of the album, if other than Artist"

As regard to specific albums that were in competition between the artists investigated in this section, we can see from the tables below that a strong reason of why Taylor Swift was the winner of the *Album of the Year* is based on her abilities to write songs and released them at the level of abilities she really has no matter what critics outside The Recording Academy might grade them.

Kanye West, Beyoncé and Kendrick Lamar used samples from other songs and maybe that's why they didn't get the award: the music of the white artists is cleaner compared to the music of the black artists who used more samples from other songs that existed already in the music industry, they were awarded and charted, and they wanted to be recognized at a high level for a music for which they paid royalties and copyrights. In addition, the black artists used more producers and lyricists in the creation of songs and albums compared to the white artists investigated in this report.

TABLE 76. THE BEAUTIFUL MIND OF MUSIC IN THE BACKGROUND				
ARTISTS	**TAYLOR SWIFT**	**KANYE WEST**	**BEYONCÉ**	**KENDRICK LAMAR**
Use of sample	3%	64%	26%	51%
Songs with no sample	97%	36%	73%	Close to 50%
Songs as sole lyricist	30%	6%	1%	0%
Songs with two lyricists	45%	11%	8%	30%

Songs with three lyricists	19%	13%	31%	24%
Songs with at least 4 lyricists	6%	67%	58%	46%
Length as sole lyricists (minutes)	206:55 minutes	18:16 minutes (Intro & Skit) 13:57 minutes (Without Intro & Skit)	16 Seconds	0 seconds

The next table contains only the albums released soley by Kanye West, no share producer for other albums.

YEAR / ARTIST	TAYLOR SWIFT		KANYE WEST		BEYONCÉ		KENDRICK LAMAR	
TABLE 77. PRODUCERS AND LYRICISTS: ALBUM AND CAREER AVERAGE (ALL ARTISTS)								
	Producers	*Lyricists*	*Producers*	*Lyricists*	*Producers*	*Lyricists*	*Producers*	*Lyricists*
2003	-	-	-	-	1.81	4.18	-	-
2004	-	-	1.09	2.95	-	-	-	-
2005	-	-	1.42[421]	2.90	-	-	-	-
2006	2	2	-	-	2.29	4.52	-	-
2007	-	-	1.92	4.28	-	-	-	-
2008	2	1.57	1.91	5.3	2.5	4.15	-	-
2009	-	-	-	-	-	-	-	-
2010	2.42	1.05	2.78	8.14	-	-	-	-
2011	-	-	-	-	2.57	4.14	1.06	2.37
2012	1.84	1.63	-	-	-	-	1.06	3.93
2013	-	-	5.9	12	3.43	4.87	-	-
2014	2.31	2.5	-	-	-	-	-	-
2015	-	-	-	-	-	-	2	4.93
2016	-	-	3.35	10.9	2.5	6.33	-	-
2017	2.2	2.66	-	-	-	-	3	6.71
2018	-	-	5.28	12.28	-	-	-	-
2019	2.22	2.22	5.09	8.27	-	-	-	-
2020	1.82	2	-	-	-	-	-	-
2020	1.41	2.29	-	-	-	-	-	-
2021	2[422]	1.85[423]	-	-	-	-	-	-
TOTAL	**2.02**	**1.77**	**2.98**	**7.44**	**2.51**	**4.69**	**1.78**	**4.48**
TOTAL CAREER (P+L)	**1.89**		**5.21**		**3.60**		**3.13**	

---

[421] The songs with 0 producers and lyricists are not part of this average.
[422] Only the new songs from this album were included in this table, in total 7 songs were considered.
[423] *Ibidem.*

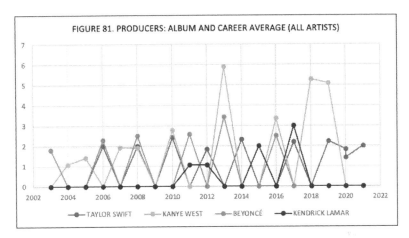

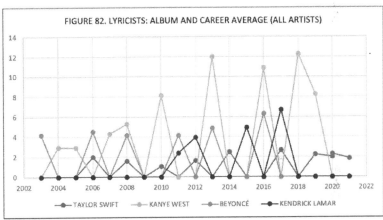

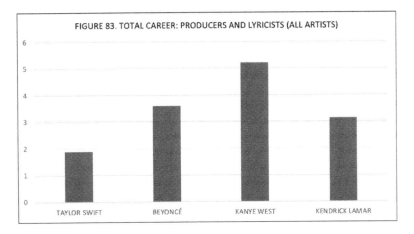

II.8.4 MUSIC REVIEW: an unfinished comparative study

Shortly after I finished this report, I decided to continue with a new chapter, *Music Review*: a comparative analysis between Taylor Swift, Kanye West, Beyoncé and Kendrick Lamar's music reviews written by various news agencies and published on Metacritic. For this chapter, I read:

- all the reviews for all the artists in a word document: 410 pages;
- the lyrics written by Taylor Swift, Kanye West, Beyoncé and Kendrick Lamar from their albums included in this report (250 pages);
- the most negative articles written in the media about Taylor Swift (99 pages);
- a number of over 500 articles written in the mass media in the UK, USA, Australia and New Zealand (over 500 from 1175 articles gathered with name of the news agency and link with the articles).

In the end, I simply did not have the energy to continue. The negative articles written about Taylor Swift and the lack of Western mass media to link the events between the artists and expose the truth (Taylor Swift a victim of Kanye West's game), plus my own disgust of the feud, kept me away from continuing this type of analysis. However, I will present two ideas that are widespread in the Western mass-media and I offer two examples for *reputation* and *Lover*: money and originality.

Money: today the journalist are mind readers, they just seem to know exactly what you think and want and they are here to tell their truth:

Consequence of Sound, Geoff Nelson: 'Besides, she, like so many before her, has a voice that sounds like money'.

The Guardian, Alexis Petridis: 'The big problem with Lover is that it's too long, the suspicion being that Swift is trying to reassert her commercial dominance by spread-betting.'

Originality:

Paste Magazine, Clare Martin (rating 5.8):

'Originality has never been Swift's strong suit':

- Paste Magazine reviewed many albums released by Kanye West, Beyoncé and Kendrick Lamar and, although their music is based on samples already awarded and included in charts in the music industry, their reviews are more generous compared to Taylor Swift's music which contains her own lyrics and musical notes. Taylor Swift has an album written by herself and many songs are created by her, Kanye West struggles to create his own song titles, Beyoncé works with an army of lyricists and producers yet they received higher grades than Taylor Swift;

'and the pulsating synth of "Cruel Summer" (thank you, St. Vincent) are particular standouts':

- in the case of Kanye West, Beyoncé (less than Kanye West) and Kendrick Lamar (to some extent), you can say this phrase to tens of songs from their catalogues with samples from other artists; for Kanye West is 'thank you' for at least 60% of his music to many artists, producers and lyricists; Beyoncé for less than kanye West, but is still there.

III. What if...

In this chapter I wrote scenarios based on the information found. These scenarios are speculative and negative. Maybe there is a possibility that these speculative scenarios have some truth and could help in making a better understanding of the events between Kanye West, Beyoncé, Jay Z and Taylor Swift.

The existence of more negative scenarios about Kanye West and Beyoncé is because of their shifting pattern of the album release in Taylor Swift's fixed pattern. Also, because of the dynamic of the events from the life of Kanye West, Beyoncé and Taylor Swift.

Why black artists are being promoted as the right winners before the award ceremony? Maybe because this a trick to put pressure on the public (to vote for them as they will win anyway and better to be already on the side of the winner) and the members (who can decide the winner) to award them: the public (with the help of the mass media) knows before the ceremony who the winner should be and if there is no black winner (the one that mass media is presenting as being the right winner) then it must be a rigged ceremony that steals the thunder of black artists; what if this is a trick to put pressure on the music institutions to award black artists otherwise they will be labeled racists and white supremacists institutions?

What if Beyoncé and Jay Z were part of the plan in 2009 for the MTV Awards?

What if Kanye West and Jay Z developed the plan for MTV Awards in 2009 without Beyoncé's knowledge?

What if Kanye West played The Bad Man (interrupted the speech) and Beyoncé the Good Woman (offered the chance to Taylor Swift to thank the fans for the award) at the MTV Awards? And if that was the plan, let's see how it could have been done in practice:

- *Step 1.* Kanye West (black man) entered the stage and interrupted Taylor Swift's speech (white woman) on the grounds that she does not deserve the award, even if it was voted by the public and that Beyoncé deserved the award;
- *Step 2.* Taylor Swift does not end the speech to thank her fans;
- *Step 3.* Beyoncé (black woman) fixed the narrative and gave Taylor Swift (white woman) her time to finish the speech (time that she received because she won Video of the Year), but first she mentioned her success: "I remember being 17 years old, up for my first MTV Award with Destiny's Child, and it was one of the most exciting moments in my life, so, I'd like for Taylor to come out and have her moment "; this is a situation where the black artist, with the award of the year, offered the opportunity to the white artist (with the negative image that she doesn't deserve the award) to finish her speech; what if the staff behind the curtain knew that Beyoncé will get the award and the plan was set up before the award ceremony?

What if Taylor Swift's career and progress was closely watched by Kanye West and Jay Z (probably with other people in their circle) and came to the idea that she would be the next famous pop artist in the USA and in the world (because she has the power to write her songs) and interfered in her narrative to destroy it or to insert in the audience's memory that Taylor Swift could not have been a successful artist without a black artist (through Kanye West)?

What if the release of Beyoncé 's album on November 12 was her idea, but also Jay Z and Kanye West were involved in making this decision (the day after the release of Taylor Swift's album, *Fearless*) and then November 18 (in the USA)?

What if Kanye West's album release pattern (November 24, 2008) was made in order to block Taylor Swift (November 11) to reach number 1 for several weeks, to reduce the popularity she enjoyed and grew every year since her debut in 2006?

What if Beyoncé (maybe got an idea from her husband Jay Z) changed her album name and included the word Fierce, which has a similar meaning to Fearless, and entered into direct and planned competition with Taylor Swift? in 2008 both artists used the same theme: *fear*, and in 2009 both artists competed for an award at the MTV VMA.

What if the release with different dates of the album *I am... Sasha Fierce* was made in order to gain ground and influence in front of Taylor Swift? what if the album release took place the day after Taylor Swift in order to insert the idea: first comes Taylor Swift with *Fearless*, but Beyoncé will come with *Fierce* and will be better than Taylor Swift, then later Kanye West will release his album in the third week and the world will forget Taylor Swift?

What if Beyoncé released the surprise album, *Beyoncé*, intentionally on Taylor Swift's birthday (December 13) as a sublime message: look who Beyoncé is and I'm coming after you (she didn't win the Grammy Awards for the *Album of the Year*);

What if Taylor Swift came up with the *1989* album (the year of her birth) to complete Beyoncé 's cycle, to reply and show who she is: an original lyricist and her first pure pop album that will eventually win the *Album of the Year* at the Grammy Awards?

What if Kanye West interfered in Taylor Swift's album release pattern a year earlier (2007), and then justified the release of the next album (2008) in the same timeframe as Taylor Swift in order to create a racial comparison: Kanye West (black man) received better reviews than Taylor Swift (white woman) and that Taylor Swift success is because she is white, not because she has better music than him? yet, Taylor Swift came with her lyrics, and Kanye West came with samples from other artists.

What if Kanye West and Jay Z knew Taylor Swift would receive the *Best Female Video Award* before the ceremony and Kanye West decided to bring a bottle of alcohol with him to cover his plan? just as he probably knew Taylor Swift wrote a song for him and said that he also wrote a song for her (I did not find information that he really wrote a song for Taylor Swift (maybe he said it as a marketing strategy, to not to be lower than Taylor Swift in the eyes of the general public), and may have known some of the lyrics: CBS[424] wrote an article with content from Kanye West published on his Twitter account: "When I woke up from the crazy nightmare I looked in the mirror and said GROW UP KANYE... ", after a few days Taylor Swift sang the lyrics of the song *Innocent* written for Kanye West and played at the MTV Awards: "32 and still growin'up now"; what are the chances for Kanye West to use words so close to Taylor Swift's lyrics? if there was a leak about the lyrics written by Taylor Swift for Kanye West, who provided the information?

What if the release of the album by Kanye West and Beyoncé in 2008, then the disagreement with the MTV award in 2009, and finally the release of the album in 2010 (for Kanye West), respectively in 2011 (for Beyoncé), was actually a long-term plan in order to present themselves as better than the white artist Taylor Swift, to diminish her popularity and creativity in the music industry?

- What if Beyoncé 's *Lemonade* album (including Jay Z) were part of Kanye West's strategy against Taylor Swift in 2016? and if this was the plan, let's see how it could have been carried out in practice:

Step 1:

- Kanye West released the song *Famous* (The Life of Pablo) where Taylor Swift is called 'that bitch'; Taylor entered the narrative created and promoted by Kanye by writing the truth: she did not know the lyrics in which she was called 'that bitch';

Step 2:

- Taylor was assailed by negative comments on social media, and the preferred term to address her is 'bitch';

Step 3:

- Kanye promised that his album, *The Life of Pablo*, will be available exclusively on the *Tidal* platform (the platform owned also by Jay

---

[424] Devon Thomas, 'Kanye West Writes Song in Honor of Taylor Swift', *CBS*, September 7, 2010, available at: https: // www. cbsnews.com/news/kanye-west-writes-song-in-honor-of-taylor-swift/, last accessed: February 25, 2021.

Z); however, on April 1, 2016, his album was made available on *Apple Music*, which led to the accusation that he cheated the audience, according to an article in Variety: „By the time Mr. West changed course and broadly released 'The Life of Pablo,' the deceptive marketing ploy had served its purpose: Tidal's subscriber numbers had tripled, streaming numbers were through the roof, and Tidal had collected the personal information, credit card numbers, and social media information of millions of deceived consumers [...] Instead, they just wanted to boost Tidal's subscriber numbers – which indeed did get a big bump from the release. Tidal may have signed up as many as two million new subscribers thanks to the album, claims the lawsuit, arguing that this could have added as much as $84 million to Tidal's valuation;"[425]

Step 4:

- Beyoncé released the surprise album *Lemonade* on April 23, 2016; Taylor Swift was caught in the negative narrative created and promoted by Kanye West; the album enjoyed success from critics being considered the best album released by Beyoncé; on Tidal, *Lemonade* was streamed 115 million times, setting a record for the most-streamed album in a single week by a female artist; what if Kanye West, through the exclusivity strategy of his album, plus the use of Taylor in his song, spread the narrative that in his album there could be something more about Taylor, which led to the growth of curious users and, in the end, some users decided to stay on the platform? at the same time, maybe the new number of users were used to justify the record number of streaming of his album, *The Life of Pablo*, and Beyoncé's *Lemonade*?

Step 5:

- in July 2016, the positive popular opinion is on Kanye's side, especially after Kim Kardashian (Kanye's wife at the time of the event) published edited parts of the phone conversation between

---

[425] Janko Roettgers, 'Kanye West Tricked Fans Into Subscribing to Tidal, Lawsuit Claims', *Variety*, April 18, 2016, available at: https://variety.com/2016/digital/news/kanye-west-tricked-fans-into-subscribing-to-tidal-lawsuit-claims-1201755580/, last accessed: February 25, 2021.

Kanye and Taylor, here the conclusion of the published videos is that Taylor knew about everything (only in March 2020 an extended of the video was released and the whole planet found out that Taylor told the truth since February 2016); Taylor's image worldwide is negative;

Step 6:

- based on her previous pattern release, Taylor releases the first song in August or September, but the *Famous* feud and the negative image obtained as a result of Kanye's song, her strategy and public image do not allow her to release a new song every two years (the last album released was in the fall of 2014, so the next album should have been in the fall of 2016), and therefore Beyoncé has no competition and has a positive image while Taylor does not release a new album and has a negative image;

Step 7 (unexpected shift of the plan and not possible to change the course of their plan):

- although *Lemonade* received the most positive reviews in her career, Beyonce does not win the *Album of the Year* (although she has 12 songs on the album, this number was not lucky) and lost in favour of the white artist, Adele;

Step 8 (unexpected shift of the plan and not possible to change the course of their plan):

- in 2018 Tidal is accused of intentionally falsifying the streaming number of *The Life of Pablo* and *Lemonade*, according to Variety: "Tidal, which has rarely shared its data publicly, had a streaming exclusive on West's album for its first six weeks of release and continues to be the exclusive streamer for Beyoncé's album. It claimed that West's album had been streamed 250 million times in its first 10 days of release in February of 2016, while claiming it had just 3 million subscribers – a claim that would have meant every subscriber played the album an average of eight times per day; and that Beyonce's album was streamed 306 million times in its first 15 days of release in April of 2016." […] "Today's report, according to MBW's translation, says that "Beyoncé's and Kanye West's listener numbers on Tidal have been manipulated to the tune of several hundred million false plays... which has generated massive royalty payouts at the expense of other artists;[426]" what if Kanye West and Jay Z's strategy to use Taylor Swift was also to increase the number of users? what if Kanye West and Jay Z used the new subscribers to falsify the numbers of streaming to make more money? let's not forget that in the conversation with Taylor Kanye admitted having big debts (millions of dollars); what if the fake number of streaming was done in order to increase Beyoncé's profile and the records obtained? what if the false plays were made this route as on the other streaming platforms (Apple and Spotify) Beyoncé would not make the numbers to have new records to celebrate and maintain relevance in the music industry as Taylor Swift does? what if the fake number of streaming and the exclusive availability of her album, *Lemonade*, on Tidal was made to show the world that she is so loved that her fans follow her on the new platform and set new records in the music industry? what if Tidal is being used to justify a false point of view that black artists are not safe on other platforms because they are ruled by white people? what if behind Tidal the black artists from this report, Kanye, Jay Z and Beyoncé, used it to their own benefit, therefore, cheating the music industry and their fans?

What if Jay Z and Kanye West are actually fighting Taylor Swift's influence over people and the music industry in which they do not accept her records and do whatever it takes to keep Beyoncé on top?

---

[426] Jem Aswad, 'Tidal Accused of Falsifying Beyoncé and Kanye West Streaming Numbers', *Variety*, May 9, 2018, available at: https://variety.com/2018/biz/news/jay-z-tidal-accused-of-falsifying-beyonce-and-kanye-west-streaming-numbers-1202804222/, last accessed: February 25, 2021; Andy Cush, 'Tidal Accused of Generating 300 Million Fake Streams for Kanye and Beyoncé', *Spin*, May 9, 2018, available at: https://www.spin.com/2018/05/tidal-fake-streams-kanye-beyonce-investigation-300-million/, last accessed: February 25, 2021; Tim Ingham, 'Tidal 'Fake Streams': Criminal Investigation Underway Over Potential Data Fraud In Norway; *Music Business Worldwide*, January 14, 2019, available at: https://www.musicbusinessworldwide.com/tidal-fake-streams-criminal-investigation-underway-over-potential-data-fraud-in-norway/, last accessed: February 25, 2021; Dagens Næringsliv's investigation can be found here: https://www.musicbusinessworldwide.com/files/2018/05/NTNU_DigitalForensicsReport_DN_Final_Version.pdf, last accessed: February 25, 2021.

What if Jay Z is willing to do whatever it takes to make sure Beyoncé is on top with each album release?

What if Kanye West, Jay Z and Beyoncé are too desperate to win the awards and be recognized more than they are in reality? what if they create all sorts of plans that in the end do not work, create more damage for themselves and blame white people?

What if Kanye West accused Taylor Swift of doing what he did in order to cover his track and other artists that he is supporting by creating a negative view about her? the end of this strategy is to create a negative wave about Taylor Swift, hoping that her fans will get sick of her negative stories that she is involved too often, and switch to his favourite artists, such as Beyoncé, because there are no negative stories about her?

In 2017 the relationship between Kanye West and Jay Z was not so good, however, in 2019 it was reported that they are again on good terms; what if this tension between them is false and was created as a solution to change the focus on a different topic considering *Tidal* was the platform where Kanye exclusively released his song with lyrics that put him and Taylor Swift in difficulty, also about the *Tidal* false plays? more, what if the new better terms of the relationship between Kanye and Jay Z (from December 2019) happened as a sublime and reply message to Taylor Swift which she could have a line about their bad relationship in one of her songs from *reputation*, 'This Is Why We Can't Have Nice Things': "but I'm not the only friend you've lost lately/if only you weren't so shady"?

What if Kanye and Jay Z are behind the feud and everything that the album patterns show in this report?

What if Beyoncé has no idea about the tricks behind the curtains even if it benefits her by having a positive image because of Kanye and Jay Z's intentional involvement?

What if the prediction of the album sales for Kanye West in 2013, Yeezus, of 500,000 copies sold in the first week was made with the purpose to encourage people to buy it as it will be popular anyway? what if the prediction of the album sales for Taylor Swift in 2014 (album *1989*), of 600,000 to 750,000 copies sold in the first week was made with the purpose to discourage people to buy it as it is a lower number than the last album, and as subtle message that she lost her fans and popularity, so there is no need to bother with her album? If we look at the number of sales in the first week of each artist before 2013 and 2014, Kanye West has a lower number of albums sales in 2010, 2011 and 2012 with below 500,000 copies in the first week, and yet in 2013 the prediction increased to half a million copies sold first week; for Taylor Swift is the opposite: in 2010 and 2012 the number of album sales is over one million, and yet in 2014 the prediction decreased to half of the last number of albums from 2012, 600,000 to 750,000. The common point of the two predictions is both were not true: in 2013 Kanye West's final album sales was below the prediction, while in 2014 Taylor's final albums sales was higher than the prediction (double to be precise). The failed prediction for the first week sales happened first with Kanye West in 2005 when his album, *Late Registration*, was predicted to sale over 1.6 million copies in the first week, however, it sold over half of the prediction, 860,000 copies; this model of prediction was used with Taylor Swift too in 2014, but with the opposite expectation; what if there are people who intentionally play with the prediction (maybe the managers paid the source of the prediction to write it according to the interests) to modify fans' intentions and get lower and higher album sales?

What if an unknown number of songs, and maybe even the name of the albums released by Kanye West, Beyoncé and Taylor Swift, is a subtle/behind the curtain message to each others; what if the information we already know about the pattern of the album release and the interference in Taylor Swift's pattern is the real evidence available to confirm the subtle messages?

What if *Lemonade* and *4:44* (Jay Z album) were produced on false statements about cheating in order to justify the albums and the world tour Part II (On the Run)?

What if only Kanye West is to blame for Beyoncé's pattern: he knew the release date of the album and planned everything on his own and set it in motion, and Beyoncé and Jay Z were as surprised as Taylor Swift and the rest of the world?

What if Kanye West thinks he is superior to white artists and, instead of creating his sounds, titles and lyrics, he uses samples to promote the idea that whites are lucky and should be honoured because he uses their music?

What if Kanye presents himself that he has such great creative powers that he does not bother using them to create new music as white producers do not have the power to understand his music, so he uses samples to show that he is still superior?

What if the black artists in this report, perhaps others outside this report, present themselves as victims of white-led music institutions to hide their lower level of originality and creativity in the music industry?

What if the reviews of the black artists are exaggerated and overrated as a strategy to change the shift of good music from the white artists to black artists and members of The Recording Academy are aware of it and this is why black artists have a lower number of nominations and awards and this is the reason of the high contrast between what the media is saying about who the winner should be (articles bought in newspapers?) and who is the real winner (based on originality and talent)?

In the following figure and table, I found a pattern that is happening in 2008, 2009 and 2016 and involves Taylor Swift, Kanye West and Beyoncé.

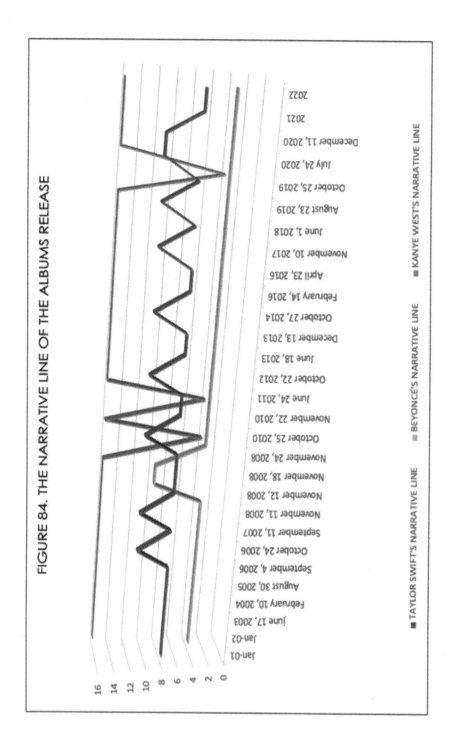

FIGURE 84. THE NARRATIVE LINE OF THE ALBUMS RELEASE

■ TAYLOR SWIFT'S NARRATIVE LINE   ■ BEYONCÉ'S NARRATIVE LINE   ■ KANYE WEST'S NARRATIVE LINE

TABLE 78. A FAMOUS ATTACK ON TAYLOR SWIFT?			
EVENT/ NAME OF THE ARTIST:	**TAYLOR SWIFT**	**BEYONCÉ**	**KANYE WEST**
RELEASE PATTERN	Fixed pattern	Fixed pattern Changing pattern Surprise pattern	Fixed pattern Changing pattern
ALBUM RELEASE NARRATIVE LINE	**2008:** She followed her fixed pattern and released her album in November 2008.	**2008:** She released the album in the same month as Taylor Swift, the second day and a week after Taylor Swift; she followed this release one time.	**2008:** A year before (2007), he changed his pattern and released the album in the same month as Taylor Swift; in 2008 he followed the new pattern for the last time.
	2016: Taylor releases the first song in August or September, but the *Famous* feud did not allow her to release a new song every two years (the last album released was in the fall of 2014, so the next album should have been in the fall of 2016). The *Famous* feud ruined Taylor's album release pattern.	**2016:** Surprise album like in 2013 (December 13, Taylor Swift birthday). Released exclusively on Tidal; Kanye's album was also exclusive on this platform.	**2016:** Released the album a couple of days before the Grammy Awards ceremony where Taylor Swift will win the Album of the Year for her album *1989*.
THE PUBLIC IMAGE NARRATIVE LINE	**2008 - 2009:** Positive before the MTV award ceremony from 2009; a little bit negative after the ceremony from 2009: Kanye told the whole world that she does not deserve the award, Beyoncé is better.	**2008 - 2009:** Positive, and also seen (through free promotion by Kanye West) as an artist that deserved the award won by Taylor Swift, the MTV ceremony was unfair with her talent and creativity.	**2008 - 2009:** Positive image before the MTV award ceremony from 2009; Negative image after MTV award ceremony from 2009 because of his view about the 'true' winner of the MTV award.
	2016:	**2016:**	**2016:**

	Positive before the *Famous* song was released; she walked to Grammy Awards while being called in Kanye's song 'that bitch'; Negative at high level after the release by his wife, Kim, of edited parts of the telephone conversation between Taylor and Kanye.	Positive at high levels, she received the highest reviews in life for her album *Lemonade*.	Little negative image, and more negative after the release of the song *Famous*, but with positive changes after the release by Kim Kardashian, of edited parts of the telephone conversation between him and Taylor.
AWARDS LINE	Taylor's music was nominated for MTV, in 2010 she won the Grammy Award for the Album of the Year for *Fearless*, in 2016 she won the Grammy Award for Album of the Year for *1989*). In both years Kanye West interfered in her narrative with a negative view about her music and character.		

Discussion about another pattern: *personal meaning of the album*

In 2013 Beyoncé and Kanye West released their albums which has full name (*Beyoncé* album by Beyoncé, and Kanye West with *Yeezus* (which is a combination of his last two letters 'Ye' with 'Jesus' (*Yeezus* from Kanye: himself, people in his circle and fans around the world call him 'Ye') to promote himself as 'Ye' (Kanye) the Jesus (God) = Yeezus as God of rap music. In 2014 Taylor Swift released her album *1989* which is the year of her birthday. What if these albums are actually connected and Beyoncé and Kanye West, through their albums, took a shot at Taylor Swift, while Taylor Swift with her year of birth, *1989*, is her reply to Beyoncé and Kanye West? Beyoncé took the shot by releasing her surprise album on Taylor Swift's birthday (December 13, 2013), while Kanye West few days before the release of his album *Yeezus,* in June 2013, in a *New York Times* interview stated about Taylor Swift VMA's moment that he doesn't have any regret about his interruption and that it was a situation where he gave into peer pressure to apologize. When asked if he'd take back the original action or the apology, if given the choice, he answered, „You know what? I can answer that, but I'm – I'm just -- not afraid, but I know that would be such a distraction. It's such a strong thing, and people have such a strong feeling about it. *My Beautiful Dark Twisted Fantasy* was my long, backhanded apology. You know how people give a backhanded compliment? It was a backhanded apology. It was like, all these raps, all these sonic acrobatics. I was like: 'Let me show you guys what I can do, and please accept me back. You want to have me on your shelves.'[427]

CONCLUSIONS based on the pattern A Famous Attack on Taylor Swift?:

- Kanye West interfered in the narrative line of Taylor Swift with a negative story about her character, while Beyoncé has a positive image about her skills and character;
- Kanye West is behind the negative stories about Taylor Swift's character and skills in 2009 and in 2016;
- Kanye West in 2016 interfered in Taylor Swift's narrative line with a negative story while Beyoncé's narrative line is involved in releasing a new album;
- Kanye West negative behaviour toward Taylor Swift is after Beyoncé released an album (2008) and before (2016, *Lemonade*) she is out with a new album.

What if Taylor Swift used samples in her songs (*reputation* in 2017 and *Lover* in 2019) to prove to Kanye West that she can do it too, is not something hard, and she does it better and has a higher popularity than him?

What if the mole in Taylor Swift's team leaked the lyrics *Dear John* to Kanye West (dark twisted games) and he decided to use them to name his album *My Beautiful Dark Twisted Fantasy* and, therefore, a strong connection was made between their albums where the audience could compare their music because both used identical words in their music?

What if Taylor Swift found out the name of Kanye West's album and she decided to use it slightly differently in her song *Dear John* in order to remind people of the person who ruined her moment, therefore, positioning herself as a long-term white victim of a black man?

---

[427] Jon Caramanica, 'Behind Kanye's Mask', *New York Times*, June 11, 2013, https://www.nytimes.com/2013/06/16/arts/music/kanye-west-talks-about-his-career-and-album-yeezus.html?_r=0, last accessed: May 28, 2018.

What if by awarding the Best Contemporary Christian Music Album, The Recording Academy lost its credibility because Kanye West's album used samples (even modified song titles that originally does not belong to Kanye West) and the album cover and not because they awarded clean music from white artists such as Beck, Adele and Taylor Swift? Here the original source of the album does not belong to Kanye West, but to the artists he sampled.

What if Kanye West and Beyoncé didn't get the Grammy Award for *Album of the Year* because of the negative strategies presented in this report to get the most recognition possible in the music industry? what if the members of The Recording Academy found out every time and, by nominating their songs and albums but not winning the category, it was the warning signal that it was not good to follow that path, that the award and the institution should not be used as a bridge for personal attacks against artists and the category of music they belong to? maybe The Recording Academy did it also with Taylor Swift: she released the album *reputation* in 2017 considered by fans and Western mass-media as a response to Kanye West's negative attitudes against her: it was nominated in one category, *Pop Vocal Album*, but did not win.

What if Kanye West uses the music of white producers to humiliate the white producers after he is being awarded with a Grammy on their music, while they did not get even a nomination?

What if Kanye West wants to prove that only a black person in his person can play the music of the white artists to a level that the white artists cannot? What if for these very reasons The Recording Academy did not nominate Kanye West's albums for *Album of the Year* and never won the *Album of the Year*?

The end of the journey: *black* and *white* music

In this report I explored a very small part of the US music industry, more precisely I investigated the contribution, greater or lesser, of black and white artists in the production and writing of their music albums. The artists investigated in this report are: Taylor Swift, Kanye West, Beyoncé, Kendrick Lamar, Macklemore & Ryan, Adele and Beck.

Below are the conclusions I reached for each purpose of the report written in *Introduction*:

1. the creativity and originality of the investigated artists:

- all artists investigated in this report demonstrated creativity and originality;
- based on the information used in this report and the interpretations made, white artists are more creative, original and have a higher level of novelty than black artists.

2. the artist(s) with a greater contribution in the production and writing of a song(s) and album (s) that have been released:

- in terms of the number of songs and the length of minutes written by a single artist, Taylor Swift has the highest level of creativity, originality and novelty; in terms of writing and producing a solo album, Beck has the highest level of creativity and originality (Beck may be even more creative and original than Taylor Swift due to the albums released but not part of this investigation).

3. whether the awards and recognition offered by the USA music industry are based on originality, creativity and novelty in music, or are offered based on the colour of the skin:

- based on the information in this report and the methods used, the white artists were awarded for their originality, creativity and novelty in the music industry;
- unfortunately, this report does not have the information necessary to determine whether the colour of the skin is the primary condition for receiving a higher recognition of the contribution to the USA and the UK's music industry.

4. what are the differences between the music recognized by receiving an award and the music that did not receive an award, but was nominated for the music award (either by the vote of the general public or by the vote of the members of the jury):

- **the major difference is the following**: the white artists wrote and produced songs based on their own musical imagination, in high contrast to the music of the black artists who used songs, lyrics and titles (more Kanye West) that have been awarded, charted and included in lists with the best songs in the music industry;
- despite the lower grades received by the white artists, the music belongs to them to a greater extent compared to black artists who paid royalties and copyrights to use samples of music already known, awarded and charted in the music industry.

5. whether the loss of the award is a direct and personal non-recognition of the black artist(s) who performed the song(s) and under whose name the song(s) and album(s) were released:

- for Beyoncé, Kanye West and Kendrick Lamar (the artists who were and were not nominated for the *Album of the Year* and lost to white artists) is a direct and personal non-recognition of their contribution in the music industry, but not to a high level of non-recognition as they used samples and were supported by many lyricists and producers in creating songs and albums, also they have lots of samples in their music, Kanye West used titles of songs from other artists; maybe the non-recognition is not as high to claim that the lack of the award is because of the colour of their skin and due to institutional racism;
- the black artists from this report and the reviews written based on their albums is also to a considerable extent on the work and

samples of other artists, lyricists and producers; while reading the reviews in magazines, the lyrics of the songs, the number of producers and lyricists for Beyoncé and Kanye West, this idea came in my mind: are they primary artists or (because of the high number of people involved in the creation of their music) participated in the music promoted with their names?

- for Kanye West, the rewards and recognition is also because of the music created by white people and used in his music and, therefore, also white people's music was not awarded and recognized with the *Album of the Year*.

6. whether the loss of the award is a direct and personal non-recognition of the black producer(s) and lyricist(s) who created a part(s) (or full) of a song(s) and the album(s):

- for the producers and lyricists who worked with Kanye West, Beyoncé and Kendrick Lamar there might be a direct and personal non-recognition as their work has a higher level of appreciation from critics on Metacritic in comparison with the music created and released by the white artists from this report.

7. reasons that might justify why white artists receive more recognition than black artists in the music industry (only the artists in this report and Grammy Awards: Album of the Year, Best Rap Album; MTV Awards: Beyoncé (Single Ladies (Put a Ring On It), If I were a Boy) versus Taylor Swift (You Belong With Me, The Man) regarding the originality of these songs:

- maybe the white artists won the *Album of the Year*, other awards and a higher support of the general public because they bet more on their musical ear and imagination than the black artists used in this report; maybe this is the way to win the *Album of the Year*, other awards and the high support of the general public: to believe in your own lyrics and instruments even if your reviews are poor, average or high, but they are truly yours, be authentic no matter what the critics consider the best and worst song(s) and album(s);

- the members of The Recording Academy seem to appreciate the: 1. music composed with real instruments than the music created with samples; 2. the artist who can perform solely on the stage; 3. the artist who can write their own songs and compose their own music at a good to high level.

In *Introduction* I wrote two arguments of black artists against the rules and awards offered by The Recording Academy. This report can provide some answers for each argument and are written below.

1. the higher recognition of music received by the white artists is not about the quality and originality of their music, but because of the colour of their skin; in other words, the white artist received the higher recognition because the institutions behind the awards is ruled by white people:

- unfortunately, this report does not have the information necessary to determine whether the colour of the skin is the primary condition for receiving a higher recognition of the contribution to the USA and the UK's music industry;
- the music released by the black artists in this report received a higher appreciation from critics; however, from my research and based on the information in this report, it seems that The Recording Academy does not take the reviews available on Metacritic into consideration and maybe because the system is based on the vote of the members (artists from various genres, experts in music) who have their own views and critics about the winning song(s), album(s) and artist(s).

2. black artists create music and white artists take advantage and profit from their creation:

- the white artists from this report have clean music and there is not enough evidence to suggest and accuse the white artists of taking advantage and profit from the creation of black artists;
- the black artists from this report (in the following order, from higher to lower level: Kanye West, Beyoncé and Kendrick Lamar) used the creation of other artists (white artists included for Kanye West, maybe more than what I was able to show in this report;

maybe for Beyoncé too), Kanye West used even titles of other songs, the cover of the album *Jesus is King* is inspired and very similar with an album cover from 1970[428]; moreover, Kanye West's album, *My Beautiful Dark Twisted Fantasy*, is inspired by the music written by white male artists (21 out of 25 male artists), so is more appropriate to say that a black artist used music created by the white artists; however, this report cannot offer a clear causal link to accuse Kanye West of taking advantage of their music; on the other hand, because the samples used (which are based on the creation of white artists) and were at the base of his album, I can suggest that Kanye West's reviews were based also on the contribution of the white artists that he sampled; it is possible that, without the samples of the music created by white artists, his recognition to not be at the higher level as it is; also, it is possible for Kanye West to profit from the music created by white artists: he used their music as publicity and strategy of marketing to gain customers to buy his album as it contains samples from white artists who have their own fan base (who might be interested in listening his songs and how their favourite songs were used); also Kanye West could profit from using the music of the white artists by dragging them in his narrative and people to link him with them and, therefore, improve his image as an artist among white people;

- it is more appropriate to say that black artists from this report used other people music and, to an extent, took advantage and profit from other artists creation because they had already a strong base of musical instruments, lyrics, theme of the song and the structure of the song from where to begin their music (which to some extent, contained samples of the music created by other artists with their own fan base);

- it is more appropriate to say that Beyoncé and Kanye West acted like sort of curators of other people's ideas and used the knowledge found in the music of other artists for which they were awarded at high level.

Other conclusions:

---

[428] Tara C. Mahadevan, 'Mystery Behind Kanye's 'Jesus Is King' Album Cover Art Solved by Third Man Records', *Complex*, November 1, 2019, available at:
https://www.complex.com/music/2019/11/mystery-behind-kanyes-jesus-is-king-album-cover-art-solved-by-third-man-records, last accessed: February 27, 2021.

- overall, Taylor Swift is highly more capable than Beyoncé, Kanye West and Kendrick Lamar to write and compose her own music;
- in the music industry there is the following conventional wisdom: 'black people need to work twice as much to get the same as white people'; I find this conception true in the case of Beyoncé and Kanye West and less for Kendrick Lamar: because of their inspiration and samples from other songs, which includes instruments, titles and lyrics and adaptation of these into a new song with a different or close musical notes, definitely cannot be achieved soley and it is a hard work which requires experts in music to create and modify the structures of the songs sampled; it seems this is a curse for using other artist's work;
- Beyoncé and Kanye West's power to create music resides to a certain level in listening to other songs, then to mix these songs with close or sometimes different musical notes and lyrics that can be connected or have some meaning to the theme of the song they intend to create (if they sing a lyric on a different note, they need a different and the right musical note to match the sound of that lyric); there are many songs in their music catalog where their (and other producers from their albums) intervention is the creation of a close sound around a sound used already by another artist;
- from the point of view of creating a song with lyrics and musical notes never heard before, Kanye West and Beyoncé have a lower level of originality, creativity and novelty than Taylor Swift;
- Kanye West and Beyoncé seems to have difficulties, (lack of musical imagination?) when it comes to solely compose and write lyrics for a full clean song never heard before, and of course to achieve highly desired global musical recognition by themselves as Taylor Swift successfully managed to achieve at global level since the start of her career;
- if the title of the greatest artist of all time is based on genuine originality, creativity and novelty brought into the music industry, Kanye West and Beyoncé are not the greatest artist of all time, and are lower than Taylor Swift;
- from my research Kanye West, Beyoncé, Kendrick Lamar do not have the ability or struggle (Kanye West) to play live a full song

using a piano or a guitar, while Taylor Swift has good, maybe advanced, skills in using them with positive praise;

- the white artists used less producers and lyricists to create music, while black artists used more lyricists and producers to create music;

- the black artists review grades are based on their own work, but also to a considerable extent on the creativity and musical ear of the artists they sampled in their songs;

- Kanye West is on the side of Beyoncé, Kendrick Lamar, Drake and Jay Z and the reason might be the following: all of them are using samples with music already known, awarded and charted in the music industry; Kanye West is acting like a person that does not like original music, and we already know he doesn't like the original music of Taylor Swift (see Harper's Bazaar interview from 2016); Kanye West's expectation of the general public and juries that award songs and albums is to prefer and love more songs that are not his own, while rejecting Taylor Swift's original lyrics and musical compositions;

- Beyoncé was rewarded in the early of her career with Grammy awards while having less favorable reviews and grades than Taylor Swift (for her debut album, *Dangerously in Love*, she won five Grammys even though *The Guardian* gave her album 40 points out of 100 on Metacritic); also her albums earned a higher number of awards and grades from critics after she used a higher number of samples, cooperated with a higher number of lyricists and producers, while Taylor Swift earned them with less to no samples, less lyricists and producers, lots of awards on her own songs;

- the black artists from this report forgot to mention on the stage the contribution of the artists that they sampled and have a song and album to promote as their own, while Taylor Swift was blamed by a journalist for being the only female on the stage at the Grammy Award in 2016 despite promoting feminism (for Beyoncé there is no mention in a bad light of her being the only female on the stage while using samples from various artists, many producers and lyricists as it was used with Taylor Swift after the *Famous* feud events);

- this report can show information that I could not see and maybe it can help to understand and fight against institutional racism;

- there are rumors that Taylor Swift writes music for money, but black artists from this report paid copyrights and royalties to have music to release;
- this report also exposed that lots of black artists, producers and lyricists are involved in making music and get better scores than the white artists; if the black artists, producers and lyricists are indeed (behind the curtain) cut their success and awards, then this report has the number of black artists, producers and lyricists who were not awarded the right recognition;
- Beyoncé and Taylor Swift about the release of their albums in 2008: I could not find information about the album's first announcement titles for both artists: I wanted to see which artist used first 'fear' to describe the theme of the album; this information is important as it can show if Beyoncé (fixed, changing and surprise pattern) entered in the same album release pattern with Taylor Swift (fixed pattern: autumn) to possible create direct competition; using same theme, *fear*, both artists expressed their own view about it and could have encouraged people to create a comparative analysis between the two artists; however, even if Taylor Swift used 'fear' first, then later Beyoncé, is not an evidence to support the idea that Beyoncé copied Taylor Swift (from the information that I had accessed: Taylor Swift wrote the song *Fearless* while on tour and was ready before Beyoncé's announcement of the name of her future album; even if Beyoncé used 'fear' first, is still not an evidence to support the idea that Taylor Swift copied Beyoncé (the only way for Beyoncé to know Taylor's Swift's album name is through existence of a mole inside Taylor's team, maybe the same person that possibly leak the lyrics of *Innocent* to Kanye West?, or maybe when the production of the CD started and a person informed Jay Z and Beyoncé?);
- black artists can shout 'unfair' only to the songs written and produced by their own mind and which exist for the first time in the music industry; for the songs they used samples (title, lyrics, instruments) they cannot do it because the success of the song and the album is given by the level of creativity of the original artist; if the original artist does not have a rich musical imagination and black artists uses the song, then they will not be successful either;

- the music created by the white artists (lyricists and producers; main artist of the album) is truly theirs at a higher level than the music created by the black artists (lyricists and producers, main artist of the album);
- based on my research, it is super hard, if not impossible, to prove that black artists did not get the desired and highly requested music recognition because of the colour of their skin; the only way to prove it is to hear or record (audio and video) a member with the power to decide the award that he/she is not going to give the award to a black artist because he/she does not like them because of the colour of their skin or another reason which show intentional racism;
- **after Grammy**: Jay Z called out the Grammys for his 2017 album, *4:44*, winning no awards, despite being a leading nominee: "Tell the Grammys fuck that 0 for 8 shit/ Have you ever seen the crowd goin' apeshit?"[429] Kanye West shared a video on Twitter of himself(?) peeing on one of the 21 Grammys he's won;[430] on what grounds both artists justified their behaviour? Jay Z's album (12 out of 13 songs) used samples, Kanye's Grammy Award (not know for which category and the name of the award) most probably is based also on the use of samples, so, through his behaviour or the person that did it, it was a huge disrespect to people whose music imagination was used in making and earning that award even if he use it allegedly to protest against the company who owns his masters; in the case of Jay Z, the lyrics from his song *Apeshit*, are for his own contribution or for the samples he used? on what grounds Jay Z can decide if the samples that he used should have been good enough to give him a Grammy? and, because he did not win an award, Jay Z is entitled and justified on good reasons to use lyrics against the awarding institution? what if his album was good, but not good enough to win an award? or maybe he was betrayed by the sample where the original artist had a lower level of musical imagination and Jay Z paid the price for using it?

[429] Ashley Iasimone, 'Beyonce and Jay-Z Call Out the Super Bowl and Grammys in "Apes—t" Video', *The Hollywood Report*, June 16, 2018, available at: https://www.hollywoodreporter.com/news/music-news/beyonce-jay-zs-apeshit-video-calls-super-bowl-grammys-1120746/, last accessed: February 25, 2020.

[430] Alicia Adejobi, 'LL Cool J drags Kanye West for urinating on Grammy Award: 'Pee in those Yeezys'', *Metro*, October 4, 2020, available at: https://metro.co.uk/2020/10/04/ll-cool-j-slams-kanye-west-urinating-grammy-award-13369300/, last accessed: February 27, 2021.

isn't it better to bet on your own imagination? just because he is a black artist it does not mean that he must receive an award, the award is also about quality, creativity, novelty and a high personal contribution which is lacking to a certain level in his album *4:44*; in the case of Kanye, what is the link between the Grammy Award and the company who owns his masters? The Recording Academy awards music, it does not hold the copyrights of his music, so his disrespect toward the awarding institution is not justified;

- Kanye West and Taylor Swift are caught in an awkward position: Taylor Swift sings her songs, but does not have the best voice in the pop industry and rumours has it she struggles to sing her own songs; Kanye West is a producer, but he cannot sing like a genuine singer; we have a lyricist who struggle to sing her songs, and a producer who uses lots of samples from other artists, struggles to create his own music and create titles of his own songs;

- it is possible that the low grades and reviews of the latest albums by Kanye West to show that he used already all the best samples available for his creative mind, or for which he could hear a new song; at the moment, and better for Kanye West, the only safe place to find something new is his own mind, it's time to show that he can also be a 'yenius' with his own lyrics, own voice and own production heard for the first time in the world as he is way behind Taylor Swift;

- by using samples, the black and the white artists offered a reheated soup, why should they receive the highest recognition for this strategy?

- there are rumours that black artists want to put pressure on the music industry to change the rules, however, everyone must follow this pressure and see if it follows to celebrate pure creativity, originality and novelty in the music industry or to celebrate the power of sampling; if everybody samples, then who creates the samples? for black artists and white artists the final aim should be quality and high personal contribution, not pressure for a larger freedom to use someone else music and shame the institution when the music is not nominated and awarded;

- owning the masters of the song is important for artists, but also is important to check the correct contribution of the artist in a song and album and see if the specific song and the album is made solely on the artists contribution or were paid copyrights and royalties to be able to have a song and album to release; artists should not own other artists masters just for the sake to show off with music created by other people, to cheat the music industry, themselves and the fans;

- Kanye West used lots of samples and paid copyrights to use it, also is possible to pay royalties (monthly) for the samples used, so his case to own the masters of the albums is complicated as implies the original creators of the music to renounce to their music in Kanye's favour, why the original artists and the owning company should abandon their creation for Kanye West if Kanye West does not bother to create his own music and also showed lack of manners and disrespected the artists used in his music and which contributed to his Grammy Awards?

- strangely, Kanye West does not mention anything about the Grammys received by Drake and Jay Z: their albums are based on the same strategy: samples and many lyricists and producers; Kanye West is focused on saying something negative about Taylor Swift, the artist who writes her songs;

- The Recording Academy loses credibility because the artists who contributed through samples to the music of black and white artists do not receive the recognition they deserve;

- for a better understanding and the general view of the good support toward the artists in the USA and UK, The Recording Academy must come with an explanation or a few reasons about the winning album and artist, information about a specific element of the winning song or album, something that the artists will better understand why they did not win and, also, to dismiss quickly the accusation of institutional racism;

- if the black artists, producers and lyricists know that The Recording Academy does not accept samples of songs to be awarded the *Album of the Year*, why they do not produce an album without samples?

- the black artists in this report used samples and their work is easier (they already have a strong base to start from, the next step for them is to think how to mix and arrange what is already created by other artists, producers and lyricists), but the rewards are smaller too; the white artists from this report took the shot for new songs and got the higher reward; is like the black artists from this report want to be recognised for other people's work because they use it: is not fair for the original artists who compose music out of nothing;

- how it comes that black artists work twice as much than white artists since they use already instruments, titles and lyrics created by other artists?
- do black artists from this report try to cheat the fans and the music industry by using other people's music as their own and want to be highly recognized for it as being the best music because they used it?
- can the black artists from this report write and produce clean and unheard music from their own mind, sell millions of copies, use at least the same number of lyricists and producers and receive the *Album of the Year* three times each?
- on Apple Music Taylor Swift has only *1989* as essential album and yet *Lover* (79 on Metacritic), *folklore* (88) and *Evermore* (85) are not included even though they have higher positive reviews with the last two albums being considered a genuine change of genre for the artist; *folklore* and *Fearless (Taylor's Version)* (82) or the old version with 73) should be included as essential albums for receiving the Album of the Year, the highest award in the USA music industry and the highest recognition of the artist, also the high impact for country music in the USA and around the planet; Kanye West (*The Life of Pablo*: 75; *Graduation*: 79), Rihanna (*Loud*: 67; *ANTI*: 73), Beyoncé (*Dangerously in Love*: 63; *I am... Sasha Fierce*: 62), Lady Gaga (*The Fame Monster Deluxe*: 78; *Born This Way*: 71), Drake (*Take Care Deluxe*: 78; *Nothing Was the Same Deluxe*: 79; *If You're Rearding This It's Too Late*: 78; *Views*: 69) have their albums as essential even if the review grade is close or lower than Taylor Swift's, also the album sales of Taylor Swift are higher than the artists in this paragraph which exposes a high level of popularity; it is time for Apple Music to be more fair with Taylor Swift's music and her recognition in the music industry should be available on the streaming platform as well;
- from what I read it seems that Taylor Swift is not allowed to be successful, she is downgraded a lot despite having more original songs than the black artists from this report; the universities should study Taylor Swift more than Beyoncé as she is more original, creative and brings novelty and has more songs solely

written and released by her; also, she has a higher impact on the American culture and people and the numbers of album sales and concerts is the evidence of how she can connect and leave a mark in the cultural life of the USA on long term; isn't strange that Beyoncé is being promoted as the black artist that has the higher impact in the USA, yet people do not bother to buy her albums as much as they do with Taylor Swift? Now the cultural impact is made by people who sell less music? How a person can be influenced by someone if they do not consume the product of that someone? Adele was accused that she received the Grammy Award because of the high number of albums sales and changed the American music culture, yet with Taylor Swift and Beyoncé we have other rules; the cultural impact is not in the eyes of the beholder, but in the wallets of the people ready to use their money and time to purchase the music of the artist and use it to live and make their own life choices which definitely create an impact in the environment of families, friends and society in the end;

- in 2021 Taylor Swift started with *Fearless (Taylor's Version)* the release of old but re-recorded albums in order to regain control over the music she created and the masters; in this album Taylor came with six more songs written many years ago, but only now they have been made public; the new songs helped Taylor to improve her value and contribution in the music industry; after the re-release of her old albums (*Red* (November 2021), *1989*, *Speak Now*, *Taylor Swift* and *Reputation*) the number of songs written will increase a lot and a large part of the figures and data used in this report will change and offer more strength to my findings; the same will happen with the new music released by black artists; however, after the publication of this report, the albums released by the artists from this report will not be investigated; this report will remain limited only to the albums already investigated.

Author note.

Thank you for taking the time to read this research paper.

Other research published under *Revi Project 88*:

On the Famous Feud (2022): In this report I investigated the *Famous* feud between Kim Kardashian, Kanye West and Taylor Swift. The mechanisms for interpreting the feud are multiple and there is still a great interest in debating the perpetrators and the victims of the feud. This report was born out of the urgent need to provide clearer, more transparent information and better-founded examples to explain the feud for the general public in a different way than what Kim Kardashian, Kanye West and Taylor Swift offered through music, interviews and other media content. This report exposes the background strategies of Kanye West, Kim Kardashian, Taylor Swift and Western mass-media to maintain popularity and fame in an ever-changing world: sacrifices, intelligence, methods of communications, side effects and a minimal view of the efficiency of their strategies in the long term. I'm gonna let you finish reading it, but *'On the Famous Feud'* is a unique and original investigation, there is no other research that explores this conflict on various levels.

The Concept of I(i)nternational R(r)elations (2022): In this paper I explored the concept of 'I(i)nternational R(r)elations', with the aim (i) to show the two techniques of writing and their representation, (ii) the meaning that is attached to each technique; (iii) the process of creation of a concept based on two terms. Through this paper: (i) I return to theorizing the concept of 'I(i)nternational R(r)elations' but from its etymological bases; (ii) the terms 'relation' and 'international' is based on a wide range of concepts that help its formation, and I want to show this formation; (iii) I contribute to the existing literature that discusses the concept; (iv) I contribute to the historical development of the interdiscipline and (v) I respond to the crisis of ideas in science.

The full experience of *Revi Project 88* is available online: